Traveling The MICROSOFT Network

Stephen W. Sagman

msn.

Microsoft Press

PUBLISHED BY
Microsoft Press
A Division of Microsoft Corporation
One Microsoft Way
Redmond, Washington 98052-6399

Library of Congress Cataloging-in-Publication Data
Sagman, Stephen W.
    Traveling The Microsoft Network/Stephen W. Sagman
       p.320 cm.
    Includes index.
    ISBN 1-55615-817-3
    1. Microsoft Network (Online service) 2. Title
  QA7.57.M52S24   1995
  025.04--dc20   95-24054
                                              CIP

Printed and bound in the United States of America.

1 2 3 4 5 6 7 8 9 QFQF 9 8 7 6 5

Distributed to the book trade in Canada by Macmillan of Canada, a division of Canada Publishing Corporation.

A CIP catalogue record for this book is available from the British Library.

Microsoft Press books are available through booksellers and distributors worldwide. For further information about international editions, contact your local Microsoft Corporation office. Or contact Microsoft Press International directly at fax (206) 936-7329.

Acquisitions Editor: Lucinda Rowley
Project Editor: Wallis Bolz

Acknowledgments

Many, many people at Microsoft Press and Microsoft Online Services have been instrumental in creating this book, and I'd like to thank them all. At Microsoft Press, I owe special gratitude to Lucinda Rowley for giving me the chance to undertake this project and Wallis Bolz for keeping it all on track. I'd also like to thank the many other Microsoft Press personnel who offered their support, including Jim Brown, Cheri Chapman, Mary DeJong, Susanne Freet, David Haysom, Rebecca Johnson, and Nikki Naiser.

At Microsoft Online Services, many people lent their support during the development of the book, including Angela Baster, Peter Bekker, Peter Bergler, Dick Brown, Judith Bruk, John Callan, Jodi DeLeon, William Foran, Harold Goldes, Liz Longsworth, Alan McGinnis, George Meng, Robert Michnick, Ann Moyle, Bassel Ojjeh, Kari Richardson, Keith Rowe, Russell Siegelman, Judy Schneider, Steve Weakley, and John Williams. I am truly grateful to them all.

Three special people were instrumental in the creation of this book. First and foremost, I'd like to thank Milton Zelman, a master graphic designer who created the wonderful look for the book, collected the imagery, and labored with immense dedication over each page. Ellen Adams, a sterling copy editor, added greatly to the clarity and style of the text, and contributed much of the Internet chapter. Mary Deaton, my wonderful technical editor, also contributed valuable material to the Internet chapter, and added her expertise throughout the book.

Finally, a loving thanks to Eric and Lola for their patience, once again.

Credits

Art Director: Milton Zelman
Copy Editor: Ellen Snell Adams
Technical Editor: Mary Deaton

Steve Sagman

Steve Sagman is the author of more than a dozen books, including *Running Microsoft PowerPoint for Windows 95*, also published by Microsoft Press. His books have sold more than a half million copies, and they have been translated into eight languages.

When he's not writing books, Steve runs The Water Mill Group, which provides user documentation, software training, and online publishing services for The Microsoft Network.

You can reach him on MSN, where he is SteveS.

*Laptop at lower right is obscured.

Contents

Table of Contents

Table of Contents

6. Postcards and Travelogues: *Using E-Mail* 116

Table of Contents

Table of Contents

Chapter One

Scenic Overlook

Welcome to The Microsoft Network

- *What is The Microsoft Network?*
- *Tour of The Microsoft Network*

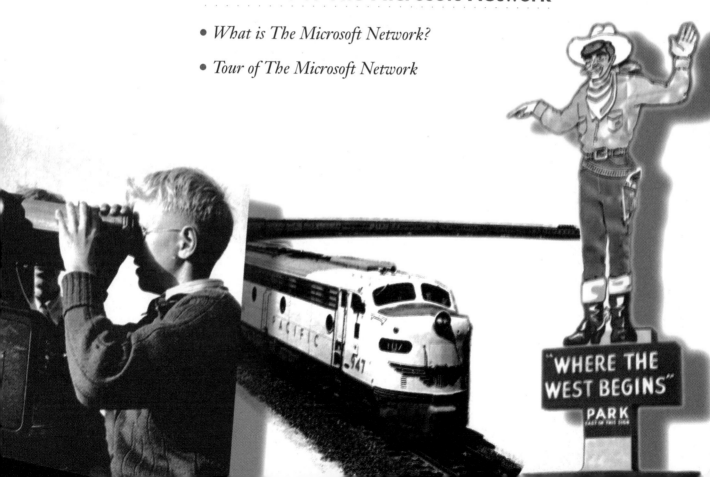

"WHERE THE WEST BEGINS" PARK

Welcome to The Microsoft Network

From all the talk in the press, you'd think everyone but you travels happily across the Internet. Strip away the hoopla, though, and few people have really ventured online—only a fraction of those who own computers with modems. So, if the online "wired" culture seems strange and forbidding, you are certainly not alone.

Remember, the whole online phenomenon is still new. The Internet has been open to the public for less than five years. The other alternatives, online services with names like America Online, CompuServe, and Prodigy, haven't been around much longer.

The main reason you hear about the Internet so much is that the Internet, and its globe-spanning network of computers, is coming together with the online services into one huge, interconnected system. The latest thing among online services is to tout the benefits of the Internet to entice people to sign up for an online service.

The Microsoft Network, the very newest online service, offers full access to

The Microsoft Network at a Glance

What An online service, which offers access to information and services, as well as access to the Internet.

Where The Microsoft Network is available via hundreds of local phone numbers all around the world.

How By signing in, you make a connection to The Microsoft Network so all the information on the network becomes available via your computer.

Why To communicate with others, participate in online communities, gather information, exchange files, and much more.

The Microsoft Network offers access to its own services, and to the services of the Internet.

the Internet right from the start. What's more, The Microsoft Network tames the wild and woolly Internet and gives it logical order because MSN is well-organized, with carefully planned communities, clearly marked roads, and every convenience for the modern traveler. The same clear structure extends to the Internet, which is otherwise vast and unruly by nature, so you don't have to venture out on the Internet blindly.

But Internet access is only one part of the package. Even before you step out onto the Internet, you will find an abundance of places to visit and things to explore on the avenues and byways of The Microsoft

Network. When you join The Microsoft Network, you get news, files, databases of information, technical support, and the chance to meet other people from all around the world through live chats and discussion groups. And you find huge libraries of files that offer everything from reference materials to demos of the latest, hot computer games. You get the chance to read a complete online newspaper from whose pages you can travel to other sites online through special electronic links. You will even find multimedia programs you can view (and hear) presented by companies who deliver information to the public or to their customers. And, of course, if every-

thing within the confines of The Microsoft Network is still not enough, you can browse the World Wide Web on the Internet, where millions of organizations and individuals are publishing their unique contributions to contemporary culture.

When you join The Microsoft Network and begin your travels online, here are some of the services to which you gain access:

Forums

All the information and services on The Microsoft Network are divided into areas called forums, which are dedicated to topics of every variety. These forums are organized under main categories within The Microsoft Network, such as Arts & Entertainment, Computers and Software, or People and Communities. Within the forums, you'll find services you can use, such as chats, BBSes, file libraries, and multimedia applications. Although each service offers information in a different way, they are all still devoted to the topic of the forum. When you find a forum that matches your special interests, you can place it in your "Favorite Places" folder so you can easily return to it.

One way to find the forums you'd like to visit is by wandering through the hierarchy of folders in which all of the content on The Microsoft Network is subdivided. For example, to find the forum on Country

Forums on The Microsoft Network are devoted to particular topics. They're located in folders and organized under the main categories.

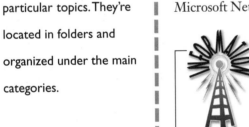

Special Events

Chats are the locale for special events at which invited guests make online appearances. For example, a health forum might host a special event at which a medical authority takes questions from participants. At events such as this, you get the chance to meet people whom you've admired, or vent your frustrations directly to others with whom you've always disagreed. Because most special event chats are open to anyone, they are a highly democratic platform, giving everyone the access that few usually obtain to key people and decision makers.

music, you'd start at the category called Arts & Entertainment, open The Music Forum, and then open the Country Club forum. There you would find files, chats, and bulletin boards with news, biographies, photos, information on tours and festivals, and listings of country artists and albums.

If you would prefer to locate a forum without roaming across The Microsoft Network, you can use the Find command to search for a forum by name or topic, and then jump directly to it.

Within forums, you'll find the services of The Microsoft Network: chats, BBSes, file libraries, and programs you can run. Here they are individually:

Chats

Chats are rooms filled with live and often lively discussions. Members of The Microsoft Network type comments right into an ongoing conversation for everyone else in the "chat room" to see.

Some chats are fun and frivolous social gatherings where members engage in the pleasure of getting to know other members. But other chats are more serious, devoted to debating important issues. They provide a place for people dealing with everything

from computer glitches to difficult personal problems to come for support.

You will find at least one chat room in just about every forum on The Microsoft Network. While a chat is meant to focus on the topic of the forum, members often stray off the subject, so you never know what you'll find in a chat until you enter. Once you arrive in a chat room, you will see the live conversation inside unfold line by line as members enter their comments. When

you're ready to make a contribution, you simply speak up by typing your message into the chat window for everyone to see.

Chats are covered in detail in Chapter 4, "Meeting the Locals: Participating in Chats."

BBSes

While chats are live, ongoing conversations, the BBSes (short for Bulletin Board Systems) are written sequences of messages that are added to as people visit forums and

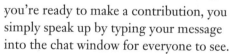

Chats are live. The participants are actually typing messages to everyone else in the chat room.

contribute something of their own. In the busiest forums, BBS conversations formulate quickly; a discussion with dozens of messages and responses can emerge in hours. But in other forums, conversations grow gradually. All the while, hundreds or thousands of people might drop by each day and review all the latest postings.

A BBS in a forum can contain many conversations on topics related to the forum. A BBS in the Travel forum, for example, might contain conversations devoted to Provence bike tours, packing two weeks of clothes in one carry-on suitcase, and which

BBS conversations are not live. They occur as people visit the BBS and add new messages to ongoing written discussions.

The Value of the BBSes

Here's an example of the value of the BBSes: imagine that you are the owner of a small business faced with a difficult issue raised by an employee. Your first stop for help might be the Small Business forum in the Business and Finance category where you can post a message asking for advice in the Home-Based Business BBS.

countries require vaccinations. You can read these conversations sequentially, following trails of messages from beginning to end, or you can follow the "subconversations" that emanate from the original string of messages like the branches of a tree. Of course, you can respond to any posting along the way, adding your comment to the conversation for everyone else to consider and respond to.

While the comments made in chats are usually spontaneous and off-the-cuff, the messages left in BBSes are often more well-considered, as people take the time to compose their thoughts in a written message. BBS messages also have the advantage of persistence. A comment or question posed in a chat reaches only the people in the chat room at the time. A message posted to a BBS reaches everyone who subsequently visits the BBS (at least until the BBS reaches its message capacity and old messages scroll off). Therefore, a BBS can be the best place to leave a question that you'd like to ask the world at large, or at least all the other people who visit the same forum. Of course, you might be lucky and get an immediate answer from someone by posing your question in the forum's chat, but you'll probably have better luck posting a query in the BBS. Many more people will see your question, and someone with the right answer will surely come along and respond in the cooperative spirit that marks most BBSes, and most online experiences, for that matter.

The BBSes are covered, along with the related File Libraries, in Chapter 5, "Seeing the Sights: The BBSes and File Libraries."

File Libraries

A special form of BBS, called a file library, offers computer files that forum visitors can download to their own computers. File libraries contain documents with information and programs that you can run. When the forum is sponsored by a computer hardware or software company, you can also find special utilities and software enhancements that work with or update the company's products. In the Shareware forum, you'll even find hundreds of handy programs written by individuals and small companies that you can try before buying for a nominal fee.

The built-in capability of The Microsoft Network to multitask, or perform two or more operations simultaneously, enables you to download software from a file library

at the same time you are reading BBS messages or participating in chats.

File Libraries are covered along with BBSes in Chapter 5, "Seeing the Sights: The BBSes and File Libraries."

E-Mail

For many people, e-mail (electronic mail) is the most important benefit of joining an online service. While company networks offer their employees the advantages of electronic mail, The Microsoft Network offers the same advantages to every member of the service. Nearly instantaneous, quick to create, and simple to store, electronic mail is a simple way to maintain important relationships.

You can freely, and privately, swap letters, pictures, and even files with other members of The Microsoft Network. And with The Microsoft Network's connection to the Internet, you can exchange e-mail with everyone else who is also connected to the Internet, including members of other online services.

File libraries contain documents and programs contributed by the forum manager, by other MSN members, and by companies who have sponsored forums on The Microsoft Network.

E-mail is universally available to everyone who hooks up to an online service or the Internet, but The Microsoft Network offers several special advantages. First, e-mail on The Microsoft Network isn't just ASCII text only, as it is on the Internet and most other online services. On The Microsoft Network, you can trade beautiful letters, formatted with a wide array of fonts, colors, and formatting. You can embed pictures you have created or scanned and files you have composed. In addition, The Microsoft Network offers a complete and customizable filing system for your messages. You can organize your electronic correspondence into folders according to any system you'd like. The system uses the same filing system to store faxes you send and receive with the Windows built-in fax software, and e-mail messages you exchange via Microsoft Mail on an organization's computer network, so all your electronic correspondence is conveniently stored in one place.

With e-mail on The Microsoft Network, you can keep in touch with family members or customers in far-off places, or business partners and suppliers just across town. If you use Microsoft Word for your word processing, you can even send e-mail right from within Word.

Sending, receiving, and filing e-mail is covered in depth in Chapter 6, "Postcards and Travelogues: Using E-Mail."

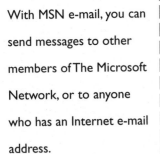

With MSN e-mail, you can send messages to other members of The Microsoft Network, or to anyone who has an Internet e-mail address.

Personal Publishing on the Web

Part of the pleasure of wandering the web is discovering the new and imaginative ways people have already used this new form of communication. Companies create web sites to advertise or promote their products. Organizations create web sites to build communities of like-minded people. And many individuals have created web pages to express themselves in fun, creative, or frivolous ways on personal "home pages." The web offers the opportunity for just about any individual or organization (with some computer sophistication, of course) to create a web site.

MSN News

The Microsoft Network's online news service, MSN News, is produced in a fully staffed newsroom at The Microsoft Network. Professional news editors sift through the news feeds that continuously emanate from the world's news wires, and present to you the latest events, weather, sports, business information, and more in an easy-to-read online format. MSN News is always up to the minute. What's more, its stories are filled with links you can follow to travel to related news, background information, or live discussions on related topics on The Microsoft Network and the Internet. For example, an article about an event might contain a link to an online encyclopedia entry about a person behind the news. This way, MSN News offers a richer experience than you can get by reading a traditional newspaper or watching TV news.

With its links to other parts of the service, MSN News can also become your gateway to various locations on The Microsoft Network and the Internet. Each day, you can make MSN News your first stop, and then travel its links to different parts of the online world.

Access to the Internet's Services

You can use The Microsoft Network to surf the web—travel from site to site on the World Wide Web—which has become one of the Internet's most popular features. Visiting the web is like reading the pages of a magazine, except that the number of pages is unlimited, and each page contains links you can click to jump to related pages. In fact, each screen on the web is called a "page," and the collection of pages at one place is called a "web site."

A truly amazing aspect of the web is that the pages, though interlinked, are very often located on different computers at remote locations around the world. Clicking a reference to a page located on a computer in Melbourne, Australia might take you to a page on a computer in Dallas, Texas.

MSN News is an online news service. Its stories contain links you can click to jump to other areas on MSN that are related to news stories or events, or to Internet sites that are related to the news.

"WHERE THE WEST BEGINS" PARK

11

The World Wide Web browser offered by The Microsoft Network is called the "Internet Explorer."

Through the Internet, each page, no matter where it's located, is as instantly and easily accessible as any other.

The Microsoft Network offers both the browser software you need to view web sites (Internet Explorer) and the connection you need to reach them. To start traveling the web, then, the only thing you'll need is a place to start. The Microsoft Network can help you there, too, by offering access to a huge, searchable database of web sites called Lycos. With Lycos, you can locate web pages by name or description.

Another, very popular Internet feature is the newsgroups, which work just like the BBSes on The Microsoft Network. The difference between Internet newsgroups and BBSes on The Microsoft Network is that anyone can read and contribute to the Internet newsgroups. Just about everyone who has access to the Internet, anywhere in the world, also has access to the Internet newsgroups. So, if you can't find an answer to a question on one of BBSes on The Microsoft Network, you'll surely find it on one of the Newsgroups.

The Internet newsgroups are organized in a hierarchy similar to the organization of forums on The Microsoft Network, so you can find a newsgroup by narrowing in on its topic. For example, if you want to read the newsgroup devoted to the topic of computer neural networks (and you do, don't you?), you can navigate through the listing of newsgroups to Computers, and then to the subcategory AI, and then to the further subcategory neural-nets—Computers/ Artificial Intelligence/Neural Networks.

You can also reach newsgroups from within many of the forums on The Microsoft Network. For your convenience, an icon in a forum leads to the related newsgroups on the Internet. To jump directly to a newsgroup of interest, you can also use the Find command on The Microsoft Network to locate a newsgroup by name or subject.

Other popular Internet features you gain access to through The Microsoft Network are FTP (File Transfer Protocol), which lets you transfer files from other remote computers to your own, and Gopher, a search facility that lets you locate and then jump to Internet sites with ease.

The Internet services available through The Microsoft Network are covered in detail in Chapter 7, "Globe Trotting: Traveling the Internet."

Microsoft Services and Support

Last, but not least, in the cavalcade of benefits you will derive from The Microsoft Network is access to comprehensive resources and support for Microsoft products, such as Windows itself. On The Microsoft Network, you'll find a forum for each Microsoft product, which offers direct access to product support and software updates. What's more, you will get the chance to discuss your use of Microsoft products with fellow users and Microsoft engineers. For instance, Microsoft Office users who are members of The Microsoft Network can connect to The Microsoft Network and gain access to expanded help and online assistance.

When you explore the Microsoft forum, you'll also find the Microsoft Developer Network, with its useful information for software developers, and the Microsoft Online Institute, where you can take courses to earn a proficiency certification in

a Microsoft product, such as SQL Server, increase your productivity, or learn a job skill.

Of course, Microsoft is not the only company on The Microsoft Network offering online support for its products. In the forums of the Computers and Software category, you'll find many other software and hardware companies who reach out to their customers with online information, services, and support.

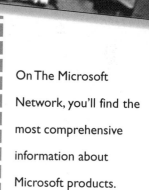

Multimedia Applications

The rich, graphical nature of The Microsoft Network makes possible complete, multimedia programs you can run right over the phone line. You'll be amazed when you first open the online version of Microsoft Encarta, Microsoft's multimedia encyclopedia. Encarta is a complete reference work, with easy searching

On The Microsoft Network, you'll find the most comprehensive information about Microsoft products.

Microsoft Encarta and Microsoft Bookshelf, an electronic encyclopedia, and a set of electronic reference works are both available on The Microsoft Network in special online editions.

through more than 26,000 articles, 5,000 photos, and 360 maps. It also offers 300,000 links between articles. Microsoft Bookshelf, another online reference work, offers seven best-selling reference books, such as the American Heritage Dictionary, 3,000 images, and more than 80,000 pronunciations. As you explore The Microsoft Network, you'll find many other reference, news-related, or pure entertainment multimedia titles created by companies who specialize in providing online information.

The Tour Starts Here

The best way to understand the value of The Microsoft Network is to see it in action. So here is a brief, guided tour which will let you experience some of the features you'll find online. Before you finish the tour, you'll get the lay of the land and visit many scenic destinations.

Before you start, you should take a few minutes and follow the instructions for installing The Microsoft Network software.

These instructions are in Chapter 2, "Planning Your Online Adventure." During the setup process, you will select a local access telephone number, choose a member name, and set up your account so you can sign in and join the tour, which begins at the home screen of The Microsoft Network, MSN Central.

- If you have not already done so, go ahead and sign in to The Microsoft Network by double-clicking the icon on the Windows desktop labeled The Microsoft Network. Then, in the Sign In dialog box, click the Connect button.

If the *MSN Today* window opens when you are connected, you can close it by clicking the Close button at the upper right corner of the window. By default, *MSN Today* will open each time you sign in, unless you choose otherwise. *MSN Today* gives you the latest updates about new services online and current activities in the forums. If a message appears asking whether you really want to disconnect, you've closed the wrong window. Don't worry. Just click No, and then click with the right mouse button on the MSN icon at the lower right corner of the screen, on the

Taskbar. Then choose Go to MSN Central from the shortcut menu that appears.

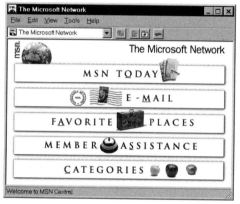

MSN Central

MSN Central is the starting screen for The Microsoft Network. You can return to MSN Central easily to start exploring a different area of The Microsoft Network. The MSN Today button on MSN Central opens the MSN Today window, which gives you the latest news about The Microsoft Network. The second button, labeled "E-Mail" opens the e-mail handling program, Microsoft Exchange, a part of Windows 95. The third button, Favorite Places, opens the special area in which you can save your most frequent destinations on The Microsoft Network and on the Internet. The fourth

button, Member Assistance, leads to assistance you can obtain on using The Microsoft Network or managing your account. The last button, Categories, takes you to the all-important first level of folders that house all of the content on The Microsoft Network.

- In the MSN Central window, click the Categories button.

When you click the Categories button, you'll see the main areas on The Microsoft Network represented as large icons with names. If you see small icons, or a list of categories, choose Large Icons from the View menu so you can follow this tour.

Before you proceed any further, you should also take a moment to make two more important changes to the way The Microsoft Network works. The first change will remove unessential windows from the screen. With an uncluttered desktop, you can easily navigate from place to place.

You can always return to MSN Central before venturing out on another pathway through The Microsoft Network.

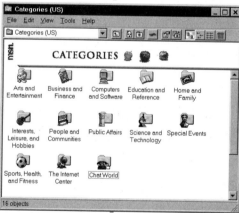

The Categories.

Using a single window to browse MSN folders keeps your desktop clear and uncluttered. Besides, you can always open a second window when you need to.

- From the View menu, choose Options. Then, on the Folder tab of the Options dialog box, click "Browse MSN folders by using a single window that changes as you open each folder." The other option opens a new window every time you change locations. Finally, click OK to close the Options dialog box.

The second change will give you a toolbar with buttons. By clicking these, you can carry out frequent tasks, such as returning to MSN Central. If you already see a toolbar running across the categories window, just under the menu bar, you can skip this step.

- From the View menu, choose Toolbar.

All the information and services on The Microsoft Network are located behind the icons you should now see in the Categories window. By double-clicking any of these icons, you can begin exploring the content tree of The Micro-

soft Network. The organization of information is called a content tree because it has large, main branches corresponding to the categories; smaller branches off the main branches corresponding to areas within the categories; and then still smaller branches that are the forums within the areas. The forums contain the services you will want to use, such as chats and BBSes.

The actual visual metaphor used to represent the information on The Microsoft Network is folders within folders. It's the same metaphor used by Windows to depict the information on your system's disks. The first folders you open are the categories, such as the category called "Computers and Software." When you open a category folder, you find more folders that partition the category into areas, such as Hardware, Software, and so on. The folders within each area represent further partitions at an even more specific level. At any level, you may also find icons which represent the individual forums within the Computers and Software category.

One way to move through The Microsoft Network is to double-click a category folder to open it, and then move another level deeper by double-clicking one of the

Cross Country

icons in the category folder. You continue clicking the folders you find represented as icons in each window until you find the forum you want. That folder will contain icons for chats, BBSes, file libraries, and other services. To retrace your steps, you can click the Up One Level button on the

 toolbar. If you keep clicking the Up One Level button, you'll return eventually to MSN Central, where you started.

To see this structure of folder within folders for yourself, follow these steps:

1. Double-click the Computers and Software category icon to open the category folder.
2. In the Computers and Software window, double-click the Hardware icon to open the Hardware folder.
3. Click the Up One Level button on the toolbar to return to the Computers and Software category. You've successfully ventured down a level and then returned back up.
4. Now, in the Computers and Software window, double-click the Computer Companies and Organizations icon.
5. In the Computer Companies and Organizations window, double-click the Software Companies icon to open the Software Companies folder.
6. In the Software Companies window, double-click the Microsoft icon to open the Microsoft folder. How did you know I'd take you there?
7. In the Microsoft window, double-click the Microsoft Windows 95 folder to open the Microsoft Windows 95 forum.

The Microsoft Window

As you will see, the Microsoft Windows 95 forum contains icons for a chat and other services. You will also find a kiosk, an

Every forum and service on The Microsoft Network is in its own folder.

You open any folder by double-clicking it. You return to the previous folder by clicking the Up One Level button.

information file you can read about the forum. The Windows 95 Technical Support area (double-click the icon labeled "Windows 95 Technical Support") contains a BBS, file library, and other services.

The shape of each icon will provide clues about the type of service it represents.

Chat icons have this background.

BBS icons have this background.

File library icons have this background.

To open any service you find in a forum, simply double-click its icon. You might want to open the Questions & Conversations chat area, for example, where you will find many different chats and can participate for a moment in an ongoing, live discussion about Windows 95 features.

1. In the Microsoft Windows 95 window, double-click the icon labeled Questions & Conversations Chat Expo.
2. In the Questions & Conversations Chat Expo window, double-click the "Windows 95 Chat Room" icon.

If nobody is in the Windows 95 chat room, you may want to return to the categories and choose Chat World. You'll almost certainly find visitors in the Chat World Lobby.

When the chat window opens, you'll see three panes inside. The conversation flows through the large pane at the left. The right pane holds a list of chat participants. The bottom pane, next to the Send button, is where you type contributions to the chat.

To learn more about one of the participants in the chat, you can double-click a member name on the list at the right. You will see the member's properties, or all the information that the member wants you to know. To contribute something to the chat, just type your message into the small pane at the bottom of the chat window, next to

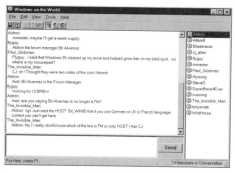

The Windows on the World chat window.

the Send button, and then press Enter or click Send. This should trigger a response from someone in the chat. You might even have been warmly greeted when you arrived. There's a camaraderie online that is often missing from person-to-person communications.

After you've spent a couple of minutes getting the feel of a chat, you can close the chat window by clicking the Close button at the upper right corner of the window. You'll be returned to the Windows 95 forum window, where you can investigate another feature of The Microsoft Network. This time, you'll take a quick look at a BBS.

● **1.** In the Microsoft Windows 95 forum window, double-click the icon labeled "Windows 95 Technical Support."

2. In the Windows 95 Technical Support window, double-click the "Windows 95 Members to Members BBS" icon.

After a moment, a list of folders will appear in a window labeled "Windows 95 Members to Members BBS (Read Only)." The "Read Only" indicates that you can't put messages here. You must first open one of the folders on the list. When you double-click any folder, you'll find a list of message descriptions called "headers." Each

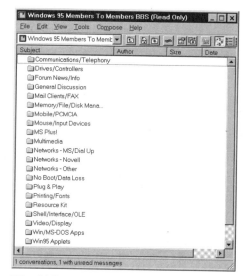

The Windows 95 Members to Members BBS window.

The Communications/ Telephony BBS.

header appears in bold text accompanied by a gray arrow to indicate that you have not yet read the message it represents.

Each of the headers on the list represents the first message of a conversation. This message may have replies hidden underneath, followed by still more replies to the replies. A BBS can contain hundreds of these conversations. You can choose any conversation whose initial message subject interests you and then follow its sequence of postings.

To see more of the messages in a conversation, you must click the small plus sign that precedes the header of the initial message. The replies to the initial message will appear. Some of these replies may be accompanied by plus signs, too. To reveal the additional messages, click their plus signs. By clicking the plus signs, you will reveal the full structure of the conversation.

To read any message, just double-click its header. This also reveals the replies to the message. After you read a message, you can use the navigation buttons on the toolbar to open other

messages selectively. Chapter 5, "Seeing the Sights: The BBSes and File Libraries," covers these controls in depth.

In addition to simply reading the messages, a BBS gives you the option to add a new message to any existing conversation, or to start a new conversation by posting an initial message. You might want to post a new message to seek an answer to a question that is pertinent to the forum, for example.

After you have read a few messages in the BBS, you can leave the BBS by clicking the Up One Level button on the toolbar twice.

travel tip

Exiting a BBS
This is important: do not try to close the BBS window the same way you closed the Chat window. The Microsoft Network will think you intend to sign off and ask whether it's OK to disconnect. Unless you plan to continue this tour another time, you'll want to click the Up One Level button to leave the BBS, instead.

Here's a little background: when you open a chat, a separate chat program starts in its own window. You can close the chat program by closing the chat window. But when you open a BBS, you are not running a separate program, so there's no need to close the BBS window to end the program. You simply return to the previous level in the content tree by clicking Up One Level.

- Click the Up One Level button on the toolbar twice to leave the BBS and return to the Windows 95 Technical Support forum.

File Library

File Libraries resemble and function a lot like BBSes, except that their messages contain descriptions of files that you can put onto your own computer, called downloading. The actual files are represented as icons within the message text. To start downloading the file, you can double-click any icon.

The Computer Games forum contains a file library filled with games, game demos, and related software. You can open this file library to get a first-hand look at how a library works.

To get to the Computer Games forum, here is a faster way of navigating through the content tree: at the left end of the toolbar, you'll see a drop-down list that

shows the name of the current folder, in this case, Windows 95 Technical Support.

- Click the text Windows 95 Technical Support, or click the down-arrow button next to the list to drop down the list.

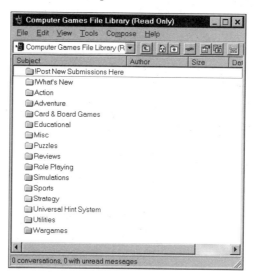

Computer Games File Library.

File libraries are like BBSes whose messages each have one or more attached files.

The drop-down list, called "Go to a different folder" shows a list of the folders you have opened on the way to the current folder. To return to a previously opened folder, just click that folder name on the list.

The "Go to a different folder" list shows the folders that are open above the the currently opened folder.

1. In this case, click the list entry "Computers and Software."
2. In the Computers and Software window, double-click the Software icon.
3. In the Software window, double-click the Computer Games icon.
4. In the Computer Games window, double-click the Computer Games icon to open the Computer Games forum.
5. In the Computer Games window, double-click the Computer Games File Library icon.

Within the File Library window, you'll see a series of folders, each of which holds files of a different type. Take a look inside the Action folder.

1. In the Computer Games File Library window, double-click the Action folder.
2. In the Action window, double-click the Demos folder.

After a moment, you will see a list of message headers whose subjects describe the files within. Each message header is

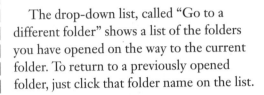

accompanied by a paper clip icon to indicate that a file is attached.

1. Double-click any message header to open it. Here, the person who contributed the file, or the forum manager, will provide a short description of the file. You will also see one or more files represented as icons.
2. Click any file icon with the right mouse button. From the shortcut menu, choose File Object.

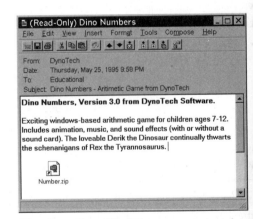

The icon in a file library message is the file you can download.

3. From the File Object menu, choose Properties. The Properties dialog box gives you further information about the file and the option to begin downloading it.

If you want, you can download the file by clicking the Download File button. The file will be placed in the file transfer queue, and it will be sent to your computer. One of the really nice things about The Microsoft Network is that you can do other things online, such as participate in chats, while your files are transferred. If you'd rather not download the file, close the File Transfer Queue window, and then click OK when a message appears informing you that there are still files in the file transfer queue.

- Close the message window, and then click the Up One Level button on the toolbar several times until you've left the Computer Games forum.

By now, you have gotten a pretty good idea of the scope of The Microsoft Network. The branches of the content tree—the pathways you can travel—seem virtually unlimited, especially when you add the thousands upon thousands of fun and interesting sites to which you can jump on the World Wide Web. To gain access to these sites, you can click one of the icons that leads to a World Wide Web site. You'll find these in forums along with the icons that lead to local information and services on The Microsoft Network.

When you click an icon for a web site, the MSN Explorer, a program you use to view and navigate among the pages of the web, opens automatically. In the vernacular of the Internet, interesting web sites are dubbed "cool," and you'll find a bunch of cool web sites via The Microsoft Network.

Here's a quick way to jump to a place on The Microsoft Network when you know its description but not its location:

1. From the Start menu, choose Find.
2. On the Find menu, choose On the Microsoft Network.
3. In the Find: All MSN Services dialog box, enter the words "cool web sites", without the quotes, in the text box next to "Containing:"
4. Click the Find Now button.

The Find command will search the forums and services of The Microsoft Network, and then display a list of matching names within the dialog box. In this

On The Microsoft Network, you can chat in one window while downloading a file in another and browsing a BBS in a third window.

23

case, you'll see an entry for a Cool Web Sites folder and a Cool Web Sites BBS. There may be more. You can double-click any entry on the list to jump directly to the area it represents.

Here is another great feature of The Microsoft Network: when you find a service you want to visit frequently, simply drag its icon to your Windows desktop. This is the area where the icons for My Computer, Network Neighborhood, and other Windows features appears. When an icon is on the desktop, you can double-click the icon to quickly connect to The Microsoft Network and jump directly to the service. To try this simple procedure, follow these steps:

1. Click the MSN icon at the lower right corner of the screen, on the Taskbar, with the right mouse button.

2. From the shortcut menu, choose Go to.

3. In the Go to dialog box that appears, enter the Go word "pubserv" without the quotes. (You can learn a forum's Go word by clicking its icon with the right mouse button.)

In the Public Service forum, you'll see an icon for the Public Service BBS.

4. Place the mouse pointer on this icon, press and hold the mouse button, and drag the icon to any visible part of the Windows desktop. The icon appears on the desktop with the label "Shortcut to Public Service BBS."

Shortcut on the desktop.

Now, for maximum drama, disconnect from The Microsoft Network.

- Click the Sign Out button on the toolbar. When you're asked whether you really want to disconnect, respond by

Dragging an icon for a service to your desktop makes the service instantly accessibly right from your desktop.

24

clicking Yes. The Microsoft Network window will close.

As you probably guessed, your next step is to double-click the Shortcut to Public Service BBS icon on the Windows desktop to see whether it takes you directly back to the Public Service BBS.

- On the Windows desktop, double-click the new Shortcut to Public Service icon. You will see the Sign-in window for The Microsoft Network.

After you enter your password, if necessary, and click Connect, you'll be re-connected to The Microsoft Network. The system will drop you directly into the Public Service BBS. By dragging an icon from The Microsoft Network to your desktop, you can make any collection of information on MSN as readily available as the information on your own computer's disks.

There is one more feature of The Microsoft Network to see on our tour. It's e-mail, the electronic messaging service, which lets you send instant messages to anyone else on The Microsoft Network, or anyone in the world who has a public e-mail address.

● **1.** Click the MSN icon on the Taskbar with the right mouse button.
2. From the shortcut menu, choose Go to MSN Central.

The MSN Central screen appears in its own window. The window in which you can see the Public Services BBS is probably also still open on the screen. Another of the features of The Microsoft Network is that you can explore two or more areas simultaneously, in separate windows. You can participate in a chat in one window, for example, while exploring a BBS in another window.

- On MSN Central, click the large E-Mail button.

After a few moments, Microsoft Exchange will open. Exchange is the e-mail handling program that works with The Microsoft Network, and other Windows programs.

You should see two panes

You can have several windows into The Microsoft Network open simultaneously. In one window, you can be participating in a chat, for example. In the order window, you can be browsing a BBS.

Microsoft Exchange handles all your electronic correspondence from within Windows, including the e-mail you send via The Microsoft Network.

in the Exchange window separated by a gray, vertical line. If you see only one pane, choose Folders from the View menu.

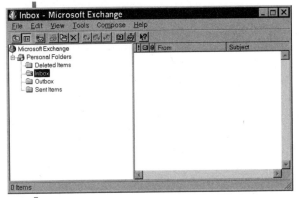

Microsoft Exchange.

The left pane of the Exchange window displays the initial folders that are provided for your use. The right pane of the Exchange windows shows the contents of the currently open folder. To open a folder, click it on the folder list.

After you have been using The Microsoft Network for a little while, you will start to accumulate incoming e-mail in the Inbox folder. The

messages you receive are listed in the right pane of the Exchange window when the Inbox folder is open. Just double-click any message to open it. After a message is open, you can click the Reply button on the toolbar to send a response.

Exchange allows you to file messages by simply dragging them from the message list to the appropriate folder on the folder list. If you do not yet have the folders you need for a useful filing system, you can simply add them. Why not create a folder for each person with whom you correspond, each project you are working on, or each company with which you do business?

Creating messages is easy, too. You just follow these steps:

● 1. Click the New Message button on the toolbar.
   2. In the To text box of the New Message window, enter the name or e-mail address of the person to whom you want the letter to go. After you've been using e-mail for a while, you'll accumulate a list of e-mail names and addresses you can keep in your personal address book file. If you don't know to whom to address a message, you can always send a message to me, Steve Sagman

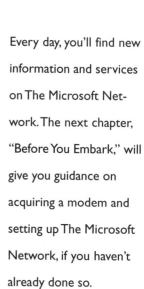

(or SteveS). I'd love to hear from you and know that you have successfully reached this point in the tour.

3. Press the Tab key twice to move the insertion point to the Subject line and type a message subject.

4. Press the Tab key to move the insertion point to the message area, and then type the body of your message.

A new message.

As you enter the text of a message, you can use the controls on the Formatting toolbar to format the text. You can change its color, font, size, and make other modifications, such as underlining it, or centering it. You will find complete instructions in

Chapter 6, "Postcards and Travelogues: Using E-Mail."

- When the message is complete, click the Send button on the toolbar. Your message will be on its way. Here's the Send button:

Until you're ready to do some more exploring on your own, you may now want to sign out by clicking the Sign out button. There's a Sign out button on every toolbar in MSN windows.

You've now seen some of the main features of The Microsoft Network, but there's still far more to explore. In many forums, you'll find special icons, which represent multimedia programs you can run. When you start one of these programs, you'll be immersed in a total visual and aural experience created by the program's provider. You are also sure to enjoy following the daily news with MSN News, the online news service of The Microsoft Network.

Enjoy your experience on The Microsoft Network, and don't forget to drop me a message to let me know how you are doing!

Every day, you'll find new information and services on The Microsoft Network. The next chapter, "Before You Embark," will give you guidance on acquiring a modem and setting up The Microsoft Network, if you haven't already done so.

Chapter Two

Before You Embark

Preparing for the Trip

- *What is The Microsoft Network?*

- *Installing The Microsoft Network*

- *Modem Speeds, Settings, and Setup*

- *Getting Ready to Sign In*

Preparing for the Trip

What is The Microsoft Network?

Get ready to embark on a fantastic journey through The Microsoft Network. You will visit exotic destinations, explore treasure troves of information, and meet new people from around the globe, all without leaving the comfort of your home.

But before you set out upon your first online odyssey, you will probably want to know where to get started and what to pack. Here's some background, a little advice on proper preparation, and a few tips to remember so your first venture online will be smooth and comfortable.

As soon as you connect your computer to the outside world by modem, you step beyond the looking glass into a universe of exploration and adventure. You may be traveling cyberspace — and "traveling" is the premise of this book — but you are also on an expedition from which you will return with treasures from around the entire world.

If you have never been online before, signing in to The Microsoft Network is an ideal first outing. The Microsoft Network (MSN) is an easy-to-navigate highway with every service available to the modern traveler. If you're a veteran cruiser of the information superhighway, you'll be amazed at the scope of The Microsoft Network, the elegant way it works, and its integration into your Windows system. As you will see, the technological features of The Microsoft Network give it capabilities you won't find anywhere else.

Preparations at a Glance

What   Before you can sign in for the first time, you must install the software for The Microsoft Network and set up a modem. It also helps to understand a little about The Microsoft Network before you jump on board.

When   While you install Windows, and before you connect to The Microsoft Network for the first time.

How   Most of the software and hardware installation required for The Microsoft Network is automatic, but there are still a few choices you can make.

Why   To make your first visit to The Microsoft Network a breeze.

The Microsoft Network is a great place to meet new people, visit exotic places, and gather free software and useful advice.

Your Introduction to The Microsoft Network

What exactly is The Microsoft Network? It's a service that brings an online community directly into your home. It offers files, news, weather, sports, travel, business information, and many more useful features that will enrich your life. It also connects you with people around the world, so you can converse on just about any topic or follow trails of public messages about shared interests, hobbies, or perhaps, favorite authors or movie actors. It even lets you participate, or simply eavesdrop on, live discussions called chats, where the participants' typed comments are delivered live to everyone else in the group. If you'd rather gather free software or get technical support on your latest computer gadget, dozens of bulletin boards are filled with helpful suggestions and useful files from other members and from the companies that have manufactured your hardware and software. You might even find a technical support engineer waiting to answer your questions live.

Designed from the start to be used with Windows, The Microsoft Network takes advantage of many of the great new features in Windows 95, so it acts just like the

The Microsoft Network works just like everything else in Windows 95, so it's logical and easy to use.

31

applications that you have already in your computer. If you know how to use Windows 95, you'll find using The Microsoft Network easy. If you're new to Windows, it can be a great place to learn all about using Windows effectively.

Is it the Internet?

Surely, you have heard about the Internet, the global web of interconnected academic, government, and commercial computer networks. The Internet started as a Department of Defense project, and became all the rage in 1991, when it was first opened to the public.

The Microsoft Network is the newest online service. It offers the best features of other services that have been available since the early 1980s.

SCENIC OVERLOOK

A Brief History of Online Services

During the early 1980s, a few firms who provided business computer services to companies by day, and personal computer services to people after hours, offered memberships and local phone numbers to anyone interested in paying to connect by computer modem. Members could scan the service for news and weather, send and retrieve files, and engage in typed "conversations" with other members, albeit slowly and clumsily. These services, *CompuServe*, *The Source*, *Genie*, and *Delphi*, recruited thousands of subscribers who sought a new way to connect to other people and exchange information, ideas, and even, in a few cases, wedding vows. To use any of these services, however, you had to memorize dozens of cryptic keyboard commands or select options from one menu after the next.

Services such as *Prodigy* and *America Online* designed their systems so people could use Windows-like software and a mouse. This big improvement in ease of use, plus a stunning drop in the price of a modem, encouraged millions of new subscribers to join the electronic community. Now, virtually all online services offer graphical software that can help people use their systems more effectively. More than 6,000,000 people are members of an online service, and thousands more join every day.

Where is The Microsoft Network?

One end of The Microsoft Network is you, your computer, and the software for The Microsoft Network that comes with Windows 95—the "client." The other end of the network is in Washington state, in a building near Microsoft's main headquarters. At this site, dozens of extra-powerful PCs act together as a huge "server," pumping information to all "clients" connected to MSN. In between the client and the server is a complex web of high-speed, dedicated telephone lines that spans the world. This web breaks signals into small information packets and sends the packets through any available pathway through the network. The other end of the network reassembles the packets into a continuous data stream. If any packet gets damaged along the route, a replacement is automatically requested and sent, so the information passes through the network successfully regardless of the condition of any particular pathway.

In technical terms, The Microsoft Network is true client-server software optimized to work over communications lines.

The Microsoft Network is not the same as the Internet, but it can be your gateway to the Internet. MSN is a separate network with connections in dozens of countries. It has its own databases of information, conversations, files, and mail system that are separate from anything on the Internet. But MSN is also connected to the Internet, so you can use many Internet services, such as Internet mail, the Usenet Newsgroups, the World Wide Web, and other features, such as FTP, which are covered in detail in Chapter 7, "Globe Trotting: Traveling the Internet."

Installing The Microsoft Network

Before you sign in for the first time, the software for The Microsoft Network must be installed and a modem must be connected to your machine. To check whether the software is

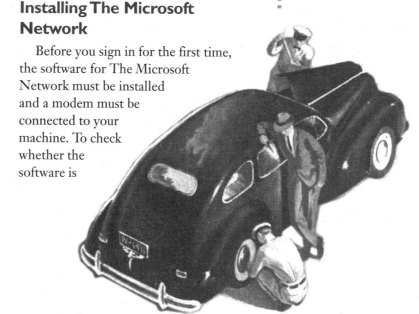

The easiest way to install The Microsoft Network is to perform a "Custom" installation when you set up Windows and choose The Microsoft Network as a component that you want installed.

already installed, look for an icon labeled "The Microsoft Network" on your Windows desktop. If this icon is not present, you'll need to follow the directions in the next section, *Adding The Microsoft Network to the Desktop*. If the icon is there, you can skip ahead to the section *Signing Up for The Microsoft Network*. If you need more information on modems or aren't sure you have one installed, refer instead to Modem Speeds, Settings, and Setup.

Adding The Microsoft Network to the Desktop

To get The Microsoft Network software ready for use, you must add it to the current Windows installation and set up Microsoft Exchange so Exchange can send electronic mail (e-mail) via the Network.

Just so you know, when you install The Microsoft Network software, you must also install Microsoft Exchange, the special program within Windows that handles your electronic mail tasks. It's represented by an "Inbox" icon on the desktop. With Exchange, you can

compose and send new e-mail, maintain an address book of favorite correspondents, and read incoming messages before filing them in folders.

To add software for The Microsoft Network, follow this procedure:

● **Adding the Software for The Microsoft Network**
 1. Double-click the My Computer icon on the desktop.

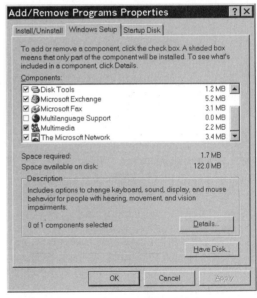

Click the box next to The Microsoft Network.

2. In the My Computer window, double-click the Control Panel icon.

3. In the Control Panel window, double-click the Add/Remove Programs icon.

4. In the new window that opens, click the Windows Setup tab. You'll see a list of components you can install or remove.

5. Check that Microsoft Exchange has a check in the box next to it. If not, click the box to install Exchange.

6. Scroll down the list and click the box next to The Microsoft Network Online Service.

7. Click OK at the bottom of the window.

The Windows Setup program will guide you through the steps necessary to install The Microsoft Network software and Exchange, including restarting the machine when necessary. After Windows restarts, you will need to sign up for The Microsoft Network.

Signing Up for The Microsoft Network

After the software is installed, you follow a simple sign-up procedure to get The MSN icon on your Windows desktop. The presence of the icon tells you that the Network is ready to use.

To begin the sign-up procedure, follow these steps:

● **Starting The Microsoft Network Sign Up**

1. Click Start on the Taskbar.

2. On the Start Menu, choose Programs.

3. On the Programs menu, choose The Microsoft Network.

Follow the instructions on the screen for the next several steps. These call MSN and get the newest local access telephone numbers. During this procedure, you'll also be asked for your name and address, and other pertinent information, including billing information and a

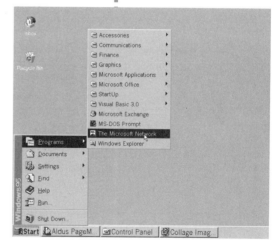

Click The Microsoft Network on the Programs menu.

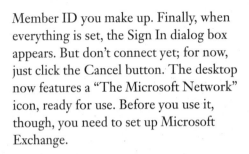

You may want to add The Microsoft Network to your existing profile if you use Exchange to send and receive e-mail on an office network.

Member ID you make up. Finally, when everything is set, the Sign In dialog box appears. But don't connect yet; for now, just click the Cancel button. The desktop now features a "The Microsoft Network" icon, ready for use. Before you use it, though, you need to set up Microsoft Exchange.

Setting Up Microsoft Exchange

Another important preparation before you connect for the first time is to make sure Microsoft Exchange is properly configured so Exchange can send electronic mail (e-mail) via The Microsoft Network.

- If The Microsoft Network is the first service you will use to send or receive e-mail, you can skip ahead to the section *Getting Ready to Sign In*. Microsoft Exchange is set up automatically for use with MSN.
- If you already send or receive e-mail or faxes through another service, such as Microsoft Mail on your local area network, or through CompuServe, Exchange is already working. But you'll need to make sure that a special profile for The Microsoft Network has been added to Exchange.

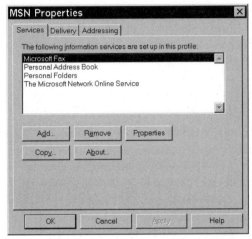

The Properties dialog box for a profile.

A *profile* is a set of directions that tells Exchange which electronic mail services to use and how to use them. The best way to understand profiles is to look at the list of profiles for Exchange that are already installed. To do so, follow these steps:

● *Examining the Microsoft Exchange Profiles*

1. On the Windows desktop, double-click the My Computer icon.
2. In the My Computer window, double-click the Control Panel icon.
3. In the Control Panel window, double-click the Mail and Fax icon.
4. On the Properties dialog box, click Show Profiles.

In the Microsoft Exchange Profiles dialog box, you will now see at least one profile, The Microsoft Network Online Service. You may also see others, such as "MS Exchange Settings." If the Microsoft Network profile is the only profile on the list, you're all set. If you also see a profile called "MS Exchange settings," this profile may already contain the settings for all the other services you use— for example, Microsoft Mail, Microsoft At Work Fax, the Personal Address Book, and the Personal Folders—so you may want to add The Microsoft Network to this profile.

You can either leave MSN in its own profile, in which it will be the only service, or you can add MSN to the services of an existing profile. If you use other services, your best bet is to add MSN to an existing profile. That way, you will not need to switch to the profile for The Microsoft Network each time you want to use MSN e-mail. The only advantage to leaving The Microsoft Network in its own profile is that it lets you store incoming and outgoing mail messages from MSN in a different mail storage file, separate from the e-mail and faxes you send and receive via other services.

To check which services are installed in another profile (for example, MS Exchange Settings), click the profile's name on the General tab of the Profiles dialog box and then click Properties.

In the new Properties window, you will see a list of the installed services. To add The Microsoft Network, follow these steps:

• Adding The Microsoft Network to an Existing Profile

1. In the Properties window for a profile, click Add.
2. In the Add Service to Profile dialog box, scroll down the list of services and then double-click The Microsoft Network Online Service.

You can also use the Properties dialog box to verify or change the settings on the Delivery and Addressing tabs. The Delivery tab contains two options: one to designate where incoming messages will be stored in your system, and one to establish the services Exchange will use when sending outgoing messages. If you want outgoing items sent to others on your local area network with Microsoft Mail rather than MSN e-mail, you might want to move Microsoft Mail to the top of the list of

Profiles are a little confusing only if you are adding The Microsoft Network after you have been using another e-mail program in Windows 95.

37

Modem stands for Modulation/Demodulation, the process of sending and retrieving digital data on lines that typically transmit only analog information like sound.

e-mail services. If the person to whom you have addressed a message is not available on Microsoft Mail, only then would the message be sent through The Microsoft Network. After all, if the recipient is on your local area network, you do not need the additional expense of sending the message through The Microsoft Network. You can prioritize services by clicking any service and then clicking the up or down arrow buttons.

On the Addressing tab, you can select which address book your system will consult first when you need someone's e-mail address. You may have separate address books for mail on your company's network, mail on the CompuServe information service, and mail on The Microsoft Network. You can also determine which address books the Network will use when it automatically double-checks the addresses on outgoing messages. For the first of these two settings, you'll probably want to choose Personal Address Book. Make sure it is also at the top of the list for the third setting. Now you can click

OK to return to the list of profiles, and click Close to close the dialog box. You can also close the Control Panel and My Computer windows.

Modem Speeds, Settings, and Setup

If you already know all about modems, and you've been using a modem with another Windows program, you can skip this section. If your modem is already working

Internal modem.

with Windows, then it's all set up for The Microsoft Network, too.

What is a Modem?

A modem is a device that connects a computer to a phone line. It converts computer data to and from the kind of information you can send and receive over standard phone lines.

External modems sit on your desk with one cable

PC Card modem.

Those Mysterious Modem Lights

External modems with front panels provide beneficial little lights. As long as you understand these lights, external modems will keep you informed about the status of the connection.

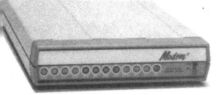

External modem.

MR: Modem Ready: Illuminates when the power is on and the modem is ready to do its thing. This light will come on after you turn on the modem.

HS: High Speed: Illuminates when the modem is working at its fastest possible speed. This light should always be on while you are connected; if it is not, you're not communicating with the Microsoft Network at the highest rate that your modem can achieve.

OH: Off Hook: Illuminates when the modem "picks up the phone" just as you'd lift the handset of a phone off its hook. This light should come on just before you hear the modem dialing.

CD: Carrier Detect: Illuminates when a connection is established. In some instances (when &C0 is part of the command that is sent to the modem when the modem is initialized), the Carrier Detect light may remain on at all times, whether you are connected or not.

TR: Terminal Ready: Illuminates when the PC has signaled to the modem that the PC is ready to send or receive data.

EC: Error Control: Illuminates when the modem's built-in error-checking is operational. Error-checking ensures accurate data over noisy phone lines.

TX or **SD:** Transmit or Send Data: Illuminates when the modem is actually sending or transmitting data.

RX or **RD:** Receive or Receive Data: Illuminates when the modem is actually receiving data.

AA: Auto Answer: Illuminates when the modem is set to answer calls automatically. This light illuminates only when you use software that allows other people to dial in to your machine. While using The Microsoft Network, you will not see this light on because you are dialing out, not allowing others to dial in.

If you don't have a modem for your PC, buy at least a 14.4 kbps model. To prepare for the

very near future, you should purchase a 28.8 kbps modem if you can afford it.

running to the back of your PC and another cable running to a convenient phone jack. Internal modems, or those which reside inside the PC, make it appear that the cable is connected directly from the phone jack to the computer.

Fortunately, or unfortunately, depending on your view, there are many different kinds of modems from which to choose, so you'll have to decide whether to buy an internal or external modem. You'll also have to choose a modem with a certain speed from among a number of manufacturers and models. But don't worry; after you purchase and connect your modem, Windows will help you set up the modem properly.

Shopping for a Modem

Without a doubt, modem shopping may be the most confusing part of getting ready to use The Microsoft Network. A modem's speed is its most important attribute. Modems transmit data at different speeds, typically at 2400, 9600, 14,400, or 28,800 bits per second. The higher the number, the faster the modem. It's easy to find both 14,400 and 28,800 bps modems (also called 14.4 or 28.8 baud modems).

As always with computer equipment, computer experts recommend that you buy the fastest you can afford. A 14,400 bps modem is fine for use with The Microsoft Network, but, if you can afford it, consider a 28.8 kbps modem (up to twice as fast) so you'll be prepared for the day soon when The Microsoft Network is available at that ultra high speed.

One caveat about 28.8 modems, though: 28,800 bps is considered to be about as fast as you can pump data through a standard phone line *when the phone line is strong and clear*. If your phone line is faint or noisy, the modem may drop back to a lower speed to ensure a reliable connection. If you do choose a 28.8 modem, make sure it's a V.34 class model (say: "V dot 34") so you can be sure the modem will be able to connect at full speed. The box, modem, or literature should say V.34 prominently. Similarly, if you buy a 14.4 kbps modem, make sure it is a V.32bis ("V dot 32 biss") model.

The price of a modem also depends on whether the modem is internal, external, or

The Microsoft Network provides access to most of the Internet's best features, including the World Wide Web.

on a PC card. Internal modems, or special-ized circuit boards fitting into a slot inside the computer, are the cheapest. An external modem, an appliance that sits on your desk, has a case and control panel so it is a little more expensive. PC card modems, or credit card-sized modems that fit into a card slot on a laptop, are the most expensive due to their miniaturization.

"PC card" is the new name for PCMCIA cards, so you may find them still advertised as PCMCIA.

There are some considerations other than price in your decision to choose either an internal or external modem. External modems usually feature a front panel with lights that tell you whether the modem is

Turning a Modem into a Speed-Dialing Demon

You've heard the leisurely pace at which your modem dials the phone. How would you like to turn your modem into a speed-dialing demon? It's easy. Simply follow these steps: While set-ting the properties of your modem, click the Advanced button on the Connection tab in the Proper-ties dialog box. In the Advanced Connection Settings dialog box, you'll see a text box labeled Extra settings. In this box, type S11=50. (That's s, eleven, equals, 50.) Then click OK to return to the Properties dialog box, and click OK or Cancel until you've closed all the dialog boxes. For most modems, the S11 setting changes the length and spacing of the touch tones during dialing.

Now sign in to the Network. If your phone system won't establish a connection at this higher dialing speed, try increasing the S11 setting gradually, in increments of five, until it works. Not every modem allows this alteration. If the dialing speed does not seem to change no matter what you do, check your modem's manual to see if there's another setting to alter the duration and spacing of your modem's touch tones.

Advanced Connection Settings `? X`

☑ Use error control
  ☐ Required to connect
  ☑ Compress data
  ☐ Use cellular protocol

☑ Use flow control
  ◉ Hardware (RTS/CTS)
  ○ Software (XON/XOFF)

Modulation type

Extra settings
S11=50

☐ Record a log file

OK   Cancel

sending or receiving data, or is in a high-speed connection. External modems are also easily transported from one computer to another. Also, in dire circumstances, when you want to terminate a connection, you can simply flip the power switch on an external modem. Internal modems often require you to reboot a computer to reset a modem. Connecting an external modem is also easy; you just plug the modem cable into a serial port at the back of the computer. To install an internal modem, you must remove the case of your PC and, sometimes, adjust little jumpers or flip tiny switches on the circuit card so the modem won't conflict with other devices installed in the computer.

Internal modems do not clutter your desk, and are always on when the PC is turned on. Internal modems travel with the computer and offer convenience, especially if the computer is a portable. Laptops are best served by conveniently small PC card modems that slip into a credit card-sized slot. (When you have to carry something around, the lighter the better.) PC card

modems are available in the full range of speeds, and some models even have little pop-out phone jacks so you can plug the phone cord right into them.

Setting Up a Modem in Windows

Fortunately, The Microsoft Windows program does everything it can to set up a modem automatically, including recognizing the brand and type, and configuring itself to make best use of the modem. You need only install the modem, and start the modem configuration program.

After you've unpacked a new modem, follow the manufacturer's instructions for connecting the modem to your PC. If the modem is external, you'll need to connect a PC-to-modem serial cable from a serial port on the PC to the serial port on the modem.

A serial port, often handily labeled "Com" or "Serial," is always a male connection that has nine or 25 pins protruding. If your PC has two or more serial ports, simply plug the cable into any unused serial port. After you plug the other end of the cable into the modem, make sure you've

9-pin serial port.

25-pin serial port.

If a modem is connected to your PC when you install Windows 95, the setup program will recognize and install the modem automatically.

42

also connected a phone cord from a wall jack to the modem's *line* jack. If you also want to use a standard phone on the same line, you can connect a phone to the modem's *phone* jack with a separate cord.

Next, with the modem plugged in and turned on, follow these steps:

● *Installing a Modem*

1. Double-click the My Computer icon on the desktop.
2. In the My Computer window, double-click the Control Panel icon.

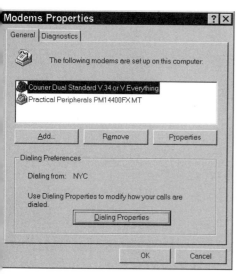

The Modems Properties dialog box.

3. In the Control Panel window, double-click the Modems icon. The Modems Properties dialog box will open, displaying a list of modems already installed.
4. In the Modems Properties dialog box, click the Add button.
5. In the Install New Modem window, make sure the Don't Detect My Modem box is cleared so Windows will attempt to find and configure your new modem automatically.
6. Click the Next button, and watch as Windows finds and queries your modem to determine its type and capabilities.
7. Click the Next button, and then click Finish on the final dialog box.

To confirm your new modem's proper setup, you can click the Diagnostics tab in the Modem Properties window. You should

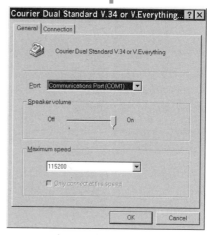

The General tab of the Modems Properties dialog box.

The default settings on the tabs of the Properties dialog box are usually the best settings for day-to-day use of your modem.

43

The Connection tab.

see that your modem is connected to the serial port.

About Modem Properties

When you add a new modem, Windows chooses the best settings it can for the modem's properties. Even if you would rather not fuss with these settings, you might still want to examine them in case there's anything obvious that should be changed. For instance, you can adjust the modem's speaker volume.

To see the properties for a modem, select the modem on the list of modems in the Modem Properties dialog box (you get to this dialog box by clicking the Modems icon in the Control Panel), and then click the Properties button. A Properties dialog box opens.

On the General tab for your modem, you can usually set the volume of the modem speaker and the maximum speed of the modem. This maximum speed is often greater than the modem's speed. The maximum speed of a 9600 baud modem might be set to 19,200, for example. The maximum speed of a 14.4 modem might be as high as

38,400. By compressing the data it sends, your modem may achieve rates of transmission higher than its rated speed.

On the Connection tab, you can change the modem's data bits, parity, and stop bits. To connect to The Microsoft Network, leave these set to eight data bits, no parity (none), and one stop bit. The three Call Preferences settings further refine how your modem interacts with the outside world. You might want to activate the setting labeled "Disconnect a call if idle for more than x minutes" in case you wander away from the PC and forget that you're racking up online time charges because you're still connected to The Microsoft Network. After you examine the properties, click OK, and then click Close to shut the Modem Properties dialog box.

Getting Ready to Sign In

Now that the software is all installed and the modem is hooked up, you're ready to sign on. You've already connected with The Microsoft Network once during the installation process, but now you're ready to connect and start using the service.

Before you can connect, you need to make a few last-minute selections. You'll only have to do this once. The MSN

The Sign In dialog box.

software will remember your settings and use them again the next time.

Choosing an Access Number

The Microsoft Network has access telephone numbers all over the world so you don't have to make a long distance call to get online. Before you can sign on for the first time, you must pick the access number that would be best for you to use. This number should be closest to your location. If you use a portable computer at two or more locations, you can change the access number when you arrive at your new location.

To choose an access number, follow these steps:

● *Selecting an Access Number*

1. Begin by double-clicking the icon for The Microsoft Network on the

windows desktop. When the Sign In dialog box opens, you'll see spaces for you to enter your Member ID and your password. You'll also see a Settings button that leads to the all-important Connection Settings dialog box.

2. Click the Settings button.
3. On the Connection Settings dialog box, click the Access Numbers button. A dialog box with a primary and backup number appears.
4. Click the Change button next to the Primary number.
5. In the next dialog box, choose your country and state or region from each drop-down list of alternatives.

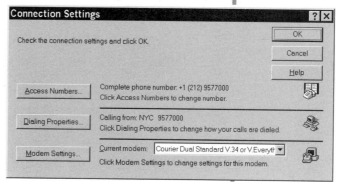

Connection Settings dialog box.

When you choose different options for the primary and secondary access numbers, MSN will try both numbers alternately until it connects.

45

The Dialing Options make it easy to dial out from a hotel or place a credit card call when you are traveling.

You may need to scroll down the list by using the small, vertical scroll bar along the right side of the list.

6. A list of local access points for the country, state, or region chosen in Step 4 appears in the third area of the same dialog box, the Access Numbers list. Choose the location nearest to you that has the highest speed your modem can handle. If you live in an area whose closest number provides a lesser speed, you'll have to decide whether to make local calls at the lower speed or make long distance calls to run at full speed.

7. After you choose a primary number, you can choose a backup number, another to dial if the first number is busy by clicking its Change button. (If the second number is also busy, MSN keeps alternating between the primary and secondary numbers until you get through.) The backup number is usually the second closest number or a local number that provides a slower speed. If your location offers only one good access number, use it for the secondary number also. MSN will keep trying until it gets through.

8. After you've chosen both numbers, click OK to return to the Connection Settings dialog box.

travel tip

New Access Numbers

As time goes by, more and more locations will offer the full range of popular modem speeds and more locations will have local access numbers, so you'll want to revisit the access number list periodically to see if a faster alternative has appeared.

Choosing Other Dialing Options

Before connecting for the first time, you'll want to visit the Dialing Properties dialog box, too. This dialog box offers settings you can use to specify your current location, and settings that specify any special dialing procedures that MSN should follow, such as dialing 9 to get an outside line before dialing the access number.

More than likely, the Dialing Properties dialog box already contains your area code and country near the top. If it doesn't, go ahead and enter them to create the settings for your Default Location.

Next, take a look at the four "How I dial from this location" options. If any of them apply to you, take a moment and enter the proper instructions. For example, if you cal from an office telephone, you may need to enter 9 to access an outside line. If you do not have a touch tone telephone, you must choose Pulse dialing rather than Tone dialing.

Finally, click the "Dial as a long distance call" checkbox at the bottom of the Dialing Properties dialog box only if you want a number dialed as long distance (a "1" will be dialed before the number) even if the number is not in a different area code.

If you travel to other locations regularly, such as a branch office or weekend location, you may want to create alternate locations that you can easily choose by entering the area code and country, and then clicking the New button next to the "I am calling from" text box. In the small Create New Location dialog box, enter a name for the location, and then click OK. Now, when you change locations, you can select the location from the drop-down list. All of the settings for that location will go into effect.

Finally, before leaving the Connection Settings dialog box, check the Current modem setting. If you have two modems, make sure the modem you want to use is selected.

Now, click OK to put all your changes into effect and then return to the Sign In dialog box.

The Sign In dialog box.

Using Remember My Password is a great convenience, but it also means that anyone who uses your computer can sign in as you.

Dialing Properties dialog box.

Recording Your Member ID and Password

In the Member ID blank, type the member name you chose when you signed up for The Microsoft Network. Next, in the Password blank, enter the password you selected.

To set MSN so you won't need to enter a password each time you sign in, click the Remember my Password checkbox on the Sign In dialog box. But beware that when this checkbox is checked, anyone who can get to this Sign In dialog box on your computer can sign in as you. If you leave the Remember My Password checkbox blank, you must enter your password each time, so only those who know the pass-word will be able to sign in with your account. Because it's easy to purchase items and ring up online charges that will be applied to your account, you may want to think twice before letting others, even family members, use your account.

Making the Connection

Once everything is correct, simply click the Connect button on the Sign In window. The MSN software will dial The Microsoft Network, verify your account, and then sign you in. You will first see the MSN Central window appear. Then, you may see the MSN Today window on top. Whether MSN Today opens each time you sign in depends on a setting you can change.

MSN will disconnect only after asking if you really want to leave.

Hold All Calls: Disabling Call Waiting

If your phone line has Call Waiting and a call comes in when you're signed in, your connection to MSN may be broken unless you disable call waiting. Most local phone companies offer a special code you can dial before placing a call to disable Call Waiting for the duration of the connection.

The MSN software can enter this code for you before it places each call to MSN. In the Dialing Properties dialog box, click the checkbox next to "This location has call waiting." Then enter the code to disable call waiting into the blank at the end of the line. You may also find the code on the drop-down list when you click the down-arrow button next to the blank.

Setting an Automatic Disconnect Interval

After a certain period of inactivity, MSN will automatically disconnect so you do not inadvertently remain online for long periods when you thought you'd disconnected, or when you are called away from the computer unexpectedly. This feature is especially helpful because MSN may be carrying out a task (such as downloading a file) in the background while you work on other projects. It's easy to forget that you're connected when you become absorbed by something else on the screen.

To set an automatic disconnect interval, choose Options from any MSN View menu after you are connected. On the General tab of the Options dialog box, you can change the number of minutes of inactivity to use as a limit before the software signs you off.

On the same dialog box, you also see an option for displaying MSN Today when you first connect ("startup"). Clear this checkbox if you want to go straight to a site on MSN without waiting for MSN Today to appear. Click OK when you finish with the Options dialog box.

Signing Out

Second in importance to knowing how to sign in is knowing how to sign out. After you finish a session on MSN, click the Sign Out button on the toolbar, or choose Sign out from the File menu. You must confirm that you really want to sign out by clicking Yes on the next dialog box.

Another way to sign out is to double-click the MSN icon on the Taskbar.

Next Stop

You've waited long enough. It's time to sign in and begin your explorations of The Microsoft Network. In the next chapter, you'll learn to navigate through MSN, travel its byways, find the features and services that await you, and make your way back home. You'll also learn how to get the best views of the many attractions you'll find, and how to earmark your favorite places as shortcuts, so you can always return to them quickly and easily.

You can also tell The Microsoft Network that you want to sign out by double-clicking the MSN icon on the Taskbar.

Chapter Three

On The Road

Navigating Through MSN

- *MSN Central*
- *Getting a Scenic View*
- *Earmarking Favorite Places*
- *The Power of Shortcuts*
- *Using Go Words*
- *Exploring MSN with the Explorer*
- *Finding Forums and Services*

2198 M

y 1205 M

URG 1902 M

N 2678 M

1138 M

Navigating Through MSN

After every travel adventure, it is always good to get home. The Microsoft Network's version of a safe haven is MSN Central. Each foray into the forums and services of MSN begins at MSN Central.

Home Sweet Home

MSN Central welcomes you to The Microsoft Network by displaying a large window which lists each of the main areas and services on the system.

MSN Today is a daily news magazine about the forums and services on MSN.

E-Mail is your gateway to Microsoft Exchange, the program that handles all your electronic correspondence. Exchange handles the e-mail to and from other MSN members, other people on your office network, and addresses on the Internet.

The other three buttons initiate your travels to the fun and fascinating gathering places—forums—where you and other visitors to The Microsoft Network can share files, have on-line "chats," participate in ongoing discussions, read articles, play games, and even shop.

Categories shows you the communities, libraries, conference rooms, and recreation centers you will find on The Microsoft Network. You begin exploring MSN by peering inside the "folders" you find there.

Member Assistance leads you to the people who can help you if you have problems using MSN. It also offers you information about managing your account.

Favorite Places lets you create "shortcuts" to the places you most like to visit. This is your personalized itinerary, and you can add to it anytime you like.

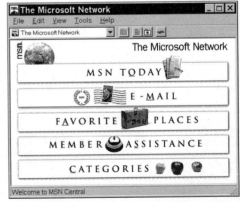

MSN Central is your starting point.

Navigating at a Glance

What The information and services on The Microsoft Network are organized in folders. To get around on MSN, you must know how to find folders, open folders, jump quickly to folders, and return to previous folders.

Where Icons for folders and services are located in every nook and cranny of MSN.

How MSN folders and services are represented by icons. Open a folder by double-clicking its icon. Inside, you will find still more folder icons or icons for services.

Why To get there, of course.

MSN users in Australia, the U.K., Germany, and France will see their own versions of the MSN Central and Categories windows.

Leaving Home

The Microsoft Network contains so many alluring spots that it's easy to get lost without a map. Luckily, the entire network is organized into groups of specially marked places called folders. Once you know how to navigate through folders, you can get anywhere on The Microsoft Network.

MSN's main folders are called categories. To get to MSN's categories, click the Categories button on MSN Central. When the Categories window opens, each category is represented by a picture, or icon, on a folder. You can open any folder by double-clicking it. If you see a list or little folders without icons, choose Large Icons from the View menu. Later in this chapter, you will learn all about views and how to switch among them.

Each category folder contains a collection of folders. For example, the category "Arts and Entertainment" contains separate folders for music, theater, and so on. If you open the music folder, you will find inside more folders for different kinds of music.

The Categories window.

During development, MSN Central was called "Home Base," so the MSN Central icon still looks like a little house.

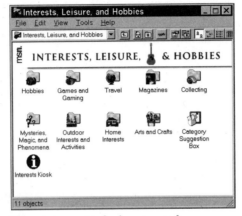

The Interests, Leisure, and Hobbies folder.

These folders contain the chats, BBSes, and other places you can visit. Above the folders, MSN displays a banner that tells you the name of the folder, forum, or service that you have open.

Finding Your Way Back Home

After you've gotten lost down one of MSN's many side roads, you may want to return to one of the folders you opened along the way. To retrace your steps, use the "Go to a different folder" list. To pull down this list, click the current folder name on the toolbar or click the down-

TRAVELERS FIRST AID

Help! *MSN Today* Covers MSN Central!

The *MSN Today* window may open every time you get connected. Until you close *MSN Today* by clicking its Close button, it may obscure a good part of the MSN Central window. To avoid this problem, you can change a setting so *MSN Today* will not open every time you are connected.

To change this setting, connect to MSN and then choose Options from the Tools menu. On the Options dialog box, clear the check box next to "Show *MSN Today* title on startup."

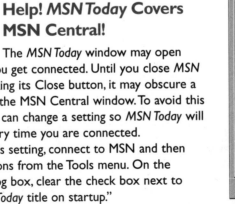

The Options dialog box.

The "Go to a different folder" list.

Click here to pull down the list.

The Toolbar

arrow button just to the right of the list. (If you do not see the toolbar, remember to choose Toolbar from the View menu.)

The "Go to a different folder" list shows the currently open folder and other folders that are open above the

currently open folder.Click a folder on the list, and there you are again. At the top of the list, an icon labeled "The Microsoft Network" represents MSN Central. To jump right back to where you started, click this icon. Another way

Making Windows Work

As you learn your way around MSN, you may find it helpful to see both the toolbar and the status bar. The toolbar runs across the top of each window and displays buttons to access special functions. For example, one button will back you up to the previous folder. By placing the mouse pointer on a button without clicking, you can trigger a yellow tool tip that pops up to show the button's purpose.

The status bar runs along the bottom of each window and tells your location and the contents of the current window.

Toolbar —

Tool tip —

Large icons —

Status bar —

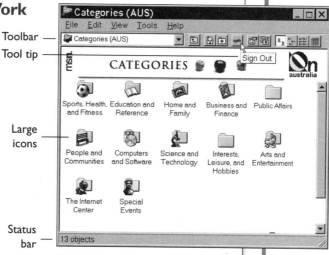

Parts of the MSN window.

As you move from place to place within MSN, you may find it most comfortable to use a combination of mouse clicks and keyboard navigation techniques.

 to teleport yourself back "home" is to click the MSN Central button on the toolbar.

travel tip

Up One Level Button

 A faster way to return to a folder you visited previously is to click the "Up One Level" button on the toolbar. You can also choose "Up One Level" from the File menu.

Using the Keyboard to Move Through the Folders

Rather than double-click icons with the mouse, you can navigate MSN with the keyboard. By pressing the arrow keys, you can highlight any folder icon. To open the folder, you press Enter. If you do not see the highlight when you first open a folder, press an arrow key. To return to the previous folder, press the Backspace key.

Managing Windows

By now, you may have open windows all over the place. Some will overlap or obscure others. To better assess your location, you will want to clean up your display.

MSN displays windows two ways: It can display the contents of each folder you open in a separate window. MSN can also display a single window that keeps changing as you open each folder.

As usual, there are tradeoffs to both approaches. You can visit several forums or services simultaneously by opening each folder in its own window. You can easily switch among the windows, arrange them side-by-side, copy and paste information from one window to the other, and so on. However, some travelers may find that opening many simultaneous windows is as confusing as trying to concentrate on several things at once.

Travel Delays

Because each icon must be sent from The Microsoft Network to your hard disk the very first time you open a folder, the icons take a little while to appear. The next time you open the same folder, the MSN software can get the icons from your own hard disk rather than from The Microsoft Network, so they appear almost immediately.

Carrying out all your excursions through MSN within the same window allows for a much simpler screen. If you really want to investigate a different area of MSN without leaving the current forum, you can open a second window by clicking the MSN Central icon in the toolbar. You can also use your right mouse button to click the MSN icon in the Taskbar, then select View MSN Central on the shortcut menu. MSN Central will appear in a second window. In this window, you can visit another area on MSN and your travels will not affect the contents of the first window.

To change your viewing options, follow this procedure:

Choosing to View MSN with a Single Window or Multiple Windows

1. From the View menu, choose Options.
2. Click the Folder tab in the Options dialog box.
3. On the Folder tab, choose one of the two "Browsing" options: "Display each folder in its window" or "Use a single window which keeps changing as you open each folder."
4. Click OK.

Help! I've Fallen Off MSN and I Can't Get Back!

It's the number one MSN travel blooper! You close a window and suddenly MSN asks whether you want to log off. Just say No, and then either double-click the MSN icon or right-click the MSN icon in the taskbar and choose Go to MSN Central.

Getting a Scenic View

Once you leave MSN Central, you can choose from any of four views for looking at the folders and services on The Microsoft Network: Large Icons, Small Icons, List, and Details.

Your personal preference will decide the view you use primarily, but you can switch among views as you work on MSN. For example, switching from Large Icons view to Details view lets you view the contents of a folder sorted alphabetically. It also lets you easily see which folders are forums and which are BBSes.

Using a single window to navigate through MSN rather than another window for each folder you open conserves all-important memory and system resources.

Changing Views

The easiest way to change views is to click one of the four view buttons in the toolbar. You can also choose from the four view commands that are listed on the View menu in any window.

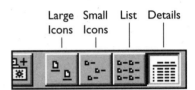

Large Icons | Small Icons | List | Details

The View buttons on the toolbar.

Large Icons view

Folders are large so the images on them are easily seen.

Small Icons view

Folders are small so you can fit more of them on the screen.

List view

Folders are listed in columns and sorted alphabetically.

Details view

Details about folders display in columns. You can sort the folders by the entries in any column.

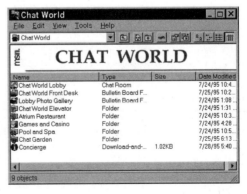

58

travel tip

Sorting Items in Details View

When you view folders in Details view, you see additional folder information arranged in columns. To sort the list in ascending order according to the columnar entries, click the button at the top of the column. For example, to sort the contents of a folder by type of service (BBSes, then Chats, then Download and Runs, then Forums, etc.) click the Type button at the top of the Type column.

Earmarking Favorite Places

As your forays into the folders of The Microsoft Network go deeper and deeper, you will happen upon sites and services intriguing enough to bring you back repeatedly. Fortunately, MSN makes it simple to collect all your favorite destinations in a folder called Favorite Places so you won't have to hunt through folders to find your way back to a site. When you connect to MSN, you can open the Favorite Places folder. Inside, you'll find all the icons you placed there as you found interesting folders, forums, or services on MSN. Simply double-click any of these icons to jump directly back to a site, even if it is deep within the folder-within-folder structure of MSN.

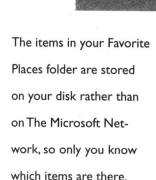

The items in your Favorite Places folder are stored on your disk rather than on The Microsoft Network, so only you know which items are there.

FIRST AID

Every Window I Open Looks Different!

Here's a helpful thought to keep in mind about views. When you browse folders by using a single window, MSN displays the contents of each folder using the same view. When you use a separate window for each new folder, each folder is displayed in the view you used when you last opened that folder. The system preserves the views you choose for particular folders.

A similar scheme holds true for the toolbars in windows. Whether a toolbar appears in a window depends on whether you had the toolbar turned on when you last opened that same folder. If you're using a single window to browse through MSN, the toolbar remains either on or off.

All you need to do while visiting a spot you would like to earmark is click the "Add to Favorite Places" button on the toolbar or choose Add to Favorite Places from the File menu. An icon for the service, called a *shortcut*, is copied to your own Favorite Places. The next time you'd like to return to a favorite destination, click Favorite Places on MSN Central, and then double-click the shortcut icon for the destination. Without any further fuss, you will be transported immediately back to the same site for another visit.

Because Favorite Places can be important to your MSN navigation, you can always get to it easily. Simply click the Favorite Places button on any toolbar or click the MSN icon on the Taskbar with the right mouse button and choose View Favorite Places from the shortcut menu.

If you decide to no longer keep a destination handy in your Favorite Places folder, simply open the folder, select the shortcut icon and then choose Delete from the File menu.

Pinpoint your favorite destinations on MSN by adding them to the Favorite Places folder.

Shortcuts to all your favorite places on MSN.

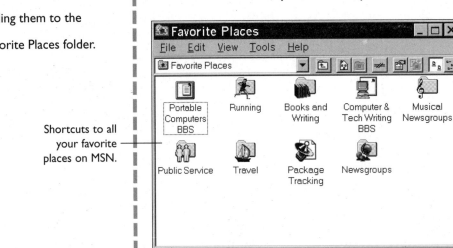

The Favorite Places folder.

The Power of Shortcuts

The icons in the Favorite Places folder are just one example of the value of shortcuts. Remember, when you are signed in and you add a site to Favorite Places, MSN places a shortcut for it in your Favorite Places folder. Then, any time you sign in, you can open the Favorite Places folder and take the shortcut.

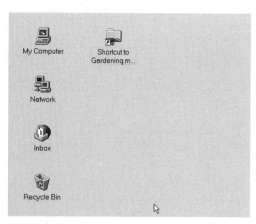

Shortcut to the Gardening forum on the desktop.

Here's something very special about shortcuts: Shortcuts work just as well when they're placed on the Windows desktop. In fact, they can lead you to a site on MSN *even if you're not signed in.* When you double-click a shortcut, no matter where it is, MSN will launch if necessary so you can sign in. Then the shortcut will jump you directly to an MSN forum or service. Shortcuts can also be stored in any folder on your system and embedded in files you have created—for instance, in documents you've typed in Microsoft Word. You simply drag them anywhere you want.

Shortcuts work from *anywhere* within Windows. By double-clicking an MSN shortcut you've placed on your Windows desktop, you can jump to folders and services on The Microsoft Network just as easily as you can jump to folders and files on your own system. MSN folders become just as accessible as the information stored in your own folders, so you're no longer limited to the finite information on your own disk.

Let's say you find some valuable information on MSN about gardening, your favorite pastime. Rather than copying information from the Gardening forum to your own hard disk, you create a shortcut to the Gardening forum.

Creating a shortcut is easy. In our example, you simply enter the Gardening forum and then choose Create Shortcut from the MSN File menu. MSN will place an icon on your Windows desktop indicating the shortcut back to the Gardening forum.

You can drag a shortcut from the Favorite Places folder onto the Windows desktop, into a document, or into an e-mail message.

You can now double-click the Gardening shortcut icon on your desktop or drag it to the folder on your hard disk where you store all your own files about gardening. When you need information about a particular aspect of gardening, you can open this folder and double-click an icon for one of your own files, or, if you do not already have the information you need, double-click the shortcut icon to the Gardening forum, instead. You will almost certainly find the information there.

Just as you can drag a shortcut from the desktop to a folder, you can also drag it to an e-mail message in Exchange or to a document you're creating in a word processor. Sending a shortcut icon in an e-mail message to someone else makes it just as easy for a friend to get to the same destination. When your friend gets your e-mail message, he or she can simply double-click the shortcut icon you've sent. Are you planning to attend the chat on gardening this evening? Send an invitation and the shortcut to a friend. At the appointed time,

Shortcut icons on the desktop are distinguishable from regular icons because they have a small, curved arrow at the lower left corner.

your friend can double-click the shortcut in the e-mail message to join you.

Using Go Words

Each folder, forum, and service on The Microsoft Network has an associated Go word. If you know a site's Go word, you can jump directly to it from anywhere on MSN. For example, the Go word for the chat in the Pets forum is "petschat." Of course, if you plan to visit a site regularly, you can add the site to your Favorite Places folder so returning to a site is a point-and-click affair.

Entering a Go Word

The fastest way to enter a Go word is to right-click the MSN icon on the Taskbar and then choose Go to from the shortcut menu. A small dialog box will open so you

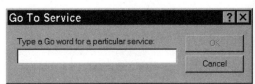

Go To Service dialog box.

can enter the Go word. Type in the Go word and then press Enter.

What's the Go Word?

To learn the Go word for a folder, forum, or service, you can check the site's Properties sheet: click its icon with the right-mouse button. The Go word appears on the first tab you see in the Properties window, the General tab.

The Microsoft Network Guide, at the back of this book, also lists the Go word for each forum on MSN.

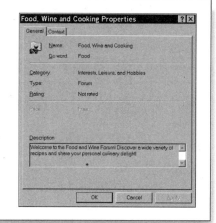

Another way to get to the Go To Service dialog box is to choose Go To from the Edit menu, and then select Other Location from the Go to submenu.

Exploring MSN with the Explorer

So far, you have seen one of the easiest and most direct ways to move from place to place within The Microsoft Network. However, you might find another approach even more helpful. Some people prefer this alternate route because it lets them better visualize the structure of The Microsoft Network. It's a little like taking the scenic drive, although it gets you to your destination just as quickly.

The Explorer, a special feature in Windows 95, provides a comprehensive view of your system and all its disks, folders and files. In one of its two panes, the Explorer shows the tree structure of folders on a disk. When you select one of these folders, the Explorer shows that folder's contents in the other pane.

With the Explorer, browsing through folders is quick and easy. The Microsoft Network is also organized in a

Viewing The Microsoft Network with the Explorer enables you to easily see the structure of folders within folders that makes up the system.

Explorer view of MSN

The Explorer's two panes display the folder list and the contents of the open folder that is open.

tree structure of folders, so you can use the Explorer as an easy way to navigate MSN, too. The Explorer presents you with an easy-to-follow view of the folders and forums of MSN, and it gives you a fast way to jump from place to place within MSN.

The Explorer shows the tree of sub-folders under a folder, and the contents of any one subfolder. If you are exploring MSN, the subfolders you see in the left pane are likely to be forums. The Explorer displays the services contained in each

forum (such as chats, bulletin boards, file libraries, and kiosks) in the right pane.

Viewing MSN with the Explorer can be accomplished three ways. To open MSN in the Explorer, follow any one of these steps:

● ***Opening MSN in the Explorer***
- With the right mouse button, click the MSN icon on the Windows desktop and select Explore from the shortcut menu, or
- As you double-click the MSN icon on the Windows desktop, press and hold the Shift key, or
- Click the Start button on the taskbar, select Programs from the Start menu, and then choose The Microsoft Network from the Pro-grams sub-menu.

When you connect to MSN with the Explorer, the system displays MSN Central in the right pane of the Explorer, and an outline structure of the folders on MSN within the left pane.

To see the contents of any folder that is in the left pane, click it once and the contents appears in the right pane. To see the subfolders in the left pane, double-click the original folder. Another way to display the subfolders is to click the small plus sign

open a chat, you must first click the forum folder which contains the chat in the left pane, and then double-click the chat icon in the right pane.

Finding Forums and Services

Once you are accustomed to the Explorer, you will come across attractions of every variety on MSN. Of course, you may prefer not to mount an expedition each time you go on-line. A special feature called "Find" can help you locate a site on MSN and then hop right to it.

Find operates under the assumption that you can describe what you are looking for in a word. Are you a fan of Betty Boop cartoons from the '40s? Then you can use Find to search for "animation" You love a Duke Ellington tune? Then use Find to search for "jazz." Find will quickly identify the forums that you might enjoy and show them on a list. You can explore these items one by one and keep coming back to the Find list for more.

After you start a search, and provide the find word, the system searches all of MSN for matches. It can even search the text of messages in bulletin boards and the descriptions of files in file libraries. It provides every refer-

Use Find to locate a forum or service by name or subject. Find is the same command you use to locate files or folders on your disks, or computers on your network.

next to the original folder. The plus sign turns into a minus sign to indicate that all the subfolders are now visible. To hide the subfolders, once again click this minus sign.

Eventually, as you open subfolders deeper within the MSN tree structure, you will get to a forum whose subfolders are actually services such as chats, bulletin boards, and file libraries. If you click the icon of a bulletin board or file library in the left pane, the contents of the bulletin board or file library actually displays in the right pane. Chats, which are services rather than folders, do not display in the left pane. To

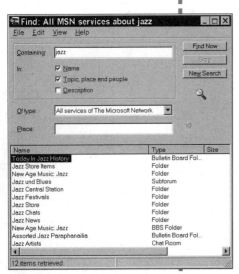

The Find dialog box.

ence to a topic, even if it is buried deep within one of the forums.

Looking for a Service

Using Find is meant to be very quick and easy. Without a lot of fuss, Find will take you to places that interest you. Find is equally helpful when you're not connected to The Microsoft Network. If you are not signed in, Find will establish a connection to MSN, and then carry out its search after you enter your usual sign in password.

As Find locates a service that matches your query, it adds the service to a list within the Find dialog box. To jump to that site directly, you simply double-click the item on the list. To start a search, follow these steps:

● **Starting a Search with Find**
1. Click the Start button on the taskbar.
2. From the Start menu, choose Find.
3. On the Find submenu, choose On The Microsoft Network. The Find: All MSN services dialog box opens.

In the Find: All MSN services dialog box, you will specify search terms. You can also refine your search to seek out services of a

certain type, such as Internet newsgroups or chat rooms. To specify search terms, follow these steps:

● **Specifying a Search**
1. In the Find dialog box, enter a search word in the Containing text box.
2. To search for a particular type of MSN service, click the down arrow button next to the pull-down list labeled "Of type," and then click a service type.
3. To search for a service that relates to a particular geographic location, enter the name of the location in the Place text box.
4. Click Find Now.

If Find cannot locate a service that matches your query, the system will display "0 items found" in the status bar at the bottom of the Find window. If a search comes up empty, click the New Search button to clear the current query and enter a different search word to match.

For example: Say you are interested in the nursing profession as a possible career and you would like to find everything on MSN about nursing. You'd like to find bulletin boards and file libraries that contain information about what it is like to be a nurse, and chats where you can ask health professionals for career advice.

To begin, select Find from the Start menu and then choose On The Microsoft Network from the Find submenu. In the Find dialog box, you enter "nurse, nursing" (without the quotation marks). This query searches for either "nurse" or "nursing."

When you click Find Now, the system will display a list of services related to nurse or nursing in the Find dialog box. Double-click any site that sounds interesting. To search only for chats on nursing, click the Of type list, then choose Chat rooms from the list before clicking Find Now.

travel tip

Investigating Found Items

If the list of found items contains several entries, you can leave the Find dialog box open, returning to it after investigating each entry.

More Complex Searches

Find allows you to be more specific or more broad in your search by entering a combination of search words. When you enter two or more words, such as "nutrition kids" (again, without the quotation marks), the Find command will locate only services that match both words. You would

uncover only services that are related to children's nutrition. Another way to specify the same query would be: "nutrition and kids."

Instead of using Find to locate services that contain only two or more words, you can use it to match any one of two or more words. In this way, you get a little margin of error.

If you enter several words, Find will locate something if it matches any one of the words. You simply enter two or more words separated by commas, such as "notebooks, laptops." You can also enter "notebooks or laptops." The Find command will locate all services that pertain to notebook *or* laptop computers.

To search by partial words, the system allows you to use wild cards in searches. In a wild card search, an asterisk stands for any combination of letters. For example, you can enter "garden*" to find all services that match gardening, gardeners, garden planning, garden information, and so on. A question mark stands for any single letter. You can enter "D?n" to find Dan, den, din, Don, or dun.

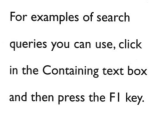

For examples of search queries you can use, click in the Containing text box and then press the F1 key.

Meeting the Locals

Participating in Chats

Participating in Chats

If you enjoy meeting people from all over the world, the gabfests in the The Microsoft Network chat rooms will be right up your alley.

A *chat* is a live conversation among MSN members. Of course, people don't actually "speak" during a chat; they type short comments and send them into the chat room, instead. The comments people send into the chat appear on the screens of all the participants, no matter where they are.

In the scheme of things, chats fall somewhere between party lines and conference calls. Most chats quickly become a jumble of simultaneous, interwoven conversations, but not every chat is so chaotic. Some chats are polite and orderly affairs, managed by a host who assigns some members roles as guests on a panel and designates everyone else—perhaps dozens or even hundreds of people—as listeners who follow along, but cannot

chime in. Chats can be purely social—like people sitting around shooting the breeze—or they can be serious conversations about topics like the war in Bosnia, or the cure for cancer or some topic of mutual concern to many people in different places.

So where do all these chats take place? Special sections of the network called chat rooms are located within just about every forum on MSN. Some chat rooms are like smoke-filled lounges, populated by weekend jocks arguing over the latest sports news. Others are intimate roundtables—

A chat is a live gabfest peopled by participants typing comments from all over the world.

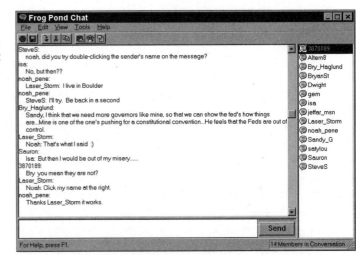

Chats let members type live messages.

Chats at a Glance

What   A chat is a live, typed conversation among two or more members of MSN from anywhere in the world. When you open a chat, the chat window shows the comments other participants have just typed. In a different area of the chat window, you can type comments that will be sent to everyone else's chat window.

Where   Chat rooms are located in most forums. Usually, you'll find the word "chat" in the names.

How   When you open a chat window, you'll find a list of members who are participating in the chat, an area that displays the comments other members have entered, and an area in which you can compose your own comments to send into the discussion.

Why   Chats give members the opportunity to communicate directly and instantaneously with other members all over the world.

Chats take place in chat rooms. You'll find a chat room in just about every forum on MSN. And you'll find many chat rooms in Chat World, one of the main categories on MSN.

small gatherings where participants compare notes about family life and share child-rearing stories. Still others are as peopled as convention halls, with participants engaged in heated political debates. In fact, there are dozens of chats taking place right now, and there are always chats in progress in Chat World so you can try one out right away. If you decide to stop in on a chat or two—and you can participate in several chats simultaneously—you might want to bring along some aspirin. Following a busy, fast-paced chat can require the concentration of an air traffic controller.

In this chapter, you'll learn how to enter a chat, find out who is participating, how to contribute comments of your own, and customize the chat window so it works just the way you would like. You'll also discover how to decipher some of the mysterious shorthand codes that you will no doubt come across the very first time you join one of MSN's many running chats.

Double-click any name

on the member list to

learn more about a

participant.

Joining a Chat

Just about every forum contains a chat icon. To open a chat window, you simply double-click the icon. A typical chat window, shown in the figure below, contains three panes. You read messages from chat participants in the *Chat History pane*. To determine who is present in the chat, you consult the *Member List pane*, a handy list of participants. In the *Compose pane*, you type

and refine your comments. Then you add them to the discussion by pressing Enter or clicking the Send button.

In a computer chat, it's perfectly OK to listen in without contributing, but you cannot eavesdrop on a conversation without the other people in the chat knowing it. Everyone in the chat can choose to be notified when someone new arrives. They can also be notified when you exit a chat, so it's just as hard to slip away without offering an excuse for leaving so soon.

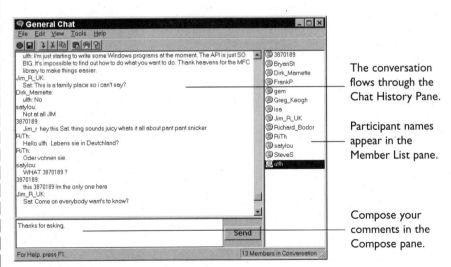

The conversation flows through the Chat History Pane.

Participant names appear in the Member List pane.

Compose your comments in the Compose pane.

A typical chat window.

Seeing Who's On

To learn more about any member of a chat, double-click a name in the Member List pane. The Member Properties window displays the autobiographical information entered into the Address Book. You can also click a name and then click the Member Properties button on the Toolbar.

Usually, everyone in a chat is a *participant*. A yellow chat bubble next to each name on the member list shows that they can freely add to the general chatter. Special icons may accompany some names, though, indicating these participants enjoy special rights.

 The gavel icon denotes a *host*, who mediates the discussion; each chat may have one or more hosts. Hosts can designate other members *spectators*, denoted by the glasses graphic, who can watch but not participate in the conversation.

If you've joined a chat expecting to participate and notice that you are a spectator who can't add to the conversation, don't be insulted. There is a good reason for this. Typically, everyone is a participant. But in some cases, like conferences with special guests, or panel discussions which may be popular, the host will relegate every member to roles as spectators, except for the special guests, who will become the only participants. *See Participating in Special Events, page xx.*

For a special event, such as an appearance by an invited guest, the host can change other participants to spectators who can listen in, but not contribute, to a discussion.

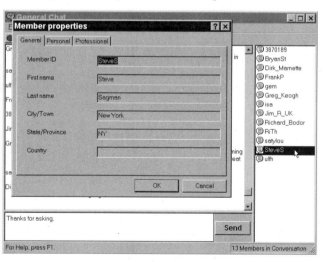

Double-click a name on the member list to see a participant's member properties.

Everyone in the chat room will see the text you send.

Chat World provides various chat rooms, and even one-on-one chats, for more intimate conversations.

SCENIC OVERLOOK

Anatomy of a Chat

These four snapshots of a chat in action show how a conversation builds as you and others contribute comments.

Chat participants.

The last line in the Chat History pane is the most recent arrival.

1. Chat is in progress.

You add comments into the Compose pane and then click Send.

2. You respond to a question.

Comments you add appear in the chat.

3. Your response appears in the chat...

Earlier comments flow out of the pane as new ones arrive.

4. ...where it is soon joined by comments from others.

Identifying Yourself in the Member Directory

MSN is one of the best and easiest ways to connect with other people who share the same views, interests, and hobbies. Modifying your Member Properties entry in the MSN Address Book gives you the chance to share personal information with others. You

might particularly want to include information about your special interests or pastimes. Others who share the same passions can find you by

Member Properties dialog box.

searching the Address Book. Who knows? You might even get invited to some swanky, on-line soiree.

To enter a personal profile, simply follow these steps:

● *Modifying Your Member Properties*
1. From Home Base, choose E-Mail.
2. In the Microsoft Exchange window, choose Address Book from the Tools menu.
3. In the Address Book window, choose Microsoft Network from the "Show Names from the" pull-down list.
4. Select your name from the list or type it into the Type Name text box that appears just above the list.
5. Double-click your name or click the Properties button in the toolbar.
6. On the General, Personal, and Professional tabs in the Properties window, enter or revise your personal information.
7. Click OK and then close the Addres Book window.

You can provide as much, or as little, information as you'd like for your member properties listing in the MSN Address Book.

Don't Believe Everything You Read

It would be nice to believe that everything people say about themselves is true. Unfortunately, you can't verify the accuracy of information in member profiles. People might, for whatever reason, adopt a different sex, age, or occupation. Brief exchanges in chat leave little opportunity to check this info. For your security, use the same common-sense precautions in computer chats that you'd use when entering into any discourse with a relative stranger.

Chat Etiquette

Over the years, on-line chatters have followed a few unwritten rules of etiquette. The rules guarantee a happy experience for everybody.

- Remember you are in an open forum. Don't lecture, advertise, or engage in an extended, private dialogue with only one other member of a chat.
- Be considerate. Don't insult others (this practice is called "flaming") for expressing dissimilar views.
- Don't type in all capital letters because IT LOOKS LIKE SHOUTING!

Contributing to a Chat

After you've gotten up the gumption to participate in a chat, go ahead and double-click the chat icon in any forum that interests you. When the chat window opens, the conversation appears line-by-line in the Chat History pane as people enter comments.

Sometimes, you may note that nothing appears in the Chat History pane. If you are the first to arrive, you can't have much of a conversation until someone else happens to drop by.

After following the flow of chatter for a moment or two, you will likely want to join the conversation. To add a comment,

Don't worry too much about typos and spelling. Everyone's forgiving of typing mistakes because they're all typing just as quickly.

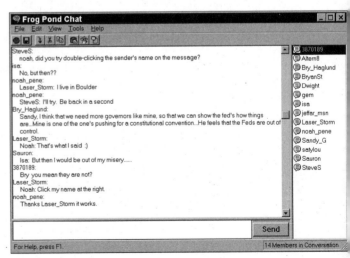

Chat window

simply type it into the Compose Pane next to the Send button. You can take your time to get it just right because your comment won't be sent until you press Enter or click the Send button. Don't wait too long, though, or the conversation "thread" might disappear. Errors in spelling and punctuation are easily forgiven in chat forums. Also, if you are responding to an individual, you will want to address your comment to that particular member by including that person's member name.

Example: BlueOx, is it cold in London today?

If you're totally stymied by what to say, you can always try: "Hello, folks!" Unless everyone is especially busy trying to keep up with a fast-moving conversation, someone will surely welcome you within a moment or two. Make sure your comment is really suitable for broadcast because when you press Enter or click Send, everything you have typed appears on the screens of all members in the chat. Also, keep in mind that anybody in the chat can save the *Chat History* and review it, print it, or send it to someone by e-mail, so your words can come back to haunt you!

If you're a loquacious sort, and you need to create a comment with several lines of information, just keep typing when the insertion point (the typing cursor) reaches the right side of the chat pane. The insertion point will automatically wrap to the next line. If you want to start a new line before you reach the right edge of the pane, don't press Enter. That sends out everything you've typed. Instead, to start a new line, press Ctrl+Enter. Pressing Ctrl+Tab will tab over to the right within a comment.

Scrolling Back Through a Chat

By using the scroll bar at the right edge of the Chat History pane, you can scroll back through the chat history. Reviewing the chat history can be helpful when you need a reminder about something that was said earlier. You can even select text in the chat history and copy it to the Compose pane to quote an earlier statement. You can return all the way to the first comment that appeared when you entered the chat room, though you can go no further. You'll never know what was said before you arrived, unless you ask. You don't get to see what is said about you after you leave, either.

The Chat History lets you review, save, or print a chat you've attended.

You can scroll back through a chat, but only to the point at which you entered the chat room.

After you've said your teary farewells, simply close a chat window to leave a chat.

Resizing the Panes in a Chat Window

To see more of a conversation, you might want to make the entire chat window taller or wider by dragging the outside borders of the chat window. You can also enlarge the size of the Chat History pane that is within the chat window by dragging the heavy, gray lines that separate the panes or by dragging the intersection of the three panes. When you change the size of the Chat History pane, the text will re-wrap within the newly enlarged pane.

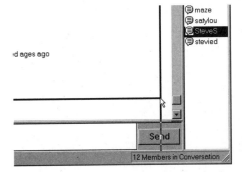

Resizing the panes in a chat window.

● *Quoting from the Chat History*
1. Scroll back to the text you want to copy.
2. Highlight the text.
3. Click the Copy button on the Toolbar.
4. Click in the Compose pane at the spot where you'd like to paste the copy.
5. Press Ctrl+V, or click the Paste button on the Toolbar.

You can also use this technique to save selected portions of a chat. You simply select them in the chat history, and then copy and paste them into a word processor such as WordPad. Then you can save the WordPad file.

Saving the Entire Chat History

Your on-line conversation might have been so lively and entertaining that you want to save the whole thing for posterity. To save the chat history to a text file on disk, choose Save History on the File menu. Then, in the Save As dialog box, change the destination for the file, if necessary, and enter a filename. Everything you've seen since entering the chat will be saved in a file. At any point, you can also clear your own chat history by choosing Clear History from the Edit menu.

Leaving a Chat

It's simple to leave a chat. When you've typed in your final good-byes and you have decided it's time to make your graceful exit, simply close the Chat window. Everyone participating in the chat will be informed that you've departed and the system will remove your name from every member's Member List pane.

Ignoring Someone

Occasionally, people participating in chats act up, speak rudely, or become just plain obnoxious. While you can't eject them from the chat room, you can ignore them. You can configure your chat display so that you need not see any of their comments. To ignore a chat member, follow these steps:

Ignoring a Chat Member

1. Click the name in the member list pane.
2. Click the Ignore button on the Toolbar. The Ignore button looks like this:

Chat Codes Demystified

To save both time and typing, the on-line community has evolved its own peculiar, cryptic shorthand. Chat participants often "say" common expressions with just a few letters. With time on-line, you will find using them becomes second nature. Here are a few of the most popular codes:

IMO	In my opinion.
IMHO	In my humble opinion (usually followed by something that's anything but humble).
BTW	By the way...
BRB	Be right back.
OIC	Oh, I see.
LOL	Laughing out loud (better than "ha ha ha").
ROFL	Rolling on the floor laughing (if it was *really* that funny).
RTFM	Read the *darned* manual.
Rehi	A greeting to someone who returns to a chat.
<g>	Grin.
<G>	Big grin.

You can ignore an obnoxious participant so you don't have to see the comments he enters.

79

Even if you create an exclusive group to filter out messages except those from certain people, everyone else in the chat can still see the comments you enter.

80

When you ignore someone, the system shows that person's member name with a line through it, indicating that you no longer see messages from that particular member. People who are being ignored don't know it unless you tell them.

You can also use the Ignore command to create an exclusive group within a larger group. The system will filter out all messages except those from the members you specify. To create an exclusive group, follow these steps:

● *Creating an Exclusive Group in a Chat*

1. In the Member List pane, select the members with whom you want to communicate.
2. Choose Select Members from the Tools menu.
3. Choose Invert Selection on the submenu.
4. Click the Ignore button on the Toolbar.

When you click the Ignore button, the system will filter out messages from everyone but your designated few. Remember, though, that members who come late to the party will not be ignored, so you must ignore them individually as soon as they arrive.

Expressing Yourself with Smileys

A phone chat has vocal inflections and a F2F (face to face) has facial expressions, but typed comments can lack the comic intent, irony, or other sentiment you intend. To overcome this shortcoming, chat participants use smileys, or emoticons as they are sometimes called. When you really mean a little bantering fun, but your comment might read as sarcastic, tack on a smiley. Here are a few of the most popular smileys. To appreciate them, just tilt your head to the left.

:-)	Smile	:-(	Frown
:->	Big grin	;-)	Wink
:-o	Surprised	:-O	Shocked

FloJ:
    Turns out you'll be the only one there!
Davide:
    Well, that's just great! :-)

You'll get all the attention. :->   Send

For Help, press F1.   20 M

Smileys in action.

If a member becomes truly disruptive, you can report that person to the forum manager. Close the chat window and then exit the forum. Now you can right-click the forum icon and inspect the forum properties to learn the forum manager's name. Send the forum manager e-mail with your complaint and he or she will send a reminder that chats are public forums with rules of appropriate conduct.

Customizing a Chat Window

Creeping lines of text aren't always easy to follow. So, to help track a chat and all its participants, you might want to customize your chat window. You can actually change the way it works.

To customize a chat window, select Options from the Tools menu. One set of options ("Notify me when members join the chat" and "Notify me when members leave the chat") adds boldface comments when members arrive or depart from a chat. Another option allows you to preserve the chat history as a disk file when you exit. One more option inserts blanks between lines so the chat history is easier to read.

The Options dialog box.

Options	✕

Notify me when
- ☑ Members join the chat
- ☑ Members leave the chat

- ☐ Save chat history before clearing or exiting
- ☐ Insert blank line between messages

OK   Cancel

Inserting a blank line between messages makes the chat easier to read, but you see fewer comments on the screen.

Participating in Special Events

Chatting informally with other members can be a lot of fun, but The Microsoft Network can also give you the chance to meet public figures, question noted authorities, and converse with celebrities and other interesting people. Special events that take place in chat rooms, like live conferences, roundtables, forums, and seminars, are a lot like regular chats except that they are rigorously controlled by one or more hosts. The Babbage Auditorium, which resides in the Special Events category (From MSN Central, choose Categories, and then double-click the Special Events icon), houses many of the special events that occur on MSN, but individual forums can host events, too.

During a special event, everyone who attends is relegated to the status of mere spectator, except for the host (or moderator) and, of course, the special guests who

are free to interact. The host usually starts things off with a brief round of introductions. The guest typically makes a short statement and then opens the floor for questions from the "audience."

To address the special guest or to ask a question, you need to open the special Ask Questions Here chat room, which is always located in the same forum as the special event. In this chat room, you can enter your question or comment. At the host or moderator's discretion, he or she will transfer questions from the Ask Questions Here chat room to the main chat room, where they can be seen by everybody and responded to by the special guest.

Many special events also provide some detailed preliminary information about the topic of the special event or about the guest. Clicking the About the Guests icon will provide this information to you. To get a sense of how previous conferences have run, you can read through the Special Events archive housed in the Special Events category. To stay current on upcoming special events, check the Calendar of Events in MSN Today by clicking the MSN Today button on MSN Central.

Upcoming special events are listed in the Calendar of Events in MSN Today.

Participating in Chats

Chat World

You are *not* looking for product support, nor counseling, nor the chance to air your grievances. You just want to chat; to engage in some old-fashioned jaw boning. Well, with Chat World on The Microsoft Network, you've come to the right place.

Chat World is a multitude of chat rooms organized like the services of a grand hotel. Take a moment to wander around Chat World and you'll find a lobby (a general chat everyone can join), a front desk (a BBS where you can leave messages for other "guests"), a restaurant, a pool, a casino, and still more places to visit, each with one or more chats to join. In the Pool and Spa, you'll find chats named Poolside Bar and The Wading Pool, for example. In the Atrium restaurant, you'll find small chats, intimate booths for two. In the Chat Garden, you'll find tables of all sizes to which you can pull up a chair.

Except for the Chat World Lobby, the chats in Chat World are not monitored. There's no host to restrict the conversation to specific topics, so you are free to discuss anything and everything with your chatting partner or partners.

And if you'd like to see who you're talking with, you can check the Lobby Photo Gallery, where your conversation counterpart may have uploaded a picture.

Guests may join a special event from the floor of a trade show, from the arena of a sporting competition, or from the studios of a broadcasting station, when they participant in special events chats.

Next Stop

Chats are fun and even addicting, but when you're in the mood for quiet time online or you're looking for a file, you'll want to visit the two other services that appear in most forums: BBSes and the file libraries. BBSes contains messages written by MSN members and forum sponsors, and file libraries contain programs, utilities, games and other software contributed by members and by companies who use file libraries to distribute software updates to customers. The BBSes and file libraries are the subject of the next chapter.

Chapter Five

Seeing the Sights

The **BBSes and File Libraries**

- *What are BBSes and File Libraries?*
- *Reading a Bulletin Board*
- *Posting Messages on a Bulletin Board*
- *Getting Files from a File Library*
- *Uploading a File*

The **BBSes and File Libraries**

After hours of lively chatting in the chat rooms, you might find yourself seeking a spot online that is a little slower paced. While a BBS (short for Bulletin Board System) is often no less social than a chat, the conversations are not "live." Instead, forum members contribute typed messages as a way to exchange ideas and information, so browsing a BBS is more like viewing a community bulletin board upon which people have placed public letters than chatting around a conference or dinner table.

On MSN, you'll find bulletin boards with everything from quiet deliberations to raging debates. The topics are as vast in scope as the number of forums on MSN because nearly every forum contains at least one BBS. You'll encounter BBSes covering everything from career transitions to the hottest TV shows. On still other BBSes, you'll find classified ads, "for sale," and "help wanted" postings.

For an even more peaceful pursuit, you can browse the stacks of the file libraries. In most forums, you'll find file libraries that contain programs written by other members. In forums sponsored by companies, you may find file libraries that offer software updates and utilities for the company's customers.

What are BBSes and File Libraries?

Online bulletin boards are comparable to their real-world counterparts. A BBS on MSN is an area in a forum in which members can post public, written messages and replies. Not only can you use a BBS to find a job, sell some furniture or find someplace to live, but you can communicate by exchanging messages with people from all over the globe. Unlike e-mail messages, though, BBS messages are available for everyone to read.

When you visit a BBS, you can:
- Follow ongoing discussions by reading the messages.
- Contribute to existing conversations by posting replies.
- Seek assistance from other members or from technical support specialists who monitor the BBS.

A file library, another area you will find in most forums, contains programs and file

BBSes at a Glance

What   A folder in a forum that contains public messages and replies on topics related to the forum.

Where   BBSes reside in almost every forum.

How   Open a BBS folder and follow the written conversations within. To contribute to an ongoing discussion, simply respond to an existing message or start a new topic by posting a new message to which others can respond.

Why   BBSes allow members to ask questions, compose replies, and offer observations in an organized manner. BBSes also provide an area in which customers can post technical support questions and receive replies from other members or from support specialists.

hat have been contributed by other members. Companies also use file libraries to provide members with software updates for their products. A graphics forum might offer file libraries of public domain clip art, while a computer gaming forum would offer a file library of game demos.

When you open a file library, you can:

- Browse the stacks to search for programs, documents, sound files, pictures, icons, and other files that you'd like to have.

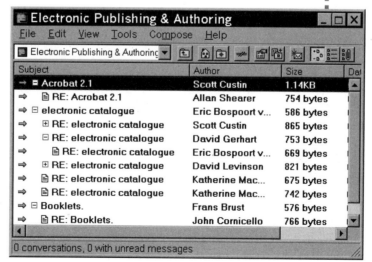

An MSN BBS

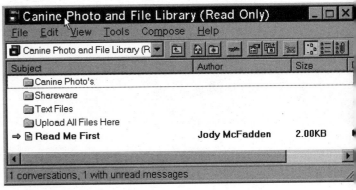

File Libraries at a Glance

What Collections of graphics files, applications, utilities or other downloadable files contributed by members or by the sponsor of the forum.

Where File Libraries reside in many forums.

How Use the same techniques to browse File Library folders and files that you use to browse the folders and files on your own disks. Choose any file to download and it will be transferred from MSN to your own disk.

Why MSN members can share their programs and utilities, and companies can distribute drivers, utilities, and updated software for the products they sell.

BBSes and File Libraries are two of the services you'll find in almost every forum. You may also find a chat, an information kiosk, and one or more files that you can download and run just by double-clicking their icons.

- Copy or "download" selected files to your own computer.
- "Upload" or contribute your own files so other members can share them.

In this chapter, you'll learn how to read and participate in BBS conversations. You'll also learn how to borrow from and add to the collections of the file libraries.

A file library may be Read Only, which means you can only take files from the library, not contribute your own.

A file library may also contain subfolders, which categorize the files it offers.

A file library

Reading a Bulletin Board

Nearly every forum folder contains a BBS. Like chats, Microsoft Network's BBSes give members the chance to swap stories, exchange ideas, and even vigorously debate each other. But unlike chats, discussions take place in written, public messages that are saved and stored in libraries of messages, rather than in live, on-line conversations. Just as every member can participate in forum chats, every member can read and respond to the messages in a forum's BBS.

Each message in a BBS either starts a new topic or continues an ongoing discussion. As members contribute to a discussion by posting a reply to a message, the BBS adds the new message to a *conversation*. You can follow the conversation from the message that began it all to the most recent reply. Each message may prompt several replies, since everyone who reads it has the option of responding. And each of the responses may spark a response. As more people reply to messages at various stages in the discussion, the conversation branches out like a tree.

Fortunately, *Conversation view* in a BBS makes it easy to follow an ever-evolving discussion by displaying the conversations in a BBS as a tree structure.

---

travel tip

BBSes with Folders

In some BBSes, the forum manager has created folders to subdivide the messages by topic. When you open one of these BBSes, you'll see a list of folders rather than a list of messages. Simply double-click any folder to view the messages inside. After you read the messages, click the Up One Level button in the Toolbar or press Backspace to close the current folder and return to the folder list.

Following a Conversation

When you double-click a BBS icon for the first time, you see the contents of the BBS in Conversation view. The subjects of the initial messages in many conversations appear as a list. If the BBS is not displayed in Conversation view, choose Conversation from the View menu.

A gray arrow points to each message in the conversation that you have not yet read. Unread messages are also displayed in boldface type.

People who read bulletin boards without ever contributing are sometimes called "lurkers." Don't let the sound of that scare you away. There's nothing wrong with reading the public messages.

A Conversation Tree Grows in Cyberspace

Here's how a conversation tree grows: **1.** Someone leaves a message in the Gardening forum asking for advice about the best mulch to use for a garden. If you visit the BBS just after the question is posted, you see this:

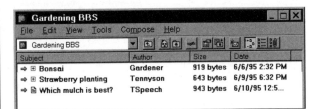

2. Later in the day, two gardeners offer their advice. Each posts a reply. The conversation looks like this:

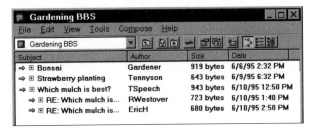

3. The next day, another gardener reads both replies. She disagrees with the second reply, and decides to post a response. After she enters her reply, others who visit the BBS find this:

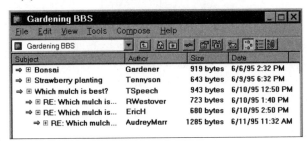

4. Finally, a real know-it-all shows up, disagrees with everyone, and decides to deliver his opinions in a reply to the original message. Here's the result:

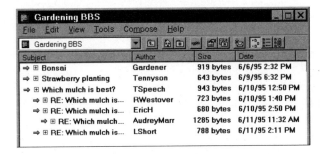

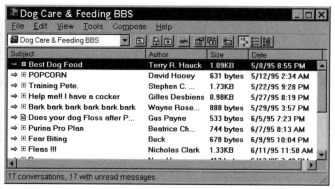

When it is first opened, a BBS is displayed in Conversation view.

Opening Messages in Succession

One way to begin navigating a conversation is to read its initial message. To do this, simply double-click the message and then use the navigation buttons on the message window toolbar to move to other messages. After you read a message, for example, you can click the Next button to open the following message. Or click the Next Conversation button to skip the rest of the current conversation and jump to the first message of the next conversation.

If, during a previous visit, you've already read some of the messages in a conversation, you will see arrows next to messages that you have not read or messages that you *have* read but that have unread replies. Unread

messages also appear in boldface. To move to the next unread message *that is visible in Conversation view*, you can click the Next Unread Message button in the toolbar. To move to the next unread conversation, you can click the Next Unread Conversation

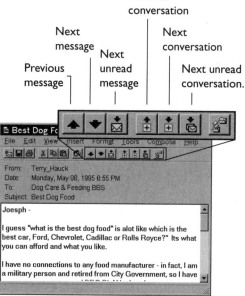

A BBS message.

The navigation buttons on the toolbar let you move quickly among the messages.

You can move along the
branches of a conversation
tree before you open any
of the messages.

button, instead. But to move directly
to unread replies that may be hidden
beneath messages that you've read,
you'll have to reopen a message
you've already read in a conversation
and then click the Next button until
you get to unread messages. A much
better alternative is to navigate
directly to unread messages by using
the techniques described next.

Navigating the Conversation Branches

Rather than open messages to
begin navigating through the conversations, you can travel the branches
of the conversations, opening only
the messages whose subjects interest you.

The small icon to the left of each
message shows if the message has
replies, and whether those replies are
in view.

When a message has replies, it is
accompanied by this icon. Click the
icon to reveal the replies.

To hide the replies to a message
and simplify the display, click this icon.

This icon appears next to a message that has no replies. A message

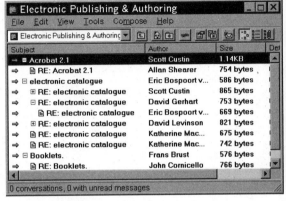

The branches of a conversation.

with this icon is the last message in one
branch of a conversation.

To travel the branches of a conversation,
click the icons in front of messages to open
and close parts of the conversation. For
example, click the Expand Replies icon next
to the initial message in a conversation to
bring the replies to the initial message into
view. And then, if any of these replies *also*
has replies, click its Expand Replies icon to
see the next level of replies. You can click
the Expand Replies icon next to any of *these*
replies to see still more replies, and so on.

After you reach the last message in one
branch of a conversation, you can return to

any previous message, choose an alternate reply and then travel down that branch of the conversation, investigating the replies to that reply. After you finish a branch of a conversation, you can close it by clicking the Collapse Replies icon in front of the first reply in the branch.

click the Expand Replies icon next to the initial message. To view all the messages in every conversation, you can even choose Expand All Conversations from the View menu.

travel tip

Opening an Entire Conversation

Here's a valuable shortcut for viewing conversations: To open all the replies under a message, press Shift and click the Expand Replies icon next to the message. Then, to hide all the replies, press Shift and click the Collapse Replies icon. With this technique, you can open one branch of the conversation after the next, read all the messages it contains, then close the branch and go on to a different branch.

To view all the messages in a conversation, you'd press Shift and

As you wander the branches of a conversation, you can either double-click any message or press Enter to read one of the messages. Then you can click the Close button or press Esc to return to Conversation view so you can move to other messages.

Rather than click icons, you might prefer to use the keyboard to navigate through a conversation. Rather than click an Expand Replies icon, you can simply move the highlight to a message with the arrow keys and then press the plus key on the numeric keypad. The equivalent to clicking the Collapse Replies icon is pressing the minus

Collapsing some of the replies in conversations hides some of the detail so you can get the big picture and see how a conversation has progressed.

Are BBS Messages Censored?

A BBS is a public setting, and, as such, it is monitored by the forum manager, who helps ensure that the forum remains decent and free from unwarranted solicitation. Forum managers will rarely resort to removing public messages from BBSes, unless they carry information that is illegal, unethical, or in some other way clearly fails to meet basic on-line community standards.

key on the numeric keypad. To expand or collapse all the replies under a message, press the Shift key while pressing the plus or minus keys.

Returning to Your Place in a BBS

When you return to a BBS after visiting another MSN destination, you'll see only the conversations that you have not yet read. To see all the messages in a BBS, (even those you have read before), choose Show All Messages from the View menu. The number of messages you'll then see

Learning About the Sender

If you're intrigued about a posting, you can find out more about its author. After opening the message, simply double-click the name of the sender on the "From" line. MSN will display the member properties information stored in the Microsoft Network address book in a Member properties window. Click OK or Cancel after you've browsed the information.

Messages you have read.

Unread messages have arrows and bold text.

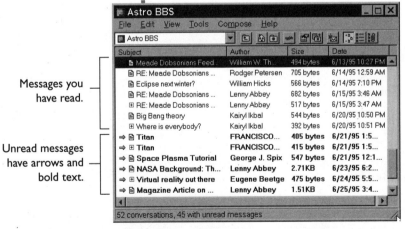

Returning to a BBS with Show All Messages turned on.

depends on the message capacity of the BBS and the length of time messages remain in the BBS before they expire. Both these options are set by the forum manager. You can't change them.

The system provides an easy way to locate your place in a BBS if you choose to show all the messages. When you read a message, its subject line changes from boldface to regular type in Conversation view and the gray arrow is removed. When you return to a BBS, you can resume your reading at the first boldface message.

Refreshing a BBS

Every few minutes, a BBS automatically updates itself to show messages that have been added by other MSN members. To check whether any new messages have arrived before the system updates the BBS, choose Refresh from the View menu.

Sorting the Messages

In Conversation view, you can sort the conversations according to the initial message. All the responses in a conversation get sorted along with the initial message. You can organize the conversations alphabetically by subject, by author, or by date, for example. To sort the conversations, simply click a button at the top of a column. To sort the messages by date, you'd click the Date button at the top of the Date column. To choose descending order rather than ascending order (sorting messages by descending date would put the most recent message first), right-click any column heading button and then choose Ascending or Descending from the shortcut menu.

List view offers another way to view and sort the messages in a BBS. In List view, messages are simply listed and sorted according to one of the columns. It's hard to follow the conversations as they have

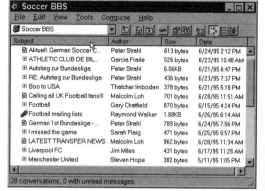

To sort the conversations by subject, click the Subject button.

unfolded, but you can sort the messages by author or date to group all the messages by author or by date contributed.

To switch to List view, click the List view button.

Saving and Printing Messages

When a BBS message has information you'd like to save, you can save the message to a file on your disk or you can print the message. To save a message, follow these steps:

Whenever you open a BBS, you see all the new messages that have been contributed since your last visit. If Show All Messages is turned on, you see all the messages on the BBS.

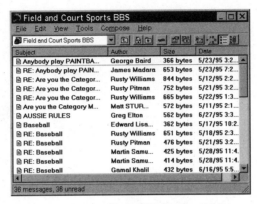

The messages of a BBS displayed in List view.

● **Saving a Message**
1. Open the Message.
2. Click the Save button on the toolbar.
3. From the "Save file as type" drop-down list, choose Text Only or Rich Text Format.

> **Text Only** The message text is saved as an ASCII text file without any formatting.
>
> **Rich Text Format** The formatting of the message is retained in the RTF file that is saved on disk. You can open the file later in WordPad and see the same formatting.

To print a message, open the message and then click the Print button on the toolbar or choose Print from the File menu.

4. On the Save As dialog box, change the destination of the message (Folder and Drive) if you'd like.
5. Enter a file name into the Filename text box.
6. Click OK.

Saving an Attachment

BBS messages sometimes come with attachments. A paper clip icon next to the message subject tells you that a file is attached. A company, for example, might attach the company newsletter. Participants in the Pets forum BBS might similarly attach the latest scanned photo file of their Schnauzer or Tabby cat. An attachment appears within a message as the icon of the application used to create the file. When the author of the message attaches a Word file, for example, a Microsoft Word icon appears in the message.

If you own the application used to create the attached file, double-clicking the icon to open the attached file causes it to automatically be saved in the Temp folder on your computer. You can later move the file to another location, if you like. To save a copy of the attached file on your disk without opening the file, choose Save from the File menu. You can only save attached files if you open the message they are attached to.

You can view only the messages in the BBS that have attached files by selecting Attached Files from the View menu or clicking the Attached Files View button on the toolbar.

Marking Messages as Read

After you work through a BBS, reading the conversations and messages of interest, you may want to mark conversations or messages as already read, even those you skipped over, so they will not appear when you next open the BBS.

To mark a *conversation* in a BBS as read, select any message in the conversation in Conversation view and then, from the Tools menu, choose Mark Conversation as Read. To mark a *message* as read, click it in Conversation view and then, from the Tools menu, choose Mark Message as Read. You can also mark conversations or mes-sages as unread by choosing Mark Conversation as Unread or Mark Message as Unread from the Tools menu.

To mark multiple messages, hold the Shift key and then click each message or hold the Shift key and click the first and last

message in the group to mark. You can also select Mark All Messages as Read so none of the messages will appear the next you open the BBS unless you've chosen Show All Messages.

travel tip

Moving Between PCs

Since the record of messages you've read is stored on your own computer, if you sign on to MSN from another computer, the messages you have read will still show up as unread.

Posting Messages on a Bulletin Board

If you have a contribution to make to a current conversation, you'll want to add a reply to the conversation thread. If you'd like to address a new topic, instead, you'll want to start an additional conversation in the BBS by creating a new message.

Posting a Reply

When you have a response to a BBS message, you can easily create a reply for

By marking as read messages whose subjects do not interest you, even if you have not read them, you can be sure that they will not reappear the next time you open the BBS.

When answering a BBS message, you should use Reply by E-mail when you'd prefer to keep your response private.

everyone to read. However, if your reply contains personal or private information, you might want to respond via e-mail. MSN makes it easy to choose either method.

To create a public reply to a BBS message, you must have the message open to which you are replying. If the message is not open, double-click it in the BBS window. To start the reply, click the Reply to BBS button in the Toolbar. When a new message window opens, the message has been automatically addressed to the BBS and the subject line has been filled with the current conversation subject. By clicking on the subject line and then typing new text, you can edit the subject line. Then click in the main message area and type your reply. When you're ready to post the reply, click the Post button at the left end of the toolbar.

To create a private reply that will not appear on the BBS, choose Reply by e-mail from the Compose menu. This opens Exchange and starts a new e-mail message automatically addressed to the sender of the message. If you choose Reply to BBS and then change your mind, you need to cancel the open reply and begin again by choosing

Reply by Email; you cannot change the type of reply once you begin typing the message.

travel tip

Forwarding a Message

In addition to replying to the sender of a BBS message, you can forward the message to another MSN member by opening the message and then choosing Forward from the Compose menu. The message will be transferred to Exchange, so you can choose a recipient for it from your personal address book or the MSN address book. The abbreviation FW will be added to the subject line when the message is sent so the recipient knows that the message was forwarded rather than written by you.

Starting a New Message

If you'd like to post a message on an entirely new topic, you must create a new message. You do not simply reply. To start a new message, open the BBS without opening any of the existing messages, then click the New Message button on the Toolbar. You can also choose New Message from the Compose menu. The new message will be automatically addressed to the BBS, with the subject line blank. Click the subject line and enter just a few, but very specific, words that will make the conversation topic clear to BBS browsers. For example, in the Building a Home forum, enter a subject like "Which attic insulation: Fiberglass or Foam?," rather than just "Insulation."

Entering and Formatting the Text

After you enter or revise the subject, you can enter the message. Click the message area and then simply start typing.

Here's something unique to The Microsoft Network: BBS messages can take advantage of the full variety of text formatting options. Users can select fonts, font sizes, font color, and many other text attributes by using the buttons on the Formatting toolbar. If the Formatting

toolbar is not visible, choose Formatting Toolbar from the View menu.

The Text Formatting Toolbar

To deliver your message with maximum punch or aesthetic appeal, you may want to format it in a bright color, a lively font, or in italics. The Formatting toolbar provides your options. This toolbar, like all toolbars, provides easier access to menu commands.

Here's how you use the Formatting toolbar. After you type text into a message, drag across the text to select it and then click on Formatting toolbar buttons to choose formatting changes. You can also select a combination of text attributes from the toolbar before entering text. When you type the text, it will take on the formatting selections you've made.

After your message is posted, others will see all the same formatting you chose while creating the message, with one important exception: If the reader of a message does not own the same font you used while creating the message, his or her system will display the

The Microsoft Network lets you format text in BBS messages and in e-mail messages that you send to other MSN members.

New message form

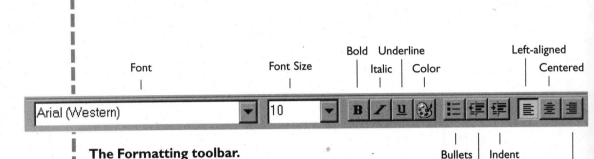

Font | Font Size | Bold | Underline | Italic | Color | Left-aligned | Centered

Arial (Western) | 10 | B | I | U

Bullets | Indent
Outdent | Right-aligned

The Formatting toolbar.

You can select text and then choose a font for it, but to choose a font for all the text in a BBS message, change the font when you begin typing the message.

message in the closest font installed. If you've used an ornate font that is not available on the reader's system, it will substitute a similar ornate font that is installed on the reader's machine. If the reader does not have an ornate font, Windows will substitute the closest font.

travel tip

Formatting Dialog Boxes

You can also format text by selecting the text, choosing either Font or Paragraph from the Format menu, and then making selections in the Font or Paragraph dialog boxes. This requires an extra step, but you can see all your formatting options in a dialog box. Another way to get to the dialog boxes is to select the text, click the right mouse button, and then choose either Font or Paragraph from the shortcut menu to open the Font or Paragraph dialog boxes.

Importing Text and Graphics

Because BBS messages can contain not only text, but graphics and files, you have several options for including information from other programs in a BBS message. You can simply copy and paste text or a picture from another program to display it in a message, or you can attach a file created in another program to send it with the message. A third option is to insert a Word document, Paint picture, or Excel graph into a message as an object. The reader of the message can double-click the object and then change it, save it, copy it, and so on. What's more, when you insert an

object, you can even link it back to the original on your system so others will see any changes you've made since you first posted the object in a message.

Copying and pasting text into a message is probably the procedure you'll carry out the most, though. If the text for a BBS message exists in another Windows application, simply copy and paste it into a BBS message window rather than retype it. You can also copy and paste graphics from other Windows applications with the same ease to copy logos, drawings, and even pictures right into your messages. Adding graphics can dramatically increase the size of a message, however, so your graphically enhanced message will take longer to open on the reader's machine than one composed of text. To keep message sizes small, either use small graphics, or use them sparingly. To copy and paste text or a graphic, follow these steps:

● Copying Text and Graphics into a BBS Message

1. Open a new BBS message.
2. Open the other application.
3. Select the text or graphic in the other application.

4. From the other application's Edit menu, choose Copy, or click the Copy button on the application's Toolbar.
5. Switch back to the BBS message window.
6. Position the insertion point at the destination for the text or graphic.
7. From the Edit menu of the BBS window, choose Paste. You may also click the Paste button on the message window Toolbar.

You can also include the text from a text file by following these steps:

● Importing Text from a Text File

1. At the spot for the imported text, position the insertion point in the message window
2. From the Insert menu, choose File.
3. In the Insert File dialog box, select the text file, and choose Text only for the "Insert As" setting.
4. Click Insert. The system will add the contents of the text file to the message at the insertion point.

When you compose a reply to a message, you do not need to "quote" the question, as you do with many e-mail systems, because others can always read the question in the previous message.

Pictures in a BBS messages will display only 16 colors even if you place a 256-color image in a message.

The smaller the original picture, the faster the message will open.

A graphic copied to a BBS message.

Adding an Attachment to a Message

To send a file with a BBS message, you can create an attachment. If you send a file as an attachment, others can save the file on their computer and open it with the application it was created in. When you send a file in a BBS message as an attachment, though, the message does not appear in the BBS until the forum manager checks and clears the file. To create an attachment, follow these steps:

● *Attaching a File*
1. Position the insertion point in the message window.
2. From the Insert menu, choose File, or click the Attach button on the toolbar.
3. In the Insert File dialog box, select a file, and choose An attachment for the "Insert As" setting.
4. Click Insert. The file is attached to the message and indicated in the message by an icon.

To save the attachment, your reader just needs to double-click the file icon and the file is saved to the Temp folder on his or her computer.

Embedding Objects in Messages

Rather than copy something to your message, you can insert a Word document, a Paint picture, or an Excel graph, among other things, into your message as an object, or even create any of these from scratch, without having to leave the message and open another application. Any application that supports embedding can be used to create an object for a message.

When you insert a new object, the application you want to use to create the object is opened for you. When you finish creating the object, close the application and the object is now in your BBS message.

If you double-click the object, the application is opened again for you to edit the object. If a reader of a message has the application you used to create the object, that person can also double-click the object and change it, save it, copy it, and so on.

You can also add an existing object to your message by inserting it from a file. If the object is large, say three or four pages of a Word document, you can display the object as an icon (much like an attached file) and the reader can see the object by double-clicking the icon to open the application. Again, the reader must have the same application the object was created in.

The main advantage of inserting objects is that they can be linked back to the original file on your computer so that when readers see the object, they also see any changes you've made since you first posted it. You can't do this with an attached file. To embed a new object, follow these steps:

● **Embedding a New Object**

1. From the Insert menu, choose Object.

2. Select Create New, and then select the type of object you want to insert in your message.

3. Choose Display as Icon if you want your reader to see only an icon and not the object itself.

4. The application that can create the object is opened for you, and you can create the object.

5. When the object is completed, choose Exit and Return from the application's File menu.

The object is now embedded in your message and the application you used to create it is closed.

● **Embedding an Existing Object**

1. From the Insert menu, choose Object.

2. Select Create from File, and then select the file you want to embed.

3. Choose Display as Icon if you want your reader to see only an icon and not the object itself.

4. Choose OK and the object is now embedded in your message.

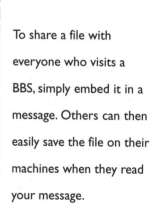

To share a file with everyone who visits a BBS, simply embed it in a message. Others can then easily save the file on their machines when they read your message.

Double-check every outgoing message before you send it, because you can't delete it and you can't get it back.

Sending the Message

When a message is ready for the BBS, click the Send button or press Ctrl+Enter. To review the message, you should close the BBS and reopen it later, or choose Refresh from the View menu. Since the message must travel through the system, it may take a few minutes for it to appear on the BBS listing. You can check to see whether your posting has really posted by choosing Refresh from the View menu.

travel tip

Check Before Sending

Double-check every message before you send it to a BBS because MSN provides no method for deleting a message you've posted to a BBS. Only the forum manager can delete messages, so once you send a message, you can't change your mind.

Reading and Responding to a Message Offline

When you've opened a provocative message to which you'd like to take some time to compose a thoughtful and considered reply, sign off MSN without closing the message window. Then, when you're off-line, reread the message, click the Reply button, and spend as

long as you need to synthesize a meaningful reply. When you click the Send button, MSN will sign back on and deliver your message.

Browsing the Stacks: Getting Files from a File Library

In addition to chats and other services, many forums also offer file libraries. These are folders that contain files available for you to copy, or *download*, to your computer. File libraries are represented by icons, just like the BBSes.

A forum sponsored by a computer hardware company might provide a file library in which it places the latest software files for its customers. Another forum, devoted to discussions of travel, might provide a file library chock full of text articles about various destinations, airfare, and vacation packages; graphics files of maps, and photo files of vacation spots. Yet another file library, in the Computer Games forum, may contain nothing but games and game demos that you can freely download and try out.

Viewing the Contents of a File Library

File library icons resemble bulletin board icons but they usually show a paper

The BBSes and File Libraries

clip in the corner. Their titles include words like "library," "file library," or "software library." To open a file library, double-click its icon.

Messages attached to the files in file libraries provide more information about these files. The file library, therefore, works a lot like a BBS. Messages typically tell on

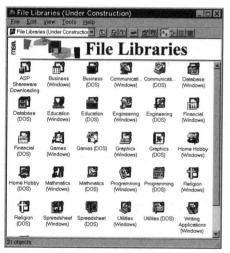

The file libraries in the Shareware forum.

what type of computer the file will run, and provide a brief description of the file contents. Some file libraries contain a simple list of messages, each with one or

more files attached, and other libraries contain folders and subfolders that organize the messages and the files they contain by type. When you enter one of these file libraries and find a list of folders rather than messages, you can open any folder by double-clicking it. You can see only the messages with files attached by choosing Attached Files from the View menu.

When you open a folder that contains a list of messages, you have a number of options. Click the buttons at the top of each column of the list to sort the messages by Subject, Author, Size, or Date, just like in the BBSes. Here, too, unread messages are displayed in boldface and accompanied by an arrow. The way File libraries operate actually differs very little from the way BBSes do, except that File Libraries are often marked "Read Only." The Read-Only designation, bestowed by the forum manager, means that you can read the messages and download the files, but not post replies or add new messages. This practice guards against computer-borne illnesses, like viruses, worms or Trojan horses.

File libraries contain contributions from other members, software from companies on MSN, transcripts of conferences held in forums, and much more.

File libraries
are much like
the BBSes
except that
the messages
in file libraries
always have
attached files.

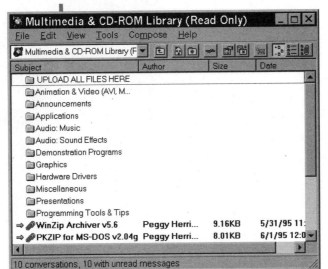

The contents of a typical file library folder.

If you are intrigued by a message subject line, double-click the message to open it and read more about the file. The message area provides a text description of the attached file, written by the person who contributed the file. The icons in the message area denote the attached files.

Learning More about Files

Before you begin downloading a file, you'll want to learn a little more about it. By checking its properties, you learn the size of the file, the expected duration of the download, the number of other people who have downloaded the file, and the charge for the file, if there is one. This last bit of information is perhaps the most important.

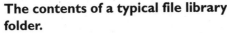

Freeware vs. Shareware

Not every file you find on-line is free. Some forums charge to download certain files. (A file's properties tell you the cost of a file. See the next section of this chapter for more info about checking a file's properties.) Other files are classified as *shareware*. Authors of these programs invite you to download and try the files out for free. If you like the file, and plan to continue using it, then you voluntarily remit a modest amount to the author. When you find a shareware program that becomes a truly valuable part of your software collection, please remember to compensate the author. Your contribution will reward the author for the value you receive and serve as an incentive for the author to create even more valuable software.

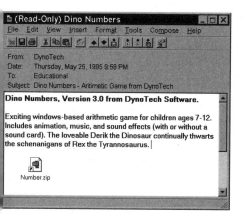

The icon in a file library message is the file you can download.

You'll also get confirmation that the file has been checked for viruses by the forum manager. To check a file's properties, follow these steps:

● **Checking File Properties**
1. Open a file library message.
2. In the message, click the file icon with the right mouse button.
3. On the shortcut menu, select File Object.
4. On the File Object submenu, choose Properties.

In the Attached File Properties window, you will see the file size, given in bytes;

approximate download time gauged by modem baud speed; status (whether the forum manager has checked the file for viruses and approved it), and the cost. You'll also see the date the file was uploaded and the number of times the file was downloaded by other members.

Selecting a File to Download

If a file description interests you (and the price is right) you can download the file by clicking the Download File button in the Attached File Properties window. Here are the steps:

● **Downloading a File After Checking its Properties**
1. Open a message with a file attachment.
2. From the Edit menu, choose File Object. (If two or more files are attached, you must first click one file icon.)

Attached File Properties dialog box.

107

For your protection,
Forum Managers screen
uploaded files for viruses.

Avoiding Viruses

Sadly, computer viruses are
a very real concern in
today's open computing environment.
Computer viruses are either mischie-
vous or malicious. They "infect" your
machine when you open a downloaded
file that has the virus embedded.

Fortunately, The Microsoft Network
is set up to screen out viruses. Before
files in the file libraries become available
to you, they are rigorously checked by
the forum manager. All files uploaded
to MSN are held out of view until they
have been approved. Only after being
thoroughly satisfied with the safety of a
file will a forum manager release the file
so it becomes visible in the file library.

3. On the File Object submenu, choose
   Properties.
4. In the Attached File Properties
   window, click Download File.

The file is added to the file transfer
queue in the Files Transfer Status window
and immediately downloaded to the Transferred Files folder. You'll find Transferred
Files within the folder called "The Micro-

soft Network." This folder is, in turn,
within the "Program Files" folder.

If you'd like to specify a destination for
the file other than the Transferred Files
folder, you can use this procedure, instead:

● ***Downloading a File to a
Specific Folder***
   1. Open a message with a file
      attachment.
   2. From the File menu, choose Save As.
   3. In the Save As dialog box, click the
      Attachments button, or, if more than
      one file is attached, click the attach-
      ment you want to download.
   4. In the Save As dialog box, choose a
      folder from the Folders list in which
      to store the file.
   5. Enter a filename for the file into the
      filename text box.
   6. Click OK.

If you checked the file properties at an
earlier time and simply want to return to a
message and download its file without any
extra steps, follow this procedure, instead:

● ***Downloading a File Without
Checking its Properties***
   1. Open a message with a file
      attachment.

2. Click the icon of the file you want to download. You can select one or more icons.
3. From the Edit menu, choose File Object.
4. On the File Object submenu, choose Download.

The file is added to the file transfer queue and immediately downloaded to the Transferred Files folder.

Managing the File Transfer Queue

When you earmark a file for downloading, the File Transfer Status window opens to show that the file has been added to the file transfer queue. This window provides a number of controls for handling incoming files. You can change the order in which the system will download files, instruct the system to automatically decompress compressed files, and change the destination folder of downloaded files. You can even tell the system to disconnect after the last file is transferred. This allows you go about your business. MSN will hang up automatically when it has downloaded all the files.

The status column in the File Transfer window shows the list of files to be down-

Download Now or Later?

Files added to the file transfer queue begin transferring in sequence immediately, but until all the files are received, your modem will be busy handling incoming data. During a download, anything else you do on MSN will be slowed down.

One solution is to pause the download until you finish all your other business on MSN, and then restart the download at the end of your session. You can even have MSN disconnect automatically after it downloading the last file. To put files on pause as they are queued, choose Options from the Tools menu of the File Transfer Status window and then, in the Options dialog box, click the checkbox next to "Pause files as they are queued."

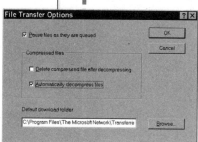

On MSN, you visit forums, read bulletin board messages, and even participate in chats, all while files are being downloaded.

loaded. At the top of the list is the file currently being downloaded; the other files on the list are pending. To remove a file from the queue, select it and click the Remove button on the toolbar. To stop a transfer in its tracks, you can even remove the file that is currently downloading.

When you pause a file by clicking it and then clicking the Pause button, the file moves to the bottom of the queue and any other pending files move up the list. Therefore, you can move a file to an earlier position in the queue by pausing

the files ahead of it. While MSN is busy downloading the next file in the queue, you can open the file that's already been downloaded and begin exploring its contents. To pause multiple files, hold down the Shift key as you click each file name, then click the Pause button. After a file has been paused, you can select it again and click the Restart button to restore its pending status. You cannot pause a file that is currently downloading.

Changing the Default Download Folder

By default, the system stores the files you download in a folder called Transferred Files within the folder called "The Microsoft Network." This folder is, in turn, within the "Program Files" folder. All files go into the Transferred Files folder unless you specifically choose a different destination folder when downloading a particular file. To change the default destination of downloaded files in the future, choose Options from the Tools menu and then, in the Options dialog box, select a new default download folder. You may want to click the Browse button next to the setting to find an appropriate folder on your hard disk.

The File Transfer Status window shows the files you have added to the queue for downloading.

Automatically Decompressing Files

Files that you can download are often files, or collections of files, that have been compressed to save disk space and transfer time. A compressed file is called a "ZIP" file, after a popular shareware compression program, PKZIP, and the .ZIP suffix that it appends to compressed files. To extract the files from a zipped file, you must use a program to decompress it. MSN can decompress the files for you automatically.

In the Options dialog box, click the checkbox next to automatically decompress files. MSN will create a folder within the Transferred Files folder for all the files it extracts from the zipped file. If you also click the checkbox next to "Delete compressed file after decompressing," the original zipped file will be deleted, saving valuable space on your disk.

Activating Transfer and Disconnect

When you'd like to transfer a file and disconnect immediately after the transfer, click the Transfer and Disconnect button on the toolbar of the File Transfer Status window. When you have paused the files added to the transfer queue during a session, and you're ready to restart and sign off, you may also want to activate Transfer and Disconnect.

Quick Downloading a File

When you want to let MSN put all its efforts into downloading a specific file, simply double-click the file icon in a file

The Downloading progress indicator.

library message. A dialog box will open, telling you the transfer time. You must also confirm whether you want to proceed with the download. If you click Yes, the file begins transferring without being added to the file transfer queue. By the way, when you use this technique, the file will download even when you have other files in the transfer queue.

When you choose to automatically decompress files, you will want to move the new folders created in the Transferred Files folder to another, more convenient location on your disk.

Contributing to a File Library

Say you've written a little utility for Microsoft Word, or you designed a beautiful quilt in CorelDRAW, or you wrote a brilliant essay on fire prevention, or you took a neat photo of the Grand Canyon that you've scanned in a GIF file. If you'd like to share your creation with the world, you can submit it to one of the file libraries on MSN. The file library in the Shareware forum, for example, is filled with programs offered by other members. You don't have to be a genius programmer to upload files.

Contributing a file is as simple as attaching it to a message in a file library. Since the forum manager will first screen the file to make sure it is virus-free and appropriate for the file library, you won't see your message with the attached file immediately. However, once it is approved, it becomes available to all other MSN members.

Uploading a File

Many file libraries feature a special folder marked something like "Upload

Compressing Files Before Uploading

To make a file smaller and faster to both upload and download, you should use a compression program such as PKZIP when you contribute a file to a file library. PKZIP can also be used to condense a suite of

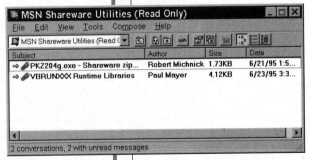

files into one. PKZIP will create a single file with the three-letter extension ZIP. Members only need to download and decompress one file to obtain the same files that you uploaded.

To use PKZIP, simply download it from the MSN Shareware Utilities library within the Software forum in the Shareware folder. The file comes with complete instructions on how to use the program.

here." In some forums, though, you'll find no special "Upload here" folder. In these forums, you will simply post your message in the folder to which you want to send your file.

To create a new message, simply open the file library and the folder to which you want to upload. Then compose a new message by choosing New Message from the Compose menu or clicking the New Message button on the toolbar.

In the Subject text box, enter a few words to describe the file. In the main message area, enter a full description of the file you are uploading. Include as much information as you would like to receive when browsing through a file library. Good details include the file's purpose, the file's recommended audience, and any special software or hardware requirements for using the file.

To attach the zipped file you've created, follow these steps:

Attaching a File to a Message

1. Position the insertion point in the message at the spot for the new file icon.

2. Choose File from the Insert menu or click the Insert File button on the Toolbar.
3. Use the controls in the Insert File dialog box to open the folder that contains the file.
4. Click the file.
5. In the Insert File dialog box, make sure the Insert As option is set to As Attachment.
6. Click the Insert button. A file icon will appear in the file.

Finally, to post your message, choose Post Message from the File menu or click the Post button on the toolbar. Remember, you won't see your new message appear until the forum manager has screened it.

Next Stop

Next, we'll turn from public communication on the chats and bulletin boards to private communication via e-mail. By sending and receiving e-mail messages, you can communicate not only with other MSN members, but with anyone around the world who has an e-mail address on the Internet.

Messages posted to File Libraries only become available after the forum manager has inspected them.

Chapter Six

Postcards and Travelogues

Using E-Mail

Using E-Mail

Your sister relocates overseas. Your business partner is on the road for months at a time. How do you stay in touch? With electronic mail (e-mail), physical distance is no longer an obstacle to fast, easy communication. E-mail messages from halfway around the world can reach their destinations quicker than messages you send across town.

You already may be familiar with the basic notion of e-mail: just like regular mail, you type a letter, address it, and send it to someone else. But with e-mail, you don't have to print the letter, address the envelope, lick the stamp, take the envelope to a postal box, and wait days for delivery. Instead, your e-mail message moves electronically to its destination in seconds, ready immediately for the addressee to retrieve and read it.

Although e-mail has been around as long as people have connected computers, The Microsoft Network adds a new twist. You can embellish your MSN e-mail with fancy text formatting. MSN lets you emphasize words with italics, for example, and give them color for impact. Other e-mail systems accommodate only plain ASCII text, which all looks the same.

Here's another benefit of MSN e-mail: You can include an attached file, like a memo from a word processor, a worksheet from a spreadsheet program, or a scanned photo from a graphics program. For example, say you are at a client's site, ready to make a presentation, but awaiting just one image to embroider the final frame. A graphic artist, connected via MSN, can send you the electronic file in seconds.

To manage incoming and outgoing correspondence, MSN relies on the same program that handles all your electronic correspondence in Windows, Microsoft Exchange. In fact, you cannot install MSN without also installing Exchange. If you already know how to use Exchange to send messages through your office network, you are one step ahead of the game. The same skills apply when you send electronic mail on MSN. But if you have never used Exchange, this chapter will take you through everything you need to know.

E-Mail at a Glance

What   An electronic mail (e-mail) system built into The Microsoft Network that enables you to exchange messages with other MSN members and with anyone in the world who has an Internet address.

Where   Everything you do with e-mail takes place in Microsoft Exchange, the universal inbox that comes with Windows 95.

How   You use Exchange to read, write, and file e-mail messages. Exchange sends and receives the messages over The Microsoft Network for you.

Why   To correspond with friends, family, businesses with whom you work, associates, fellow employees, and even the boss.

Exchange is the "universal inbox" that handles all your electronic correspondence, whether it's a fax with Microsoft Fax, e-mail on The Microsoft Network, or interoffice mail on your company's computer network.

What is Microsoft Exchange?

All your work with MSN e-mail takes place within Microsoft Exchange, the e-mail program that comes with Windows 95. You can use Exchange to compose new mail, retrieve incoming messages, send messages, and check on messages you have sent.

Because Exchange is a separate program from MSN, you can also run it when you are not signed in to MSN. Without tying up the phone or running up connection charges, you can handle many of your mail tasks. You can create messages offline, and then connect to MSN; after you connect to MSN, Exchange will send and retrieve everything at once. When you are not on-line, you can also take care of tasks you would not really want to do while connected, such as organizing your mail in the electronic filing folders that are built into Exchange.

The Microsoft Exchange filing system lets you categorize and store all the mail you send and receive. In a single folder in Exchange, for example, you can keep all the correspondence about a specific project. You can set up as many folders as you need and move e-mail messages among them.

Starting Exchange

On the Windows desktop, an icon simply labeled "Inbox" represents Microsoft Exchange (although technically, it's your outbox, as well). When you are not connected to MSN, you can double-click the Inbox icon to start Exchange. And when you are signed in to The Microsoft Network, you can click the large button on MSN Central labeled "E-mail" to start Exchange, too. Either way, Exchange will start in its own window.

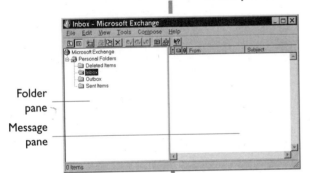

Folder pane
Message pane

The Exchange window.

Reading Your Mail

Just like the Windows Explorer, the Exchange window has dual panes. The system displays a list of folders in the left pane and the contents of one of the folders in the right pane. These folders are the special folders that are set up within the Exchange filing system. You won't see them among the other folders on your system when you explore your disks.

118

By default, the Inbox folder in Exchange is open first, and the messages it contains appear on a list in the right pane. To view the contents of another folder, you must click it. (If you see only one pane containing the message list, choose Folders from the View menu or click the Show/Hide Folders List button, the second button from the left on the toolbar. If you see only folders, the message pane can be found by clicking the line to the extreme right of the window and dragging it to the left.)

travel tip

The Exchange Toolbar

If the toolbar is not displayed, click the View menu and choose Toolbar. Most of Exchange's commonly used commands have buttons on the toolbar.

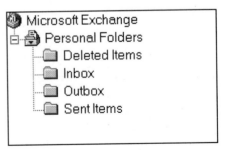

Close up of the Folder pane

Using E-Mail

When you first start using Exchange, the system displays four folders on the folder list. These folders are Deleted Items, Inbox, Outbox, and Sent Items. Incoming messages go into the Inbox folder. The Inbox, then, is the place to look for messages that you have received. Messages you have composed, but which you have not yet mailed, go into the Outbox folder. If you compose messages off-line, these messages remain in the Outbox until you next sign in to The Microsoft Network. After Exchange sends messages, it files them in the Sent Items folder. As you can imagine, messages that you choose to delete go to the Deleted Items folder. Of course, you can always add more folders to organize your mail systematically. You will learn all about customizing the Exchange filing system later in this chapter.

When you open Exchange, you will probably want to check your Inbox first. Exchange usually has this already open and waiting, with the messages displayed in the right pane. If not, simply click the Inbox folder in the left pane, or click the Inbox button on the toolbar. Any messages you have received are listed in the right pane and sorted by date and time received.

> ### travel tip
> ### Bold Means Messages Waiting
>
> *After you open Exchange, you know immediately if you have new e-mail without opening the Inbox folder. Bold type is the way Exchange tells you that you have unread items waiting. If new mail has been received, a picture of a letter appears at the right end of the taskbar, and the Inbox folder name is boldfaced on the folder list. When you open the Inbox, all new, unread messages are boldfaced, too.*

To open a message, simply double-click the message header (the message description on the list in the Inbox window) or, using the arrow keys, scroll to the message header, highlight it, and press Enter. If your insertion point is in the Folder pane, you need to move it to the message pane using the Tab key. Every message opens in its own window. If the message is especially long or involved, you may want to sign off from MSN to take your time to read it. Remember, Exchange is separate from MSN, so you can sign off after getting your

Exchange is a separate program from The Microsoft Network, so you can use it to read, write, and file messages even when you're not signed in. When you do sign in, Exchange will send and receive your e-mail.

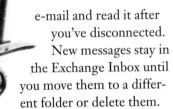

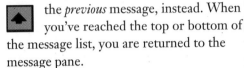

e-mail and read it after you've disconnected. New messages stay in the Exchange Inbox until you move them to a different folder or delete them.

After you read a message, you normally close the message window by pressing Esc or clicking the Close button at the upper right corner. If you have several waiting messages, though, you might want to take a shortcut to the next message in the Inbox. Just click the Next button on the toolbar.

The Next button, which opens the *next* message on the message list, has

a large downward arrow on it. The Previous button, beside the Next button, opens the *previous* message, instead. When you've reached the top or bottom of the message list, you are returned to the message pane.

Sorting the Messages

The messages on the message list are easily sorted and organized. You just decide which criteria you want to use to sort the messages: such as by sender or by subject, and then click the button at the top of the corresponding column in the message pane. To quickly review mail received from each person, you might want to sort the mes-

With Remote Mail, you can get a list of waiting messages without having to retrieve them all. See page 142.

Special Icons on the Message List

The message headers on the message list display plenty of information about each message, such as the sender's name, the subject, and the date and time the message was received. You may also see an exclamation point [!] at the beginning of a message line, indicating that the sender made the message "important" to call your attention to it; or a paper clip [@], which indicates a message has an attached file, such as a graphic file or a word processing document; or a down arrow [↓], which indicates that a sender of the message has given it a low importance. When you open a message with an attached file, the file will display as an icon in the message text. Double-click this icon to launch the file or click the icon with the right mouse button for other options.

Using E-Mail

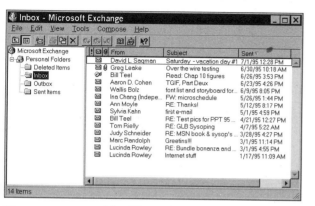

Messages sorted by Time Sent.

sages by sender; you do this by clicking the From button at the top of the From column. To reverse the order of the messages, click the column heading button with the right mouse button. From the small shortcut menu, choose Descending (largest to smallest, Z-A, or latest to earliest) rather than Ascending (smallest to largest, A-Z, or earliest to latest). A small arrow appears on the From or Subject button to alert you to how the list is being sorted.

Learning Even More About a Message

Exchange maintains far more information about each message than it shows you on the Inbox list. To reveal some of these hidden details, click a message with the right mouse button and then choose

Properties from the shortcut menu. The Properties dialog box displays when the message was sent, when you retrieved it, and whether the sender designated it as high, normal, or low importance. You also see whether the sender requested receipts for when it was read or delivered. A read receipt tells the sender when you actually opened the message in your Inbox. A delivery receipt tells the sender only when the message was sent, not when you received or opened it. The

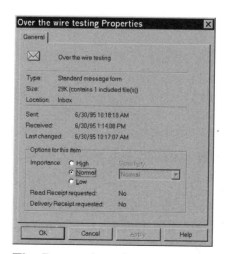

The Properties of a message.

Each e-mail message has properties that you can reveal by right-clicking the message on the message list and then choosing Properties from the shortcut menu.

FIRST AID

TRAVELERS

Time Zones

When a message has come from a time zone halfway around the world, you might wonder how to interpret the message's "time sent." For your convenience, MSN translates all times to your local time. So, if someone sends a message to you from London at noon his time, and you are in Chicago, the Properties dialog box for the message tells you it was sent at 6:00 AM.

To determine the proper time to display, MSN checks the time zone that you entered when you set up Windows. To check or change your time zone, double-click the digital clock in the taskbar and then change the settings on the Time Zone tab of the Date/Time Properties dialog box.

If you don't want the original message quoted in your reply, choose Options from the Tools menu of Exchange and, on the Read tab, click "Include the original text when replying" to remove the check mark.

sender may also have set a sensitivity level to alert you to the importance of the contents.

travel tip

Flagging a Message

To remind yourself that a message you have already read is important, view its properties, and then change its Importance to High. Now, for your handy reference, an exclamation point precedes the message header.

Replying to a Message

Replying to an e-mail message is easy. With message open, click the

Reply to Sender button. This opens a new message that is pre-addressed to the sender. You simply type in your reply text, and then send the message. Your answer goes right back to the sender.

There are several ways to compose a reply. If you were the only recipient of the message, click the Reply to Sender button or choose Reply to Sender from the Compose menu. If you were one of several recipients, you may click the Reply to All button, instead, or choose Reply to All from the Compose menu. All the recipients of the original message will receive your reply.

To keep your electronic conversation intact, Exchange will always copy into the new message the original message to which you are replying. The insertion point (the

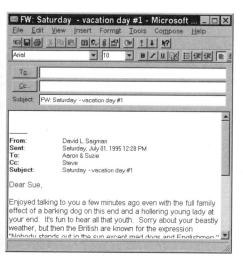

The message to which you are replying appears below your answer.

typing cursor) appears above this text, so you can enter the reply at the top of the message. The person who receives the message will be able to see your response along with the original question. A reminder like this is especially helpful when you get back an answer like, "No, I don't think so."

After you enter a reply, you can send it by clicking the Send button at the left end of the toolbar, or by pressing Ctrl+Enter. If you are off-line, the system transfers the message to the Outbox where it will wait until the next time you

Learning about the Sender

Because the address book on The Microsoft Network stores profiles of members, you can check there when you receive e-mail from a name you do not know.

A member profile, called "member properties," appears when you double-click the "From" name in the message window or when you click the name with the right mouse button and select Properties from the shortcut menu. If necessary, Exchange will connect to MSN to check the main address book on The Microsoft Network for the member information.

When the system displays a member's properties, you can click Add to Personal Address Book at the bottom of the properties dialog box to place the sender's information in your own address book.

The address book is an excellent source for all kinds of member information. If you plan to maintain the correspondence, you can transfer the sender's e-mail address to your personal address book, so you will have it on hand for the future.

Press Ctrl+R to create a reply to a message you are reading. Press Ctrl+F to forward the message to someone else.

connect to MSN. Of course, if you are connected, the system sends the message without delay.

Creating a New Message

Creating a new message is as simple as replying to an existing message. The only difference is that you must choose an address for the message yourself. To start a new message, take one of these steps:

Starting a New Message

- Click the New Message button on the Exchange toolbar. Or,
- Choose New Message From the Compose menu. Or,
- If Exchange is not open and you are not connected to MSN, click the MSN icon on the taskbar with the

You can copy the e-mail addresses you use the most into your personal address book. All other addresses are in the main address book on The Microsoft Network.

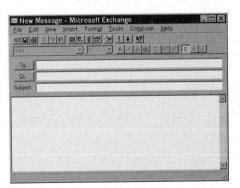

The New Message Form.

right mouse button and then select Send Mail from the shortcut menu.

When you start a message, a new message form opens. It's ready for you to enter an address and subject, and type in everything you want to say.

Addressing a Message

The best way to address a message to another MSN member is to pull the address directly from your personal address book. Since you have probably compiled your address book by culling entries from the main Microsoft Network address book, you can be certain that the addresses in it are valid and that your mail will be delivered correctly. Later in this chapter, you will learn how to transfer addresses from the main Microsoft Network address book in case someone you want to correspond with is not yet in your personal address book.

The personal address book contains a listing of all the people and organizations you have chosen to add. As your friends, family, and business associates also become MSN members, this resource is certain to grow. Since MSN features an Internet gateway through which your e-mail can reach electronic addresses worldwide, the address book can contain addresses for

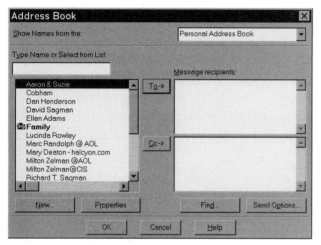

The Address Book window.

are connected to MSN, the entire address book for The Microsoft Network. Don't worry if your personal address book is skimpy at first; that will surely change as you spend more time online.

Once you have opened the address book, the fastest way to obtain an address is to start typing the member's name into the "Type Name or Select from List" text box. If you prefer, you can also scroll down the list of members to find an entry, but this is only practical when the list is still short. When the address book becomes large, with hundreds of entries or more, you may prefer to use Find, which is covered next, to jump directly to an entry.

When you locate the name you need, just double-click it to add it to the recipient list. A second option is to click the name once, and then click the To: button in the middle panel, between the two lists. If you click a name, and then click the Cc: button instead, the system adds the name to the list of recipients who will receive a copy of the

When you have the e-mail address you need in your personal address book, you can always type just a name into the To: text box of a new message. Exchange will get the corresponding e-mail address from the address.

everyone with whom you correspond electronically, even if they are not MSN members.

To browse your personal address book, click the To: button on a new message form. The address book will open in its own window. You can then select Personal Address Book from the list under Show Names From The.

Searching Your Personal Address Book

The Address Book window displays either your own personal address book or, if you

Using the Find command to search through the main Microsoft Network address book while you're online lets you find other members by name, by interest, or by any of the other properties listed on the property sheets.

message. You can double-click as many names as you need. The system will add each name to the recipient list. Your message will be sent to everyone on the list.

If you change your mind after adding somebody to the To or Cc recipient list, you can remove a name from the list by clicking the name and then pressing the Delete key on the keyboard. When the recipient list is complete, click OK to return to the New Message window.

Using Find

When your address book list is too cumbersome to browse from A to Z, or when you want to search the address book by name, you can use Find. To start a search with Find, follow these steps:

● *Using Find*

1. On a New Message form, click the To: button.
2. In the Address Book window, click Find.
3. In the Find dialog box, enter any part of a name.
4. Click OK or press Enter.

If Exchange finds matching names, it displays them in a new version of the member list called the "Search Results" list, indicated by the "Search Results" label at the upper right corner of the dialog box. This list is a subset of the entries in your address book. It shows only the entries that match the search text you entered. To see the entire address book list once again, click "Search Results" and then choose "Personal Address Book" from the drop-down list.

travel tip

Checking an Address

While you have the address book open, you can check the e-mail address of someone by clicking that person's name on the member list, and then clicking the Properties button in the dialog box. You will see the e-mail address of the member plus all the member properties information stored in the personal address book.

After you finish with the address book and return to the New Message form, you will see the name you've chosen underlined in the To: text box. The underline signifies that the name has been found and verified in the address book. You can double check the e-mail address of the intended recipient by double-clicking the name in the To: box.

Browsing The Microsoft Network Address Book

Your personal address book is useful only after you have begun accumulating names in it. If you make a habit of adding the name of every person who sends you a message, your address book will fill quickly. But if you need to address a member who is not yet in your personal address book, you can search the main Microsoft Network address book.

● *Searching the MSN Address Book*
  1. Sign in to MSN.
  2. Open Exchange, or click the E-mail button on MSN Central.
  3. Click the New Message button on the toolbar to start a new message.
  4. On the New Message form, click the To: button.
  5. On the Address Book dialog box, click the down arrow button next to the "Show names from the" drop-down list box at the upper right.
  6. Choose Microsoft Network from the drop-down list.
  7. Enter the first few letters of a name into the "Type Name or Select from List" text box, or click the Find button to search for a name.

Entering a Recipient by Name

If you know a recipient's name, you can type it directly into the To: box of a New Message form. Before Exchange sends the message, it will compare the name you have entered with all the names in your address book. If it finds a match, Exchange transfers the correct e-mail address from the address book, and then sends the message. If it does not find a match, Exchange gives you the chance to create a new entry in the Address Book. If you are connected to MSN at the time, Exchange will also check the address book for The Microsoft Network.

If Exchange still cannot find the addressee, you should choose the option to create a new entry in your personal address book. On the other hand, if Exchange finds two or more possibilities that seem to match the name you have entered, it shows them to you and asks you to select one.

Entering and Formatting the Text

Before you enter the main text of a message, you should first type a few meaningful words into the Subject text box. Try to encapsulate your topic in just a few

Your personal address book will have a subset of the entries in the address book for The Microsoft Network.

Don't forget to enter a message subject.

words, so the recipient can easily determine the purpose and priority of the message without opening it.

To enter your message text, first move the insertion point from the Subject text box to the message area with the Tab key, and then start typing. You need not worry about running out of space. You can type for as long as you have the stamina for it. In fact, your message can measure as much as two megabytes in size, so you can type thousands of pages if you need to. Most likely, you will probably type only a few lines of text and no more. Correspondence via e-mail is notoriously pithy and concise. The two-megabyte limit becomes a consideration only when you attach long files to messages.

Initially, the system displays the words you type in a standard font and color. However, unlike other mail programs that let you send only plain text, MSN e-mail allows you to style the text any way you want. You can select fonts, paragraph formatting, and colors at will. The only limitation to your absolute creative abandon is the rule that the message recipient must have the same fonts installed. Otherwise, the recipient's system translates your fancy fonts to the

closest approximation available. This may result in a less than beautiful display. Even so, your formatted message will still look better than one transmitted in plain, vanilla ASCII text.

As you enter a new message, you can choose from among the same formatting options offered by WordPad, the word processing accessory that ships with Windows. In WordPad, you first select the text by highlighting it, and *then* choose a formatting option. To display a word in boldface, select the word and then click the Bold button on the formatting toolbar. (If you do not see the Bold button, a button

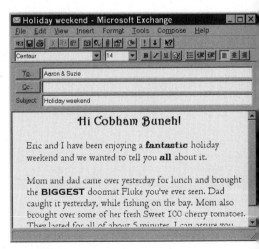

Message with styled text.

with a large "B" on its face, choose Formatting Toolbar from the View menu.)

The Formatting Toolbar offers all the text formatting options provided by the Format menu. You can have fun with your text: change colors, use dramatic fonts, and emphasize words with boldface. However, exercise restraint.

Nobody **wants** to *read* a *letter* that looks **like this**!

Sending the E-mail Message

As you've learned, actually sending the message you've toiled over couldn't be easier. Just click the Send button at the left end of the toolbar, or press Ctrl+Enter.

When an outgoing message leaves your computer, the system places a copy in the Sent Items folder. Once the message moves to Sent Items, you cannot stop it from being transmitted. Just as you cannot retrieve anything dropped into a post box, once your letter is deposited in the Sent Mail folder, it is too late to get it back.

If you are *not* connected to MSN when you opt to send your message, and you discover the outgoing message still waiting in the Outbox folder, you can reopen the message and make changes. You can even delete the message before it is ever sent.

To open a message in the Outbox folder, click the Outbox folder in the left pane of the Exchange window. Then double-click the message in the right pane. After making changes, you must click the Send button again, otherwise the message will stay in the Outbox folder. After you click Send, the message header is shown in italics. An italicized message in the Outbox will be sent as soon as possible.

To delete an outgoing message, you simply click the message in the Outbox folder, and then press the Delete key on the keyboard.

Special Delivery Options

Before you send a message, you can tag it with special delivery options. You may designate the message as "important," or "personal," or you can request that the system send you a receipt when the addressee reads the message.

For your convenience, most of these options are available on the toolbar. The toolbar features a Read Receipt button, and high and low importance buttons.

If a message listed in the Outbox is not italicized, it will not be sent. Open the message and click the Send button again.

Use the properties of a message to mark it as urgent or low priority for the reader.

If you would like a receipt message sent back to you when the message is delivered or read, you can choose one of these options while composing the message by clicking 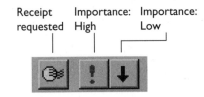 the Properties button on the toolbar. This opens the Properties dialog box. On the Properties dialog box, you can click the boxes next to Read Receipt and Delivery Receipt. You can also click one of the three Importance buttons: High, Normal, or Low. The Sensitivity drop-down list features four

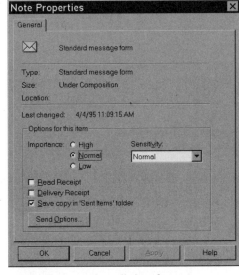

Note Properties dialog box.

options: Normal, Personal, Private, and Confidential. These options are summarized below.

Read Receipt The system sends a confirmation message when the recipient opens your e-mail.

Delivery Receipt The system sends a confirmation message when your e-mail is delivered.

Importance The system signals the importance of a message by placing a symbol in the Importance column of the recipient's Inbox.

High Exclamation point

Normal No symbol

Low Down arrow

Normal The recipient can read, modify, and forward the message.

Personal	The system displays "Personal" in the Sensitivity column.
Private	The system displays "Private" in the Sensitivity column. The recipient cannot alter your original when replying to, or forwarding, the message.
Confidential	The system displays "Confidential" in the Sensitivity column.

Forwarding a Message

Occasionally, you may want to pass on a message you have received to someone else with whom you correspond. With Exchange, you can easily forward a message and even augment it with an explanatory comment or two. To forward a message, follow these steps:

Forwarding a Message

1. Open the message.
2. Click the Forward button on the toolbar.
3. On the new message form, click the To: button and select one or more recipients from the address book.
4. Type in a note, if you want, at the top of the message.
5. Click Send to forward the message.

The system automatically starts the subject line of a forwarded message with FW. If the current message subject is "New storyboard," for example, the forwarded message subject would read "FW: New storyboard."

Including a File

Many times, you will find it helpful to include a file in an MSN e-mail message. You may want to:

- Send text that you have saved to disk. You certainly do not want to have to retype it.
- Add a special embellishment to your text. If your computer has multimedia capabilities, you might want to attach a sound file (recorded with the Sound Recorder Windows accessory) to your text.
- Send an application file, such as a word processing document or a spreadsheet.
- Include in a message a picture you have created or a photo you have scanned, perhaps your 8 x 10 glossy!

Before you forward a message, you should always consider whether the message author intended for anyone else to see the message.

131

If the recipient of a message has the software needed to play or view an included file, he or she can simply double-click the icon to launch the file. If the file is a MIDI composition, the tune will play, for example.

To incorporate a file, you can follow two basic approaches. You can attach the entire file to the e-mail message, where it displays as an icon within the message text. Or, assuming that Exchange can show the type of information that is in the file, you can copy the body of the file into the e-mail message. With this second method, you could create a picture in the Paint accessory, and then copy it into an outgoing e-mail message, where it displays.

Pasting Information into a Message

The fastest, easiest way to place something into a message is to copy and paste it there. Perhaps you have text in a document, a section of numbers in a spreadsheet, a slide in a presentation program, or a bitmap in your paint software that you want to add to a message. All of these are especially good candidates for a simple copy and paste.

To copy and paste a selection from a file, follow these steps:

● *Copy a Selection into a Message with Copy and Paste*

1. Open the file in the original application. For example, if your file is a bitmap, open your paint program.

2. Select the information you want to transfer, and choose Copy from the Edit menu.
3. Switch back to Exchange, where you have opened a new, outgoing message window.
4. Position the cursor where you want the data to appear and click the mouse button.
5. From the Edit menu of Exchange, choose Paste, or click the Paste button on the toolbar.

Inserting a File into a Message

Inserting, or copying, an entire file into a message gives the recipient a real item with which to work. You can provide your addressee a memo file to edit, a picture to modify, a presentation to deliver, or a sound, video, or music clip to play.

The inserted file appears in the message as an icon. Your recipient can double-click the icon to launch both the application that created the file and the file itself. He or she can also save the file to a disk.

Here, too, you have choices: if you want to include a file that you have saved to disk, you can simply insert it into a message. But if you want, you can create a file in another application "on the fly" while you are composing a message. Here are the two procedures:

● Inserting an Existing File into a Mail Message

1. While working in a new outgoing message form, click the Insert File button on the toolbar.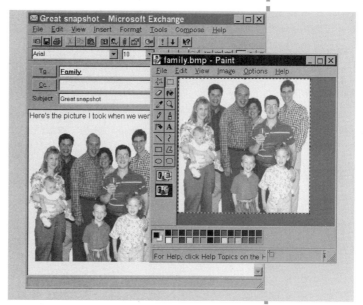

2. In the Insert File dialog box, open the folder containing the file, and then double-click the file.

If the file is a text file, you might want to click the file once, choose "Text only" for the "Insert as" option, and then click OK. This would copy the text of the file into the new message rather than create a file icon.

Here's another way to insert an existing file:

● Dragging and Dropping a File into a Message

1. Start by double-clicking the My Computer icon, and then open the disk and the folder that contains the file.

2. Drag the file icon from the folder window to the message area of the New Message form.

If you want to create a new file rather than use an existing file when you choose Insert File, follow these steps:

Paint picture in e-mail message.

● Creating the File to Insert

1. While working in a new outgoing message form, click the Insert menu, and then choose Object.

2. On the Insert Object dialog box, choose an object type from the list.

3. Click the box next to "Display As icon" if you want the object to appear as an icon in the message. Otherwise, the object will display as a

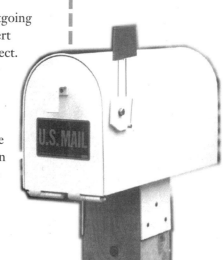

The recipient of a message with an embedded graphic can select the graphic in the e-mail message, and then copy and paste it into a Paint program or into another program, such as a word processor.

picture. For example, a Microsoft Power-Point slide will look like the real slide rather than the PowerPoint icon.

Now, depending on the application with which you will create the object:

- The application will open in its own window on top of the New Message form, or
- The controls of the other application will appear in place of those in the New Message form.

4. Use the controls and procedures of the original application, whether they are in a separate window or within the New Message form, to create the object.

5. If the other application is in a separate window, choose the "Exit and Return to mail message" command from the application's File menu. If the other application's controls are in the New Message form, choose Send from the File menu.

The object you have created will appear within the New Message

form. You can click the object, and then drag its handles to change its size or shape. You can also click the object and drag it to some other point within the text of the message.

When you insert a file into a message and send the message, a paper clip icon indicating the attachment appears next to the message in the Outbox and later in the

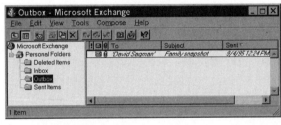

Outgoing message with an attachment.

Sent Mail folder. The same paper clip icon appears in the recipient's Inbox.

Managing Your Mail

As you've seen, Exchange offers tools to create and view messages. It also offers a complete filing system to store messages, as well. *Personal Folders* in Exchange provide a way to organize e-mail messages into logical groupings, just as the folders on your disk give you the means to organize your files.

The starter set of personal folders that comes with Exchange—the Inbox, the Outbox, the Sent Items, and Deleted Items folders—appears in the left pane of the Exchange window. You may want to think of these folders as the working set you use while reading and composing messages day to day.

When you start accumulating mail, you should leave only the most recent messages in your Inbox—the messages to which you might still respond, for example—and move the others to folders for long-term storage. Since an ever increasing number of messages in the Inbox folder will make it difficult to browse the folders, archiving old messages into storage folders is a good idea.

When you create new folders, you can label them in any way you like. You can even insert folders within folders to categorize your e-mail in greater detail. For example, you can set up a general folder for a company with which you work regularly. Within the company folder, you can then create a folder for each person at the company with whom you trade e-mail.

Creating New Folders

To create a new folder within an existing folder, follow these steps:

● *Creating a New Folder*
1. Click the existing folder to open it.
2. From the File menu, choose Create Folder.
3. In the New Folder dialog box, enter a name for the folder.
4. Click OK or press Enter.

To create a folder at the same level as the Inbox, Outbox, Sent Items, and Deleted Items folders, click the Personal Folders icon at the top of the folder list, and then follow steps 2 through 4, above.

To rename a folder you have added, click the folder with the right mouse button, and then choose Rename from the shortcut menu. Replace the existing name in the Rename dialog box with your new choice.

Click here...

...to reveal the subfolder.

The folders in the Inbox allow you to organize both the mail you have received and the mail you have sent.

Unless you create new folders so you can move messages to them, all the messages you receive will remain in the Inbox folder, and all the messages you send will remain in the Sent Items folder.

You can add as many folders as you would like. When you view the folder list, you can reveal and hide subfolders at will so the display of folders is not overwhelming. Simply click the plus sign next to a folder to reveal the sub-folders it contains. Click the minus sign next to a folder to hide its subfolders.

Moving Messages to Folders

After you create folders for storing messages, you can move a message between folders by dragging it. You can even select several messages by holding down the Ctrl key while clicking messages, and then you can drag them all together to a different folder.

travel tip

Selecting Messages

To easily select all the messages from one sender, sort the messages in the Inbox by sender. Once the messages are collected this way, you can easily select them by clicking the first message from someone, holding down the Shift key, and then clicking the last message. When the messages are all selected, you can drag them all to a folder.

Another way to move messages is by selecting the messages, and then clicking the Move button on the toolbar or choosing the Move command from the File menu. When the Move dialog box opens, you will see the same folders that appear on the folder list. Double-click any folder, or click a folder, and then click OK.

You can use these same techniques to move entire folders full of messages. Simply drag a folder from one location on the folder list to another location. To place a folder within another folder, for example, stack the folder on top of the destination folder, and it will disappear inside.

Deleting Messages

To remove old messages you no longer want to save, select the messages, and then press the Delete key on the keyboard. Deleted messages are moved to the Deleted Items folder from which you can retrieve them until you exit Exchange.

You can also move messages to the Deleted Items folder by dragging them there. To delete an entire folder of messages, drag the folder to the Deleted Items folder.

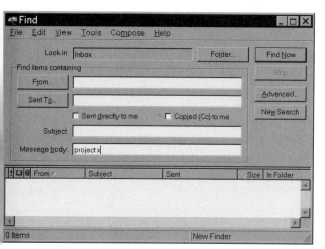

The Find dialog box.

Finding a Message

Filing messages in folders will certainly help keep you organized. With the Find command, Exchange gives you additional help in retrieving particular items. By using Find, you can search through folders for messages from certain people, about certain subjects, and even containing specific text.

To use Find, choose Find from the Tools menu of Exchange. When the Find dialog box appears, enter text to match in one of the "Find items containing" text boxes. To look for messages from a certain sender, for example, click the From: button, and then choose a name in the Select Names dialog box. To find all messages that contain a certain word, enter that word into the "Message body" text box.

When you click Find Now, Exchange will search the folder shown in the "Look in" text box. If it locates a match, Find displays the match within the Find dialog box. To jump directly to a found message, double-click it on the list.

If a search pulls up too many matches, you will want to narrow the search further. Click the Advanced button on the Find dialog box, and then enter very specific criteria, such as the range of dates during which the message was received.

travel tip

Sorting the Found List

If a considerable number of messages matches the search information you entered, you can sort the found messages on the list in the Find dialog box. You might want to click the Received button at the top of the Received column, for example, to sort the messages by date and time received.

If you delete a message by mistake, you can retrieve it from the Deleted Items folder until you exit Exchange, when the messages are permanently deleted.

Maintaining the Address Book

As time goes by, you will gradually compile an address book of the e-mail addresses of your favorite correspondents

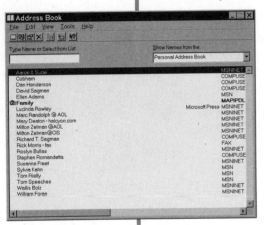

and business associates. Each time you receive a message from someone new, you can add the sender's address to your personal address book. At any time, you can also work in the address book directly, adding, editing, and deleting entries.

The Address Book.

With the Find command, you can even search the body of messages in Exchange for certain words.

The address book can store so many details about people—such as pertinent office telephone numbers, mailing addresses, departments, and even pager or cellular phone numbers— that you may want to make it the primary "Rolodex" on your system. Your modem will even place a call for you if you click the Dial button next to an entry in the address book.

To open the address book, click the Address Book button on the Exchange toolbar or select Address

Book from the Tools menu. When the Address Book dialog box opens, the system will display your personal address book, an alphabetical list of entries stored in a file on your own system. Your personal address book is a small fraction of the entire address book for The Microsoft Network. It may even include addresses not included in the Microsoft Network address book that you can reach from within MSN, such as addresses on other e-mail services, Internet e-mail addresses, and addresses on your organization's e-mail system.

Examining an Entry

Each entry in the address book has a set of properties. The e-mail address is one of

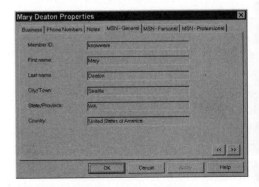

The Properties for an MSN address book entry.

these properties, and the postal address and telephone number are two more. To examine the properties of an entry in the address book, double-click the entry, or click the entry, and click the Properties button on the toolbar.

A typical address book entry has four or more tabs in its Properties dialog box. The number of tabs depends on the type of address. For example, an MSN address entry from the main Microsoft Network Address Book has six tabs: three filled with general information such as the indiv-idual's postal address and telephone number, and three filled with detailed autobiographical information that has been transferred from the address book for all of The Microsoft Network.

Editing an Entry

While an address book entry is open, you can modify information in the white-back-ground text boxes. Shaded text boxes contain fixed information pulled from the main Microsoft Network address book. You cannot change these bits of member-provided information, such as the date of birth.

After you have entered or changed the information, click OK in the Properties dialog box to store the changes.

Adding a New Entry

The best time to add an entry to your personal address book is the first time you receive a message from someone new. Just double-click the sender's name and then click the Add to Personal Address Book button on the sender's Properties dialog box. This transfers all the information the system has about the sender to your personal address book. If the incoming message is from the Internet, the system adds only the return Internet address to the address book.

You can also transfer entries from the Microsoft Network address book to your personal address book individually. Here are the steps:

● **Copying an MSN Address Book Entry to the Personal Address Book**
  1. Open the address book in Exchange.
  2. Choose Microsoft Network from the "Show Names from the" pull-down list at the upper right corner.
  3. Find an entry in the Microsoft Network address book.

Double-click any entry in the address book to check its properties.

Transfer entries from the Microsoft Network address book to your personal address book so you can examine them without signing in.

139

You can transfer the information about someone from the main Microsoft Network address book to your personal address book by clicking the Add to Personal Address Book button.

4. Click the Add to Personal Address Book button on the toolbar, or double-click the entry, and then click Add to Personal Address Book on the member properties dialog box.

When someone you meet gives you an e-mail address, you can add it to the address book manually by following these steps:

● *Adding an Address Book Entry*
1. Open the address book in Exchange.
2. Click the New Entry button on the toolbar or choose New Entry from the File menu. 🖳
3. On the New Entry dialog box, choose the type of address you want from the list. Choose The Microsoft Network Member, for example, to enter the e-mail address of another MSN user.
4. Enter the information you have into the New Properties dialog box and then click OK or press Enter.

After you finish modifying the address book, close it to save the information.

Creating a Personal Distribution List

If you regularly send e-mail to a designated group of individuals or organizations, you can simplify addressing tasks by creating a personal distribution list. When you send a message that has the name of a distribution list in the To: text box, the message will be sent to everyone on the distribution list.

You may want to create a family distribution list, for example, or a list of all your customers. The family distribution list might be named something simple, like "The Adamses." If you then address a newsletter to "The Adamses," the newslet-

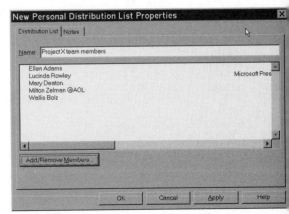

New Personal Distribution List Properties dialog box.

er will go out to everyone in your family whom you have added to the list.

To create a personal distribution list, follow these steps:

Creating a Personal Distribution List

1. Open the address book in Exchange.
2. Click the New Entry button on the toolbar, or choose New Entry from the File menu.
3. On the New Entry dialog box, choose Personal Distribution List from the bottom of the list.
4. In the New Personal Distribution List Properties dialog box, enter a list name in the Name text box.
5. Click the Add/Remove Members button.
6. On the Edit New Personal Distribution List Members dialog box, double-click each entry to add to your new personal distribution list, then click OK.
7. When you return to the New Personal Distribution List Properties dialog box, click OK to save the list.

In the address book, the system displays names of personal distribution lists in bold, and accompanied by a personal distribution list icon.

Updating Your Own Entry in the MSN Address Book

Whenever you are connected to MSN, you can edit your personal entry in the Microsoft Network address book. By changing your entry, you can control the information people have about you when they check your member properties.

To modify your entry, follow these steps:

Modifying Your Entry in the MSN Address Book

1. Connect to MSN, if necessary.
2. Open Exchange.
3. Open the Address Book in Exchange.
4. In the Address Book dialog box, choose Microsoft Network on the "Show Names from the" drop-down list.
5. Find and then double-click your personal entry.
6. Enter any changes you want.
7. Click OK.

With a personal distribution list, you can address e-mail to a group of people by entering the name of the list.

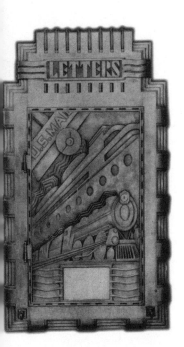

Changes to your entry in the Microsoft Network address typically appear within 24 hours. If others have copied your entry from the Microsoft Network address book to their personal address book, those entries will not be updated automatically. If you are not connected to MSN when you attempt to modify the Microsoft Network address book, Exchange will sign in automatically.

Checking Your Mail with Remote Mail

Some people get an impressive amount of mail. Others get very few messages. However, the mail they do get often comes with long files attached. If you are among these people, you will benefit from a special feature of Exchange called Remote Mail.

Remote Mail is a way to manage waiting e-mail messages. You need not retrieve every message from the MSN mailbox and shuttle it to your Inbox in Exchange. Remote Mail simply makes a connection to MSN and retrieves only the headers of waiting messages (the information you always see listed in the Inbox folder). Then it displays the headers on a list in the Remote Mail dialog box. From this list, you can select certain messages to retrieve, some to leave for later, and others to discard. With Remote Mail, you will never be burdened with unwanted e-mail again.

You can share as much information as you'd like about yourself, or as little, by modifying your entry in the address book for The Microsoft Network.

142

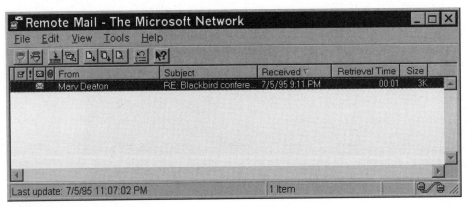

Remote Mail dialog box.

You can zap it before it ever makes its way onto your PC.

Imagine that you are minutes before an important presentation and you need an updated slide. Fortunately it's only a computer away, waiting in your mailbox on MSN. Unfortunately, there are eleven other long messages waiting there also.

Since you do not have the time to download all the messages just to get the one you need, you use Remote Mail to retrieve only the message headers. From the header list, you select the message you need and Remote Mail transfers only that message to your Inbox. The rest of the messages can wait. After Remote Mail retrieves the message with the attached slide, you place it in the presentation. The presentation is a smash and you're the hero.

To start Remote Mail, follow these steps:

Starting Remote Mail

1. Open Exchange and choose Remote Mail from the Tools menu. If you have an e-mail service other than MSN installed, such as CompuServe mail, you will need to choose The Microsoft Network profile from the cascading menu.

2. Click the Update Headers button on the toolbar to instruct Remote Mail to connect to MSN and retrieve the headers of waiting messages.

3. When Remote Mail shows you a list of waiting messages, select one or more messages to retrieve and click one of these buttons on the toolbar:

   Mark to Retrieve
   Transfers the message to your Inbox.

   Mark to Retrieve a Copy
   Copies the message to your Inbox and leaves the original in your mailbox on MSN. The message will be waiting the next time you connect.

   Mark to Delete
   Deletes the message from your mailbox on MSN without retrieving it to your Inbox.

4. Click the Transfer Mail button on the toolbar to initiate the actions you've chosen.

Remote Mail will then handle all the e-mail according to your instructions, which

Remote Mail lets you connect to check your waiting e-mail without automatically transferring all of it from MSN to your Inbox folder in Exchange.

143

With Remote Mail, you can read the subject of a message and then mark the message for deletion. You never have to retrieve mail that does not interest you. So long, junk e-mail!

includes connecting to MSN if you are not already signed in. The system will place the messages it retrieves in the standard Inbox of Exchange.

Filtering Messages on the Remote Mail List

After Remote Mail retrieves the list of waiting messages, you can filter the list. You may want to see only messages from certain people or only messages that contain certain text in their subject lines. To filter the list, follow these steps:

● ***Filtering the Remote Mail List***

1. From the View menu of Remote Mail, choose Filter.
2. On the Filter dialog box, enter text into the From and/or Subject text boxes. You can enter text into both text boxes to refine the filter to messages about a certain subject *and* from a certain person.

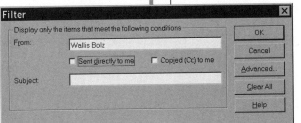
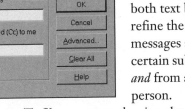
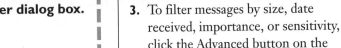

The Filter dialog box.

3. To filter messages by size, date received, importance, or sensitivity, click the Advanced button on the

Filter dialog box and make selections on the Advanced dialog box. Then click OK.
4. Click OK on the Filter dialog box to put the filter into effect. While the filter is working, you will see a filter icon on the status bar at the bottom of the Remote Mail window.

After you have filtered the Remote Mail list, the system will display all message headers again if you choose Filter from the View menu, click the Clear All button on the Filter dialog box, and then click OK.

Special Options for Remote Mail

Remote Mail can disconnect from MSN after retrieving message headers, then re-connect when you click Transfer Mail. This allows you to minimize connect time while still retrieving all your mail. It can also remain connected the whole time while you select message headers and choose whether the messages will be retrieved or deleted. If you'd like, you can also set Exchange to remain connected after Remote Mail has transferred messages so you can respond without having to re-connect. You might also want to remain connected after retrieving mail so you can go on to other parts of the service and do other things.

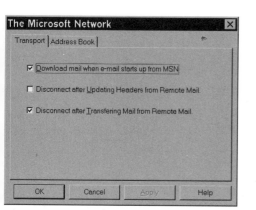

The Microsoft Network Options dialog box.

To choose these options, select Options from the Tools menu of Remote Mail. On the Transport tab of the Options dialog box, click the boxes next to "Disconnect after Updating Headers from Remote Mail" if you'd like to mark headers while offline and then sign in again after you've told Remote Mail how to handle your waiting messages. The other option, "Disconnect after Transferring Mail from Remote Mail" will sign you out automatically after you remote mail is transferred.

Compacting Your Mail Storage File

From time to time, you should compact the file in which your personal folders are

stored to both save disk space and enable Exchange to open faster.

To compact your mail file, follow these steps:

● *Compacting Your Mail File*

1. From the Tools menu of the Inbox, choose Services.
2. On the Services dialog box, click Personal Folders.
3. Click the Properties button.
4. On the Personal Folders dialog box, click Compact Now.
5. Click OK to close the Personal Folders dialog box.
6. Click OK to close the Services dialog box.

Next Stop

Next up is a close look at the Internet services you gain access to when you join The Microsoft Network. You'll learn about Internet mail, browsing the World Wide Web, the newsgroups, and other Internet-related topics.

Globe Trotting

Traveling the Internet

Traveling the Internet

Reaching the Internet through The Microsoft Network is an alternative to making arrangements with a local Internet "access provider."

Exploring the Internet is quick and easy if your starting point is The Microsoft Network. The "Internet," also known as "The Net," "Cyberspace," and the "Information Superhighway," is a huge network of computers around the world. These computers range from individual PCs to small company machines to vast networks of computers at large universities, corporate sites, and commercial information services.

The Internet offers many of the same services as The Microsoft Network to anyone who connects to it; usually you connect by purchasing some Internet software and establishing an account with a local Internet access company. Just like MSN members, Internet users can post messages on bulletin boards, exchange e-mail, and engage in chats. But because the Internet links people and services at companies, organizations, universities, libraries, and other online services such as CompuServe and America Online, the number of people and the amount of information you gain access to on the Internet is staggering. Scientists have never measured the total amount

of data on the Internet, but estimates of several hundred Terabytes (trillions of bytes) fall short by far.

There are different types of "sites" on the Internet, and you can get to any of them using MSN. World Wide Web sites provide graphical pages where you find links to other pages from all over the world. File Transfer Protocol, or FTP, sites

SCENIC OVERLOOK

Who Started the Internet?

When the US Department of Defense started the Internet in the '70s, they envisioned a reliable worldwide computer communications service that could survive even a nuclear attack. Fortunately, the world has become a safer place, and the Internet is open to commercial sites as well as the educational and scientific institutions who first used it during the '80s. Now, anyone has access to the Internet through an online service, such as MSN, or through a local company called an Internet "service provider."

The Internet at a Glance

What A vast, globe-spanning system of computers tied together for communications. The Microsoft Network has a connection to the Internet, so you can follow the Internet Newsgroups, and send Internet e-mail.

Where The BBS-like Internet newsgroups, and everything else relating to the Internet, is in The Internet Center, one of the main MSN categories.

How You can browse and participate in the Internet newsgroups the same way you follow along with, and contribute to, the MSN BBSes.

Why To extend your travel experience to other computer systems.

MSN gives you Internet e-mail, the World Wide Web, the Internet newsgroups, and other Internet features.

re libraries of software and other files that ou can download to your computer, much ke you do files from an MSN file library. A gopher" site (named after the University of Minnesota mascot, where this kind of nternet site was invented) is like a World Vide Web site because it gives you access o many other sites all over the world, ncluding World Wide Web sites. Gophers ere originally designed to help students nd faculty who were not expert Internet sers locate research information on a nultitude of computers, without having to now each computer's name.

There are also two very important ervices provided by the Internet, mailing lists and newsgroups. Mailing lists are communities of people with a common interest who exchange mail daily on their interest. Newsgroups are like MSN bulletin boards. We'll cover both of these services in detail in the pages that follow.

Stopping By the Internet

When you travel on MSN, you'll find many forums that have icons that lead you straight to the Internet. You'll know that the stop is an Internet site because it will have the Internet icon, rather than a forum,

Newsgroups work just like the BBSes on The Microsoft Network. The messages in newsgroups are organized into conversations you can read. The biggest difference is that the messages in a newsgroup come from all across the Internet.

or chat, or BBS icon. When you are using the World Wide Web, you need a "browser" to view the information. Internet Explorer from Microsoft is a web browser. Other Web browsers you may have heard of include NetScape and Mosaic. Actually, the Internet Explorer is a form of Mosaic, licensed by Microsoft and enhanced for use with The Microsoft Network.

travel tip

World Wide Web without MSN

You can also access the World Wide Web without MSN, if you have an Internet account through a company that sells access to the Internet. There may be several access providers in your community, and you can locate them by looking in the Yellow Pages under Computers. When you access the Internet via an access provider, you need

software on your machine that lets you enter instructions about where to go. You can find out more details about using Explorer itself by choosing Help from the Explorer menu.

Getting to the MSN Internet Center

The Internet Center is one of the icons you see when you choose Categories at MSN Central. Simply double-click this icon to open The Internet Center folder. The Internet Center folder probably includes these other folders:

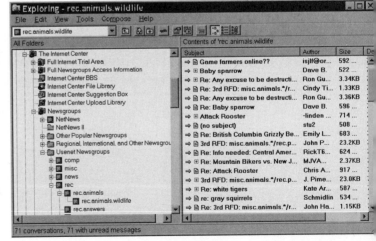

The newsgroups are just like BBSes: messages in folders.

Newsgroups and Full Access Information. This is the central repository of the newsgroups. Navigate this folder to discover topic areas that might interest you. Inside the Newsgroups folder, you will find Netnews, NetNews II, and Usenet newsgroups. This folder also contains a document that explains the process for receiving access to the entire newsgroup feed. By default, members don't have access to the "alt" category. Due to the occasionally sensitive or sexually explicit nature of the discussions in this category, MSN has restricted access to it. However, you can request access to the alt category by using a special electronic form.

Core Rules of Netiquette. This information, provided by MSN, offers some rules of the road for using the Internet. If you are unfamiliar with the Internet, you should take a look at this document.

The Internet Cafe. This area features MSN members engaged in live chats about the Internet, its complexities and many advantages.

All Internet-related services are located in The Internet Center, one of the main MSN categories.

The Internet Center BBS. This area contains the bulletin board system, which contains messages sent among MSN members about the Internet Center.

File Libraries. The Internet Center File Library has files that relate to Internet connections and file transfers. For example, in the file library you will find Wincode, a program to translate

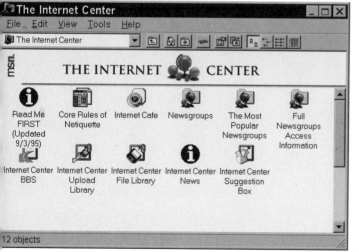

The Internet Center

The Internet Center is your first stop on the road to the many services of the Internet

certain encoded messages that you may encounter in newsgroups that contain binary files, as well as file viewers for several graphics format files. You cannot upload directly to this library because it is read only. You can, however, upload to the second library in this area, The Internet Center Upload Library. After checking out a file and deeming it suitable for mass consumption, the Sysop places it in the Internet Center File Library, so other MSN members can share it.

Read Me First. A document that includes MSN's disclaimer about the uncensored content of some newsgroups.

The Most Popular Newsgroups. This area contains the senior sysop's top ten newsgroup picks of the week.

MSN Producer's Picks. These are some great Internet sites that the folks at MSN think you should take a look at. The selection will change frequently, so stop by often.

Member 2 Member Cool Links. MSN members get the chance to let you know which they think are the coolest things on the Internet by creating shortcuts to Web sites, FTP sites, or other Internet locations in this folder.

The Internet Center Suggestions Box. This area lets MSN members send their rants and raves about MSN to the sysops.

Exploring the World Wide Web

The World Wide Web is a hypertext-based information service developed at CERN (The European Center for Nuclear Research), a high-energy physics research laboratory in Geneva, Switzerland. Originally developed to promote the exchange of research materials between physicists at numerous locations, it currently provides millions with access to complex documents that contain both text and graphics. Many Internet users know the World Wide Web from Mosaic or Netscape, the most popular "browser" application packages used to view information on the World Wide Web. There are other application programs which can access the Web as well.

Traveling the Internet

The World Wide Web, or Web for short, is the most exciting, and fastest growing, segment of the Internet. This is where almost anyone can create a "page" for themselves, and welcome all passers by into their "home" for a visit. Home pages, or single screens of text and graphics, were originally something the scientists, academics, and students using the Internet built for themselves as a way to get easy access to their favorite reports and documents. Today, there is no accurate count of how many pages exist on the Web, but it could be in the millions.

What's so cool about the Web? The Web is the graphical user interface of the Internet: pages have richly formatted text, colorful pictures, and links: links to other pages all over the world. Some pages have sound and video, too, but these are pretty novel, still.

Internet Explorer is a Web browser that you an use with the Microsoft Network. The Explorer is available to any MSN member who can download it from MSN. It is also included in Microsoft Plus, a package of special Windows 95 tools and utilities you can purchase where you purchased Windows 95.

A Web browser converts the information sent from a Web site and displays it as a Web page with text and graphics.

What's This About Nervous Words?

Hypertext is not nervous words. Hypertext describes the ability to give a word or graphic in an electronic document a hidden code. When readers of the document then click that item, the system takes them from the current location to another location or document. These special text codes are sometimes called links, hotspots, or jumps. On The Microsoft Network, they are called shortcuts. Shortcuts can take you to other locations on MSN or to other locations on the Internet. A shortcut can take you around the world to a computer in Taiwan or Israel.

You can download the

Internet Explorer from

The Internet Center on

The Microsoft Network.

Restricting Children's Access to Adult Material

Microsoft is one of the organizations supporting the Information Highway Parental Empowerment Group, which is dedicated to providing controls to lock out material that parents would prefer to keep from their children. While this group develops control techniques they can provide to parents, Microsoft has provided an immediate solution. To gain access to the full array of Internet newsgroups, including the Alt newgroups that some find offensive, users must specifically request full access by filling out an onscreen form. To find this form, look in the Internet Center folder under Full Newsgroups Extended Internet Access Information folder.

Installing Internet Explorer

Installing Internet Explorer puts the necessary software on your machine to run the browser, but it also changes the list of access phone numbers you use to sign in to MSN. When you install Explorer by downloading it from MSN, the Explorer is put on your desktop for easy access when you are not on MSN. After Explorer is downloaded and installed, the setup wizard updates your list of MSN access numbers, disconnects MSN, and restarts your computer and reconnects to MSN to do the final installation steps.

MSN has two types of network connections: one that accesses only MSN and one that access both MSN and the Internet. When you want to use Internet Explorer, you have to choose the connection which accesses the Internet and MSN network.

To check which network you are using, or to change networks, follow these steps:

● Changing Networks

1. On the desktop, double-click the MSN icon.
2. Click the Settings button in the Sign In dialog box.
3. Click Access Numbers.
4. In Service types, choose either The Microsoft Network or The Internet and the Microsoft Network.

5. The list of access numbers changes, depending on which service you select.

6. Choose a location and an access number, and then choose OK until you are back in the Sign In dialog box.

Now when you connect to MSN, the correct network will automatically be selected.

Surfin' the Net with Internet Explorer

If you double-click an Internet icon in an MSN forum, Internet Explorer opens automatically. If you find a shortcut in a forum to a site like the

Garden Net, for example, you can double-click it to open Explorer and see this set of Web pages for avid gardeners.

The Explorer window is a lot like the MSN window. It has a menu across the top,

The GardenNet Web Page

So, How do I Make Myself a Home Page?

To make a home page, you need to learn to write in another language and you need access to a server on the Internet. The language is called HTML, hypertext markup language, and it is what makes it possible to create shortcuts and display pictures on the Web. Right now, writing HTML is not as easy as using a word processor, but with practice you can have your own page on the Web. Check your local store for books on using HTML, or use Lycos to search for guides to HTML on the Internet itself. If you don't have a server, you probably want to talk to an Internet access provider about renting space on their server.

Switching from The Microsoft Network to the Internet is seamless. When you click an Internet icon, the next window opens to display an Internet site rather than an MSN forum.

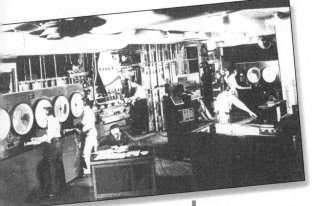

The Explorer works just like all most MSN windows except that it displays pages on the World Wide Web rather than forums on The Microsoft Network.

scroll bars to move up and down or side-to-side in the window, and a title bar across the top. Just like MSN windows, Explorer also has a toolbar. The first two buttons on the toolbar are Open and Open Start Page. Open lets you specify a new Web page to visit and Open Start Page returns you to your own "home" page. We'll talk later about setting up a start page.

Just as in MSN, there is a button to take you to a list of your favorite places on the Internet and a button to click when you want to add the current page to your list of favorite places. Your favorite Web pages are in the list on the Favorites menu of the Internet Explorer, not in the Favorite Places folder of MSN.

In the Explorer window, you'll also find a few unique items: one is the address box,

Open   Back   Stop

Windows 95 icon.

Open Start Page   Forward   Refresh

Address Box

The Forward and Back button let you move through pages you have already visited. The Stop button stops a page that is currently loading, perhaps because you changed your mind once you saw some of the opening text. The Refresh button reloads the page you are currently viewing; this is sometimes necessary because a glitch in the telephone lines may cause a page to become corrupted or distorted.

the location where you can enter the address, or universal resource locator (URL), for a Web page in order to open that page directly. The other is the Windows 95 icon near the upper-right corner. This animated icon is there to let you see when Explorer is surfing through the thousands of Internet computers looking for the page you requested.

Microsoft Internet Central on the Web

To give you a feel for Web surfing, start with the home page Microsoft has given everyone who uses Internet Explorer. On the desktop, double-click the Internet Explorer icon. Explorer is already set up to open Microsoft Internet Central first, when you open Explorer. You'll find out in a minute how to change this to another page.

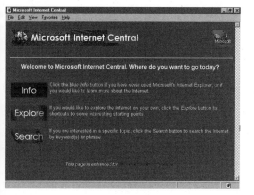

Microsoft Internet Central.

Microsoft Internet Central gives you three options: you can learn more about using the Internet under Info, begin your journey under Explore, and find pages with information on a specific topic under Search. Click Info to begin.

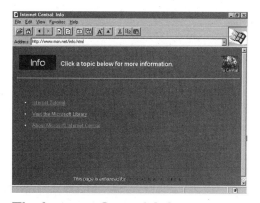

The Internet Central: Info page.

On this page, you'll find no buttons to click. Instead, you click the words themselves to move to another location. Internet Tutorial is a shortcut and the words are probably a light bluish, green. Many Web pages make words, rather than buttons or pictures the "hotspots" to indicate a link to another page. You can change what color the hotspots are before you click them and after you click them by choosing the Options command from the View menu of Explorer.

The Appearance tab is where you set the colors you want for shortcuts, text, and the background of a page. This is also where you can turn off the display of pictures on pages so that pages load more quickly.

E-mail messages sent to Internet addresses cannot have the fancy text formatting you can use in messages to other MSN members.

Remember we said you could change which page is displayed when you first open Explorer? Click the Start Page tab. If you are on a page other than Microsoft Internet Central, you can change the address of your start page to the page you are on by clicking the Use Current button. To change back to Microsoft Internet Central, choose Use Default. Use the What's This help in the Options dialog box to learn more about how you can change the appearance and behavior of the Internet Explorer.

If you've never surfed the Web before, you might enjoy taking the Internet

Tutorial on the Info page of Microsoft Internet Central.

Each page of the Internet Tutorial has a Next Page and a Previous Page button to help you move through the lessons. Anytime you want to return to Microsoft Internet Central during the tutorial, just click the To Central icon in the upper-right corner of the page.

Finding Places on the Internet

The Internet is so vast, and so full of information, you can lose many happy hours just moving from one page to another. So, what if you don't have many hours to spend? What if you need a piece of information now, not two hours from now? Chances are, you can find it quickly by searching with the tools provided by Microsoft Internet Central.

If you are not already on the Microsoft Internet Central page, click the To Central icon or select the Open Start Page button if Microsoft Internet Central is your start page.

Now, click that green Search button. Microsoft Internet Central uses a sophisticated search tool called Lycos to help you find information on the Internet. Devel-

There are never any spaces in an Internet e-mail address.

The What is the Internet? page.

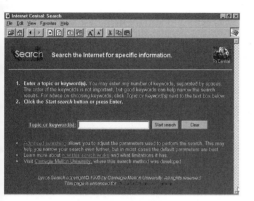

The Internet Search page.

oped at Carnegie Mellon University, Lycos can look at Web pages, ftp sites, and lots of other kinds of Internet sites to find what you need. The Search page is where you can type one or two words to begin your search. You can get help in deciding which words to enter if you click the Topic or keywords shortcut. If you need to do a more sophisticated search or control what kinds of files Lycos searches for, you will want to click the Advanced searching shortcut. Clicking the How this search works shortcut will give you detailed information about Lycos.

travel tip

The Back Button

Whenever you move from one page to another in Explorer, you can always retrace your steps by clicking the Back button on the tool bar. If the page you want to return to is dozens of pages behind you, you might find the page listed at the bottom of the File menu, or you can choose More history from the File menu and see the History window, full of shortcuts to the last dozens or hundreds of pages you stopped at. You can decide how many pages are saved in History in the Options dialog box. Choose Options from the View menu, and then select the Advanced tab to set this number.

Opening Web Pages Using an Address

If Web pages can be opened buy clicking icons in a forum, why do you need the address box? Because not every cool page in the world is a MSN shortcut. You may read about a page in a magazine and want to go see for yourself. You might want to open a Web page when you are not in a forum, or you might want to use the Internet Explorer using an access provider other than Microsoft Network.

Lycos is a system that keeps track of all the sites on the World Wide Web so you can search through them easily.

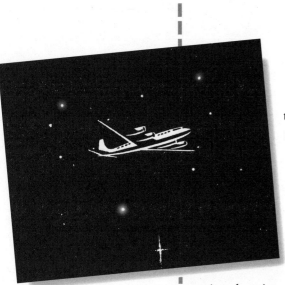

When you do any of these things, you need to give Explorer an address. Web pages are located by your browser according to the address of the Internet server on which they reside. This address is expressed in a series of words or numbers that, together, make up the unique location of a page. For example, Microsoft has a Web page. It resides on a server at Microsoft. The universal resource locator address for this page is:

www.microsoft.com.

Check the information box below to understand what each segment means.

When you type an address into the address box, you always begin it with the letters http (hypertext transfer protocol). For example, if you want to view the home page for Garden Net, you type

http://www.olympus.net/gardens/welcome.htm

into the address box, and then press Enter to locate and open the page.

You can also use the address box to learn a page's address when you get to it from a shortcut in MSN. MSN makes it much easier to view a Web page when someone includes it in a forum as a shortcut!

Creating Shortcuts to the Web

Putting your favorite Web sites on the Favorites menu is handy, but it's even nicer to be able to create a shortcut to a favorite

Be sure to type in the Internet address exactly as it's given to you, or the Web "server" will not be found.

The Parts of an Internet Address

Indicates this is a Web server. All Web pages have this in their address.

Indicates this is a commercial domain, or a company. Other designations are .EDU for education, .ORG for organizations, etc.

www . microsoft . com

Periods are used to separate parts of the address.

Indicates the name of the "domain" where this server resides is Microsoft.

site and let your friend know about it by including the shortcut in a piece of e-mail.

Creating a Shortcut

1. Open the page you want the shortcut to
2. Choose Create Shortcut from the File menu of Internet Explorer. The shortcut is placed on your desktop.
3. Move to your desktop and select the shortcut.
4. Click the right mouse button, and then choose Copy from the shortcut menu.
5. Move to the place you want the shortcut and choose Paste.

The shortcut is now wherever you put it. You never have to remember that URL!

Downloading Software from the Internet

One of the first uses of the Internet among scientists and academics was sharing software they had developed or data files of research results. To do this, a special "protocol" or communication method had to be developed that allowed the files to move across the network from one computer to another. Called FTP, or file transfer protocol, this method is what

```
Welcome to ftp.microsoft.com
File  Edit  View  Favorites  Help
Address ftp://ftp.microsoft.com/

Welcome to ftp.microsoft.com

Name                Size    Modified        Type
bussys                      Jul  3 14:52    Folder
deskapps                    Oct  7  1994    Folder
developr                    Dec 21  1994    Folder
dirmap.htm          8KB     Mar 31 15:29    File
dirmap.txt          5KB     Mar 31  9:32    File
disclaimer.txt      1KB     Aug 25  1994    File
index.txt           1KB     Oct  5  1994    File
KBHelp                      Jul 24  9:51    Folder
ls-lR.txt           5994KB  Jul 31  4:04    File
ls-lR.Z             763KB   Jul 31  4:04    File
LS-LR.ZIP           585KB   Jul 31  4:04    File
MSNBRO.DOC          28KB    Nov 28  1994    File
MSNBRO.TXT          23KB    Feb  8  1994    File
peropsys                    Oct  7  1994    Folder
Services                    Jul 21 12:39    Folder
Softlib                     Jul 27 13:33    Folder
```

The Microsoft FTP site.

allows you to download a particular piece of software, perhaps a demonstration of garden design software or an upgrade to your word processing package.

Many FTP sites, or locations where files are stored for downloading, are now available via Web pages. Rather than having to learn the commands to type in order to ask for a particular file on the network server, you simply click a shortcut and the file is downloaded to your computer.

Many software companies have FTP sites, as do universities, government agencies, local school districts, libraries, and others. Lycos will find FTP sites as well as Web pages when you use it to do a search. For a sample of an FTP page, let's look at Microsoft's.

Shortcuts can lead to Web sites, or even Web pages within sites.

The Usenet Newsgroup Categories

Most of the newsgroups available on MSN are part of Usenet, a set of newsgroups organized into a tree structure with eight main categories. You'll see the tree structure when you open the Usenet newsgroups folder on MSN. Within any of the eight categories, you will find many topics, and sometimes subtopics within the topics. Usenet now supports more than 7,000 newsgroups, each dedicated to its own particular topic. More are added just about every day. The eight major categories of newsgroups are:

comp This category includes topics of interest to both computer professionals and hobbyists, including information on computer science, software sources, and hardware and software systems.

misc This category includes groups addressing themes not easily classified into any of the other headings, or which incorporate themes from multiple categories. Subjects include fitness, job-hunting, law, and investments.

sci This category includes discussions marked by special knowledge relating to research in, or application of, the established sciences.

soc This category features groups primarily addressing social issues and socializing. Included are discussions related to many different world cultures.

talk This category includes groups who are largely debate-oriented and features long discussions without resolution or conclusion.

news This category features groups concerned with the newsgroups system, its maintenance, and software.

rec This category spotlights groups oriented towards hobbies and recreational activities.

alt This category features anything and everything. If there's no place for it in any of the other categories, it ends up here.

The files available are listed in columns. If the listing is for a folder, the name will be bold and the Type column will indicate it is a folder. Opening a folder reveals either more folders or files themselves. The size of each file, and the date on which it was last modified, is also listed.

When you locate the file you want to download, simply click the file's name. The Internet Explorer may open the file or immediately start downloading it to your hard disk. You may also see a Confirm File Open message cautioning you to be aware of the potential for acquiring a virus. Occasionally, an Unknown File Type message appears if the Internet Explorer cannot recognize the file. If either one of these messages appears, you're given the option to save the file to your hard disk or specify the program you want to open the file with.

To save the file to your disk, choose Save As. To open the file now, choose Open File. To cancel the whole operation, choose Cancel.

Exploring the Newsgroups

While the Internet Explorer lets you browse the World Wide Web, MSN helps you access another popular feature of the Internet: Newsgroups, the Internet's version of MSN bulletin boards. Members of the Internet community post information in these newsgroups just the way MSN members post information in the BBSes, sharing their knowledge and opinions freely, fiercely, and even dogmatically, on a variety of topics. With MSN, you automatically have access to the Internet newsgroups through MSN's Internet Central.

Newsgroups are a popular form of communicating with the combined intelligence of the Internet community. Newsgroups often take off where MSN BBSes end. For example, if you don't find the information you need about a new laptop

New newsgroups are formed all the time, so you'll want to check back periodically in case a newsgroup has appeared that's right up your alley.

computer in the Portable Computers BBS on MSN, you might want to check the Internet newsgroup called "comp.sys. laptops," which translates to computers/ systems/laptops.

travel tip

Favorite Newsgroups

By opening a newsgroup and then clicking the Add to Favorite Places button on the toolbar, you can add a newsgroup to your Favorite Places folder.

Users who read and post to the newsgroups range from the absolute novice to the unequivocal expert. Posting a question to a newsgroup will produce either a flood or trickle of answers, depending on the popularity of the group. In some groups, a single question might elicit 20 answers in the space of five minutes. Other, less-popular groups might receive only one or two posts a week.

Users post "articles" or "messages" to newsgroups the same way MSN members post messages to a BBS. The system then broadcasts the articles to all the other interconnected computer systems that carry the newsgroups. There is

no limit to what you can discuss in this setting—topics range from stock analysis information to international politics. Some newsgroups are "moderated." Moderators insist that their newsgroup discussions remain focused and on target. Members of this type of news-group send articles to the group's moderator, who periodically reviews the posts, and then either posts them individually to the newsgroup, or posts a composite digest of the articles for the past day or two.

Finding a Newsgroup

You can browse the categories of newsgroups until you find a newsgroup to read or you can use the MSN Find command to locate a newsgroup by name.

To use Find, follow these steps:

● *Finding a Newsgroup*

1. Click the Start button on the Taskbar.
2. Choose Find from the Start menu.
3. On the Find menu, select On The Microsoft Network.
4. In the Find: All MSN Services dialog box, choose Internet Newsgroups from the "Of type" drop-down list.
5. In the Containing text box, enter a word you think will match a word in

the title of a newsgroup. If you do not know the newsgroup's title, or are unsure, enter a word under Description that you are quite certain will be found in a description of the group.

6. Click the Find Now button.

If the Find command locates newsgroups that match your query, it displays them on a list in the Find dialog box. Just double-click the name of a newsgroup on the list to jump directly to that newsgroup.

Participating in the Newsgroups

To enter the newsgroups, follow these steps:

● *Entering the Newsgroups*

1. At MSN Central, click the Categories button.
2. In the Categories window, double-click the icon for The Internet Center.
3. In the Internet Center window, double-click the Newsgroups and Full Access Information icon. To see a small selection of popular newsgroups instead, double-click the icon labeled "The Most Popular Newsgroups."

4. In the Newsgroups window, double-click the icon for the type of newsgroup that you want to enter. When you enter a newsgroup area, the system displays all the newsgroup categories available in that area.
5. Double-click a category to see its newsgroups.
6. Double-click a newsgroup to open the newsgroup and see its articles.

Some newsgroups, such as comp.os (computers/operating systems) have multiple subfolders. And if you choose comp.os.ms-windows, you have yet another layer of subfolders to choose from. It can be several layers before you actually reach the messages.

Newsgroups work much like the BBSes on MSN. Once in a newsgroup, you read messages, navigate messages, and reply to messages exactly as you do within a BBS on MSN, selecting and following conversation threads that interest you. Chapter 5, "Seeing the Sights: The BBSes and File Libraries" provides full information about using the MSN BBSes.

Newsgroups are just like the BBSes on MSN. People post "articles" to newsgroups.

165

When you reply to a message in a newsgroup, everyone who follows the newsgroups will see your reply.

Toolbar buttons let you file messages, print messages, and cut, copy, or paste selections from messages into files or e-mail. Buttons also take you to a previous conversation, the next conversation, or the next unread conversation.

If you see an interesting message and would like to post a reply to the newsgroup, you can click the Reply to BBS button on the toolbar. This will trigger a message window preaddressed to the newsgroup, with the text of the post to which you are responding in the body of the message. If you want to send a private reply to a single newsgroup member, then you can select Reply by E-mail from the compose menu. This triggers a message window with correspondence preaddressed to the author of your current newsgroup message.

If you would like to download a newsgroup message for later referral, you can select the message you want to read and press Enter. From the File menu, choose Sign Out. The messages you select remain open. To save a message to your hard disk, choose Save As from the File menu while the message is open.

Exploring Mailing Lists

A mailing list is a discussion group that communicates entirely by e-mail. There are lists for all sorts of interests: from aeronautics to vampires and beyond. Some mailing lists are discussion lists to which any of the lists' subscribers can contribute, while others limit who can participate. Discussion-oriented mailing lists can be moderated or unmoderated. Other mailing lists simply broadcast announcements from some source to all interested parties. With your Internet gateway provided by MSN, you can join a variety of mailing lists.

Mailing list mechanics are fairly simple. A software "mail exploder," housed on the list organizer's, or moderator's computer, sends mail to all members of the list when it receives mail. On some lists, the moderator will approve mail to be sent to all list members. Thus, to send mail to all members, you need only write to one address: the list address.

Many popular books about the Internet list hundreds of mailing lists to which you can subscribe. When using a mailing list, you should adhere to the same rules of netiquette that apply to newsgroups and the MSN BBSes: Use a meaningful subject line. A subject of "help" particularly when received by those on more than one list, is not likely to elicit much of a response. If you are responding to a previous post, quote appropriately, putting your comments in context, while avoiding crafting messages that are too long. Some mailing systems mangle the information that is at the top of the message with your address, so include your "signature" at the bottom, with at least your e-mail address. If you have a response, consider responding directly via e-mail if you think no one on the list will be interested. Watch your temper. If you think you should wait or tone down your note, you most likely should. Don't type in all capital letters. Finally, use prevailing courtesy. If someone helps you out, a thank you will be appreciated.

Note that in all cases, you subscribe and unsubscribe from a list not by sending e-mail to the list itself (which means it goes to all the members of the list), but to a special address that deals with subscriptions. Sending mail to the list itself marks you as a "newbie" or novice who hasn't taken time to carefully read directions. It also irritates list members (numbering into the hundreds) who receive useless mail. When subscribing to a list, you will receive information on how to unsubscribe. Be sure to keep it and use it.

If you need help on subscribing to a list, you can usually send mail to a special address called "listserv" containing the word "help" in the body of the message. If you were having trouble subscribing to the mailing list at nerdnosh.org, for example, you'd send e-mail to listserv@nerdnosh.org with "help" in the message.

To find mailing lists at an Internet site, send mail to majordomo at that site (example: majordomo@ netcom.com) with the word "lists" on a line by itself. Majordomo manages the mailing lists at one site only, so you must search site by site. You can also get information about *all* the mailing lists known to all the listservs by sending the command `list global`. You will get back e-mail with the names of more than 5,000 mailing lists. If you would like more information about a particular list, then you send the LISTSERV a message

If you want to subscribe to a mailing list, be sure to send your "subscribe" message to the correct address for subscriptions, not to the mailing list itself.

Remember, the text formatting you apply to outgoing messages in Exchange is not transmitted to E-mail addresses on the Internet.

with the command `info` and the name of the list about which you are curious.

Sending E-mail to Internet Addresses

The Microsoft Network provides a gateway through which you can both send and receive e-mail to and from the millions of e-mail addresses on the Internet. It also gives you your very own Internet e-mail address, which is simply your member name followed by "@msn.com." My Internet address is steves@msn.com because my MSN member name is SteveS. As you can see, an Internet address does not have to be capitalized properly. The Microsoft Network Internet e-mail addresses are not case-sensitive.

Microsoft Exchange, the same program that handles e-mail among MSN members, also handles e-mail between MSN and the Internet. Unlike e-mail messages to MSN members, messages to Internet addresses cannot have fancy text formatting nor attached files

because the primary data currency of the Internet is straight text.

Addressing Internet E-mail

When you are sending e-mail to another MSN member, you can address the message to the member's name. But with Internet electronic mail, names alone are no longer adequate. You must address the message to the full electronic address of the person. Usually, this address has two parts: the person's e-mail name, followed by the company, organization, or commercial service to which they belong. The @ sign goes in the middle.

Let's say you need to send a message to your friend who is "tommys" on a computer system called "rocket.com." When you compose the new message in Exchange, you would enter into the To text box this address: tommys@rocket.com.

If you need to send e-mail to a certain Internet address often, you can enter the address into your personal address book in Exchange. When you create an address book entry and choose an address type, select "Internet Address" under "The Microsoft Network." *See Adding an Address Book Entry, page 140.*

Your Own Internet E-mail Address

It's only the coolest possible item you could have on a business card: your very own Internet e-mail address. Your membership to MSN makes it happen. When you join MSN, you get your own Internet address. It's simply your member name followed immediately by "@msn." My MSN member name is SteveS, so my Internet address is steves@msn.com (the letters in an Internet address do not have to be capitalized).

Sending data files or even software programs is possible across the Internet, though it supports ASCII for electronic mail. Binary is the blanket term that means any file that contains data outside plain letters and numbers. This includes programs, compressed files, and archive files produced by programs like PKZIP.

A standard has been established for encoding binary information for Internet e-mail. The standard, MIME, or Multi-purpose Internet Mail Extensions, is not a program you use directly when using MSN. Instead, MS Exchange can decide what sort of encoding your outbound messages require and automatically encode binary files for you. MS Exchange will also automatically decode inbound messages from sources that support MIME. In the following section, you will learn more about other forms of encoding you may encounter when using the Internet.

When you tell Microsoft Exchange you are ready to send a message, it compares the address with the addresses in your Exchange address book. If the mail is going to a user on MSN, your message will be routed to that user's mailbox. However, if your mail must be handed off to another computer or network through the Internet, Exchange will check the computer portion of the address and decide how to route the message before sending it on its way. When your message arrives at its destination, a mail server at the destination computer places it in the appropriate mailbox, where it awaits the recipient to logon and read it.

Decoding and Encoding Files

If you receive a message that looks like it is written in a foreign language, it could

By using your new Internet e-mail address, anyone, anywhere in the world, can send you e-mail messages. Members of other online services, such as America Online, CompuServe, and Prodigy, can also exchange e-mail messages with you.

be encoded, using one of several methods. One common practice on many Internet newsgroups is to uuencode messages. Uuencode allows users to exchange binary data (files containing programs and pictures), and not just text. MIME is another popular encoding technique for attaching binary data to regular, text e-mail. Both methods perform the same overall function (that is, they allow you to safely transmit binary data safely through e-mail).

The Internet Center File Library contains an executable program called Wincode, a Windows 3.1 program that converts binary files (EXE, COM, GIF, etc) to text files (and vice versa). Wincode

Wincode is a shareware program you can use to translate a uuencoded message into a file.

currently supports both uuencoding and MIME coding. This conversion allows you to dispatch and receive binary files via e-mail or any other text-based communications system. It provides a swift and effortless way to disburse programs to people all over the world. Of course, if your associates are fellow MSN members, you can simply attach a file to an MSN e-mail message.

Wincode is distributed as "freeware," but it is not Public Domain. SnappyInc. retains the copyright to the program, and they charge a fee for the "Help" file. Though not required for Wincode to function correctly, you may want to get it anyway, since ordering the Help file also entitles you to future updates and e-mail based support.

To use Wincode, download Wincode from the file library and then, if necessary, expand the ZIP archive into a temporary directory. Start Windows, choose Run from the Start menu, and type in the full path of the INSTALL.EXE program. The INSTALL program will copy and expand all the files to a directory you specify (overwriting older files), upgrade your WINCODE.INI (if necessary), and creates a Start menu entry called Snappy Inc.

A message that needs to be decoded.

To decode a file, start Wincode, and then follow these steps:

Decoding a File

1. From the Wincode File menu, choose Decode or select the second icon on the Wincode Toolbar. A 'File to Decode' dialog box will appear.
2. At this point, you can select the 'Options...' button to re-check the settings Wincode will use to Decode the file(s), clicking OK or Cancel to return to the File to Decode dialog box.
3. Click through the Directories list to locate the file(s) you wish to decode.
4. Select the file or files to decode. To decode all the files in the folder, click the All Files button.
5. Click OK to begin decoding. Wincode will display the Decode progress in it's main Window and will list the Decode method in the Hint Bar.

To encode a file, follow these steps:

Encoding a File

1. Select Encode from the Wincode File menu or select the first icon on the Wincode toolbar. A File to Encode dialog box will appear.
2. Click through the Directories list to locate the file(s) you wish to encode.
3. Select the file or files to encode.
4. Click OK to begin encoding. You may press ESC to cancel at any time.

ROT13 is another text scrambling method used on the Internet. Many people use it when their messages contain potentially offensive material. In the Read Message and Compose Message windows of the Newsgroup folder, the Tools menu has a command to encode or decode ROT13 text.

To see your message displayed in ROT13, simply pull down the Tools menu and select ROT13 encode/decode. The system will automatically encode your message in ROT13. You can send any message this way, putting the responsibility of decoding your message on the recipient.

If you encounter a strange message in a newsgroup, do not fret. In the Read Message Window, select ROT13 encode/decode from the Tools menu. If the message is ROT13 encoded, it will be translated to readable English. If it is not ROT13 encoded, then you can try using Wincode to decode it.

If MSN recognizes than an incoming mail message is uuencoded, Exchange will decode the message automatically.

Places to Go, Things to See

MSN Guide

- *The Guidebooks*
- *Places Worth Visiting*
- *Listings*

MSN Guide

Unlike most computer products, which go through long development cycles, The Microsoft Network is an ever-changing, ever-improving product with new sites worth exploring each day. To try to describe the best online destinations in a book, therefore, is like shooting at a moving target. A hot spot one moment is eclipsed by an even hotter spot the day later. Add to that all the interesting places that appear each day on the Internet, and there's an endless avenue of exploration available every time you sign in.

Still, early in the life of The Microsoft Network, special areas are developing already into uniquely beneficial, fascinating, or fun destinations that you'll want to take time to explore. You'll read about a few of the early highlights on The Microsoft Network, and get a few suggestions for interesting places to examine when you first sign in. These areas are sure to be well worth the stop.

Of course, when you join The Microsoft Network, you're likely to find many

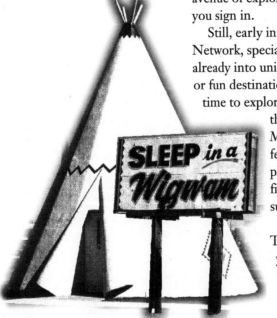

more interesting sites that will join this short list. To get some help in finding them, check MSN Today, which will keep you abreast of the newest offerings on The Microsoft Network. Another way to keep up with the changing landscape of MSN is to visit the Microsoft Press forum (Go MSPress), where you'll find our latest update to the MSN Guide.

The Guidebooks

You'll find another set of valuable resources right online at the MSN Today screen. These resources, called guidebooks are prepared by the producers on staff at The Microsoft Network, who help shape the way independent companies present their information on MSN. The producers have an intimate knowledge of new and upcoming MSN features. They also maintain the guidebooks by providing updated information about the most recent additions to the service. When you open a guidebook, therefore, you'll not only find entertaining information about MSN and its newest features, but also shortcuts you can double-click to jump directly to the sites that are described. The guidebook

The guidebook for kids.

...hat covers new content for kids is called ...Kids & Co, for example. It's fun for kids to ...ead, and it takes them to new or changed ...reas on MSN.

MSN Today will be such a helpful ...esource as you explore The Microsoft ...Network that you might want to check it ...ach time you sign in. If you want, you can ...hoose "Show MSN Today title on startup" ...n the Options dialog box (choose Options ...rom the View menu). Until you change this ...etting again, MSN Today will open ...utomatically every time you sign in.

Places Worth Visiting

No travel guide would be complete ...vithout a few recommendations for espe- ...cially interesting places to see. Here are ...ome forums worth taking the time to visit.

Arts and Entertainment

ArtForum

ArtForum magazine will be sponsoring a forum for those inter- ested in fine art. Some of the first services to appear in the forum will include news about art, art-related press releases, international gallery listings for the travel, and access to art databases for researchers and collectors.

NBC on The Microsoft Network

Exclusively on the Microsoft Network, NBC is offering online information about its many news, sports, and entertainment programs on both television and radio. When you visit the NBC area (Go NBC), you'll find forums for NBC News, NBC Entertainment, NBC Sports, CNBC programming, and forums for many of your favorite NBC TV shows, such as The Tonight Show with Jay Leno. During the 1996 presidential elections, you're sure to find comprehensive coverage in the NBC News area, and during the 1996 Olympics, NBC Sports will provide a multitude of online information to accom-

To find any forum, use the Find command on the Windows Start menu and then search "On The Microsoft Network."

pany its broadcasts of Olympic events from Atlanta.

The Microsoft Network is also the online back channel for America's Talking so you'll be able to interact with the hosts and guests on shows via MSN chats in the NBC forums.

Books and Writing

Readers and writers will enjoy the Books and Writing forum (Go Books), where they'll find areas for student writers, new writers, and working writers, such as

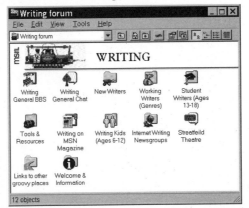

The Writing folder of the Books and Writing forum.

screenwriters, PR and advertising copywriters, poetry writers, mystery writers, and

many more. The Books and Writing forum offers everything from book reviews to files explaining copyright issues for budding authors.

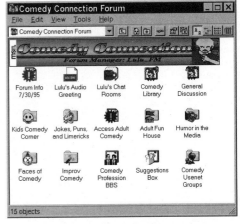

The Comedy Connection Forum

Comedy Connection

An especially entertaining stop is the Comedy Connection (Go Comedy), where you can exchange jokes, limericks, stories, and improvisations with other MSN members. You'll also find cartoons, information about clowning and magic, adult humor, and humor in the media, among many other topics.

A forum may appear in more than one folder if its content fits multiple categories.

off

176

MIDI Music

Musicians will want to check out the MIDI & Electronic Music Forum (Go MIDI), where members of the forum are collaborating on original music compositions in the MSN Stars! Area. You'll be able to download many music selections from the music libraries.

RockNet

Avid Rock music listeners will want to visit RockNet (Go Rocknet) with its rock newswire that is updated 4 times daily, charts, concert and record reviews, independent commentary, and many special features, including Dead Only, of course.

Interests, Leisure, and Hobbies

Cooking Light Magazine

The senior editors of Cooking Light magazine and well-known authors of cookbooks will participate in regular chats in the Cooking Light forum on topics such as developing menus and planning meals. You'll get the chance to ask specific questions on techniques for cooking for a healthy-living lifestyle.

Home and Family

Parenting in the 90s

Led by a clinical psychologist, the Parenting in the 90s forum discusses parenting issues for MSN members. In the Parenting forum, members can share their experiences and learn from others, as well as discuss issues such as parenting special children and adoption.

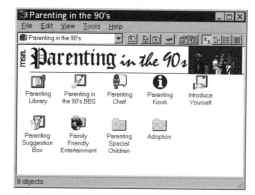

The Parenting in the 90s forum.

People and Communities

Women's Wire

The Women's Wire forum offers women advice, files, chats, and other services

MSN Today will keep you informed about new forums and services on The Microsoft Network as they appear.

Remember to add your favorite forums to the Favorite Places folder, or drag the icons of your favorite forums to the desktop to create shortcuts.

devoted to health and fitness, career and finance, and fashion and shopping.

SeniorNet

In the SeniorNet forum, you'll find offerings such as SeniorNet News, Pathways to Learning (computer instruction tailored for the needs of seniors), and Living Archives, a library to which seniors can contribute their unique histories.

Planet Out

Planet Out is a worldwide, online community for lesbian, gay, bisexual and transgendered people. Planet Out, founded by Tom Rielly, co-chair of Digital Queers, is an engaging, well-edited service which

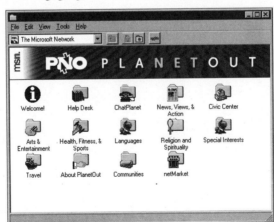

provides a safe, fun home for LGBT people, regardless of whether they're out of the closet. Planet Out debuts on The Microsoft Network, followed by other platforms later in the fall. The company is privately held and based in San Francisco, California, U.S.

Planet Out will start with five major content areas: the Civic Center; News, Views & Action; Arts & Entertainment; Sports, Health & Fitness, and netMarket. Planet Out houses many leading gay organizations including: DQ, Digital Queers (int'l); Frameline, The San Francisco International Lesbian and Gay Film Festival;•GLAAD, The Gay and Lesbian Alliance Against Defamation (U.S.); HRCF, The Human Rights Campaign Fund, (U.S.); NGLTF, The National Gay and Lesbian Task Force, (U.S.); IGLHRC, The International Gay and Lesbian Human Rights Commission (int'l); !OutProud!, The National Coalition of Gay, Lesbian, and Bisexual Youth (int'l); PFLAG, Parents, Families, and Friends of Lesbians and Gays (int'l); Victory Fund, The Gay and Lesbian Victory Fund (U.S); YAO, Youth Assistance Organization (int'l).

The New Age Forum

The New Age Forum (Go New Age), sponsors a gamut of forums including the Holistic Health area, in which you'll find information about a range of holistic activities, pursuits, and products. In separate folders, you can learn about movement therapy, energy techniques, retreats and spas, natural healing, body work and massage, and much more.

In the New Age Forum, you'll also find folders for Whole Earth, Whole Food, Whole Spirit, Divination, New Age News, the New Age Coffee House, the New Age Marketplace, New Age chats, and more.

Public Affairs

C-SPAN

C-SPAN will be using its forum on MSN to offer a variety of services, including the texts of bills currently being considered in the U.S. House of Representatives, and the voting records of congressmen. You'll also find an updated schedule for programming on both the C-SPAN and C-SPAN2 channels.

Science and Technology

EarthWatch

EarthWatch, a non-profit organization, which mounts learning expeditions to the far reaches of the globe will provide live coverage of their latest ventures via The Microsoft Network. MSN members will be able to participate "virtually" in exploratory missions to exotic locales, chat with the scientists who are at the site and receive periodic updates about the the progress of expeditions.

To learn more about a forum, double-click the kiosk icon in the forum's folder. The kiosk contains a helpful document prepared by the forum manager.

Small business owners can communicate with customers and suppliers via The Microsoft Network.

The Small Office/Home Office forum.

Small Office/Home Office

For small office/home office (SOHO) businesses, MSN has dedicated itself to providing a wealth of information, services, networking opportunities, tips, events, and comraderie, all designed to help them run small and large businesses efficiently and profitably.

Small business professionals will find "vertical market" information in areas such as law, insurance, medicine, real estate, and multilevel marketing. They'll also find legal, tax, accounting, and insurance information and services, as well as conference and convention assistance, and budget travel and meeting arrangements. The Small Business

Administration will offer information, training programs, and loan opportunities. And small business owners will be able to shop at home for office supplies, package pickup, and other services.

Especially unique are the two "SOHO Advisors." Janet Attard and Alice Bredin are authorities in the realm of small business advice. Janet is known for her "Business Know-How®" online forums and Alice for her "WorkAnywhere, Inc." Alice is also syndicated nationally on National Public Radio's "Marketplace" broadcast and she writes a weekly column for the newspaper, "Newsday."

These two advisors will be available to MSN users as sources of knowledge and advice, and also as guides to what is available in the SOHO area. Both are in daily touch with those companies who will provide information and services in the area, so they'll be able to point out useful products, services, and sources of information when asked.

Sports

Special Events

The New York Times Special Services has created a series of wonderful multimedia titles containing coverage of major sporting events such as the Americas Cup, the US Open (golf) in Southampton, and Wimbledon. Expect to see more such titles in the Special Events category on major golf, tennis, skiing, and sailing events. Each title offers regular reports directly from the events, photos, background information, interviews, and more.

Outside Online

Climbers, campers, hikers, and others should check out the Outside Online forum with its emphasis on the Pacific Northwest outdoors lifestyle.

ESPNet SportsZone

Sports news, box scores, trades, standings, team-related information, and more will be part of ESPNet's SportsZone forum.

Microsoft

Not surprisingly, some of the greatest places to visit on The Microsoft Network have been created by Microsoft, itself. Some of the most popular CD-ROM titles from the Microsoft Home division have been adapted for use online as preview versions, including Microsoft Encarta and Microsoft Bookshelf. These titles offer

many of the features of their CD-ROM counterparts, including text articles, photos, and sound files. The dictionary in Microsoft Bookshelf will pronounce any of the words you look up, for example. You actually hear the word as it's spoken. But they do not offer the video clips and certain other features that cannot be readily sent over the phone line.

The Microsoft forum.

One of the first Microsoft features you should check is Microsoft Encarta, in the Education and Reference category. Encarta is a full-scale encyclopedia with more than 26,000 articles, 5,000 photos, and 360 maps. You can browse the pages of the encyclopedia, following onscreen links that

you click to jump from article to related article, or you can use the powerful search capabilities in Encarta to zero in directly on a topic you'd like to explore, such as wildflowers.

MSN News is staffed by professional editors and journalists who will place the news in context by providing shortcuts to related information on MSN.

Another Microsoft title you'll enjoy is the online version of Microsoft Bookshelf, which features a dictionary, thesaurus, atlas, almanac, and three other complete reference works. Again, you can use a powerful search facility to locate a topic, term, or word, and jump from reference to reference within the same reference book, or in another reference book.

The MSN News newsroom.

Each day, MSN News will bring you current stories from the world's news, sports updates, financial information, and everything else you'd expect from an online news service. You'll find MSN News on MSN Today.

As you'd expect, you'll find complete information on both Windows 95 and Microsoft Office 95. Software developers will find the Microsoft Developer Network in the Microsoft folder. For those who are or plan to become software developers, the Microsoft Online Institute conducts online training on Microsoft products, programming, and support.

Listings

Though it was compiled before the official launch of The Microsoft Network, this guide should give you a good overview of the many forums and services you'll find on MSN. Go words and descriptions may have changed, services may not yet have opened for business, and, of course, many new forums will have opened since. Each forum listed offers a host of services, such as BBSes, chats, file libraries, kiosks, and more. An alphabetical index to the Guide begins on page 280.

To get the revised and updated MSN Guide, visit the MS Press forum (Go mspress).

Forum managers: Please forward revisions and additions to the MSN Guide to SteveS.

Arts and Entertainment

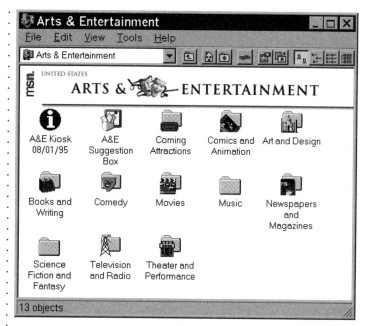

21st Century
Go **21**

21st Century Online Network is committed to being a global resource, providing individuals with leading edge interactive tools, information and media essential to creating a productive and sustainable future.

21st Century Business
Go **21business**

21business

21st Century Online Magazine
Go **21magazine**

21magazine

21st Century Special Events
Go **21Special**

Here you will find our exciting line-up of special events, conferences and guest moderators covering a fascinating wide range of topics about the next century. Tune in to the Future Now.

Adult Contemporary
Go **Radioac**

A format specific forum for Adult Contemporary radio.

Albion Books
Go **albionbooks**

Publishers of Netiquette by Virginia Shea and other fine computer networking books.

Albion Channel
Go **Albion**

The Albion Channel delivers the frontiers of cyberspace to your desktop.

Albion D&R Library
Go **Albion D&R Library**

Albion D&R Library

AOR/CR
Go **Radioaor**

An area for the AOR and Classic Rock users.

Art and Design
Go **Design**

Art Revue
Go **Art Revue**

Art Revue

ArtLine - Fine Arts
Go **ArtLine - Fine Arts**

ArtLine - Fine Arts

Bass Players Arena
Go **Bass Players Arena**

Bass Players Arena

BookLinks
Go **booklinksfolder**

Look for the latest edition of BookLinks, an annotated collection of shortcuts to book-related resources available via MSN.

BookLinks Archive
Go **booklinksarchive**

Bookport
Go **bookport**

Supporting Internet access to books.

Books and Writing
Go **Books**

British TV Series
Go **SFF_British**

SFF_British

Buckminster Fuller's Centenary
Go **21buckyanniv**

Celebrate Buckminster Fuller's 100th Birthday!

CHR
Go **Radiochr**

Format specific forum for CHR radio.

College Radio
Go **Radiocollege**

An area dedicated to College Radio.

Comedy and Humor
Go **Comedy and Humor**

Comedy and Humor

Comedy Connection
Go **Comedy**

Comedy Connection provides users of every age group a place to share and discuss all types of humor and comedy including jokes, puns, limericks, stories, poetry, improvisation, and art appealing to children, adults, and a general audience.

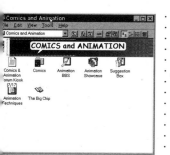

Comics and Animation

o **Comics**

Commercial Radio

o **radio**

Professional Radio Broadcaster's Forum. Topics include Program-ming, Sales, Engineering, Promotions and everything Radio!

Country

o **Radiocountry**

A format specific forum for Country radio.

Cyberspace Business with Jayme Canton

Go **21cyberbiz**

The latest info on business in cyberspace.

Faces of Comedy

Go **comedyfaces**

This area is for the discussion and distribution of information about clowning and mime.

Fairgrounds

Go **fairgrounds**

Where the Online BookFair takes off.

Future Vision Showcase

Go **21Future**

21Future

Genres

Go **Genres**

Genres

Globarium

Go **Globarium**

Globarium

Guitar/Bass Repair

Go **Guitar/Bass Repair**

Guitar/Bass Repair

Guitars, Etc.

Go **Guitars Etc.**

GUITARS ETC.

Hollywood Highway

Go **hhwy**

Here are links to movie discussion groups on the Internet.

Humor in the Media

Go **comedymedia**

This area is for the discussion of humor and comedy in cyberspace, music, print media, radio, television, and movies.

Improv Comedy

Go **comedyimprov**

This area is for the discussion, distribution, and roleplaying of Improv Comedy.

Jokes, Puns, and Limericks

Go **generalhumor**

This area is for the sharing of humorous cartoons and art, jokes, puns, limericks, poetry, and stories which appeal to a general audience.

KidSpace

Go **KidSpace**

KidSpace will explore residential design issues for the young — ranging from baby space to shared quarters to shared custody. While primarily for parents, there's a section for kids to share room tips and ideas.

Languages

Go **Languages**

Languages

Leaders in Personal Growth

Go **21grow**

Explore the expanding field of Personal Growth.

Links to other groovy places

Go **Links to other groovy places**

Double-click on any of this folder's shortcuts to go directly to other MSN forums and sevices.

Lulu's Back Chat Room

Go **luluback**

This is the back room of Lulu's Chat Lounge for those of you who would like to meet in smaller groups to share stories and humor.

Lulu's Fruit Cellar Pub

Go **lulucellar**

This area is where users can find small intimate tables in the Fruit Cellar Pub of Lulu's Lounge.

Media

Go **SFF_Media**

SFF_Medi

MIDI and Electronic Musicians Forum

Go **MIDI**

Movies

Go **SFF_Movies**

SFF_Movies

Movies

Go **Movies**

Musician Referral Center

Go **Musicians, Guitarists, Bassists Keyboardists, Vocalists, and more.**

NBC

Go **NBC**

NBC

New Age for Teens

Go **New Age for Teens**

New Age for Teens

New Writers

Go **new**

An area where writers can learn the basics of preparing and marketing their work, with the support and friendship of other writers around the world.

News/Talk

Go **Radiotalk**

An area for News/Talk radio users.

Nickelodeon

Go **Nickelodeon**

Nickelodeon forum.

Oldies/70's

Go **Radiooldies**

A format specific area for Oldies radio.

Online BookFair

Go **bookfair**

Come celebrate the convergence of books and online media with major publishers and booksellers.

Ooze News

Go **Ooze News**

Ooze News

Police Blotter Rappers in Jail

Go **Police Blotter Rappers in Jail**

Police Blotter Rappers in Jail

Radio Engineering

Go **Radioengineering**

A non-format specific area for Radio Engineers.

Radio Listener's Forum

Go **listen**

This forum is part of the Commercial Radio Forum. Without listener's opinions and input, commercial radio stations would end up playing their formats to themselves. So tell us what you think. Ask any questions, any ideas are welcome!

Radio Production

Go **Radioprod**

Radioprod

Radio Programming
Go **Radioprog**

A place for professional radio Program Directors and Music Directors to discuss techniques. Includes a message base and chat room.

Radio Promotions Idea Area
Go **Radio Promotions Idea Area**

Radio Promotions Idea Area.

Radio Sales
Go **Radsales**

Radsales

Reading
Go **Book**

A place to talk about your favorite books and authors...and, sometimes, a place to meet your favorite (or not-so-favorite) authors.

RockNet
Go **RockNet**

An up-to-the-minute rock & roll newswire provided by over 100 contributors world-wide. Plus message boards, Dead area, reviews, comments, pictures & sound.

Science Fiction and Fantasy
Go **SFF**

Star Trek TV Universe
Go **SFF_STUNIV**

SFF_STUNIV

Star Trek Universe
Go **SFF_STMovies**

SFF_STMovies

Star Wars Universe
Go **SFF_Star Wars**

SFF_Star Wars

Stimulocity
Go **Stimulocity**

Stimulocity

Student Writers (Ages 13-18)

Student Writers (Ages 13-18)
Go **student**

An area for writers between the ages of 13 and 18, with teachers welcome to visit.

Television and Radio
Go **TV**

The Music Forum
Go **Music**

The place to be for Music lovers on MSN!

Tools & Resources
Go **tools**

Reviews of writing books and software, sources of tools for writers, software demos, and vendor support.

Urban

Go **Radiourban**

An area for Urban radio users.

USA's Top Recordings

Go **USA's Top Recordings**

USA's Top Recordings

Weekly Music Columns & Reviews

Go **Weekly Music Columns & Reviews**

Weekly Music Columns & Reviews

Working Writers (Genres)

Go **working**

A place where professional (and soon-to-be-professional) writers can discuss specific writing genres such as fiction, nonfiction, screenwriting, multimedia, and computer books. More sections will be added as new members come online.

Writing

Go **Writing**

Writing

Writing Kids (Ages 6-12)

Go **writingkids**

An area for young writers between from ages 6-12.

Business and Finance

Accounting and Auditing

Go **Audit**

Audit

Accounting Bookstore

Go **Accounting Bookstore**

Accounting related books

Accounting Office

Go **CPA**

Online virtual office for accounting professionals.

Accounting, Tax & Finance

Go **Accounting, Tax & Finance**

Accounting, Tax & Finance

Advertising & Marketing

Go **Advertising & Marketing**

Advertising & Marketing

Advertising, PR & Marketing

Go **Advertising, PR & Marketing**

Advertising, PR & Marketing

After Hours

Go **Minority Business After Hours**

Minority Business After Hours

Alice Bredin Working At Home

Go **Alice Bredin Working At Home**

Do you run your own home-based business or work from home for your corporate boss? Or do you want to? This forum has the tools and information to help you get started and thrive. *Working At Home is brought to you by WorkAnywhere, Inc., and its president.*

All About Law School

Go **Law School**

A forum where prospective, current, and former students of the law from around the world can interact.

AMA Marketplace

Go **MARKET**

The American Management Association offers a wide variety of products to help you manage your business and your career.

American City Business Journals

Go **Business Journal**

Business Journal

American Management Association

Go **AMA**

AMA's source for information on how you can sharpen your skills, keep up on the latest business developments, and network with colleagues and business experts.

American Management Association Red-Hot Topics

Go **RHT**

Look in here for recent surveys and items on today's hottest business issues and let us know what you think.

AMERICAN VentureCapital EXCHANGE

Go **AVCE**

The AVCE is where entrepreneurs can list a one page summary of a venture that is seeking capital (start up or expansion). Potential providers of funding can review the listings and contact the entrepreneurs directly to get their full business plan.

Antitrust & Unfair Competition

Go **Antitrust**

A sub-section of The Law Office focused on legal issues relating to antitrust and unfair competition.

Artex International

Go **Artex International**

Artex International

Auditing

Go **Auditing**

Auditing

Austin Business Journal

Go **Austin Business Journal**

Austin Business Journal

Baltimore Business Journal
Go **Baltimore**

Baltimore

Bankruptcy Law
Go **Bankruptcy**

A topic focused on bankruptcy issues both from the creditor and the debtor perspectives.

Bar Equipment
Go **Bar Equipment**

Bar Equipment

Bar Review
Go **Bar Review**

Bar Review

Benefits
Go **Benefits**

Benefits

Birkman
Go **Birkman**

Birkman

Biz/Finc Storage
Go **Biz/Finc Storage**

Biz/Finc Storage

Bonds Online
Go **Bonds Online**

Bonds Online

Book of Lists
Go **Book of Lists**

Book of Lists

Books, Stationery & Software
Go **Books, Stationery & Software**

Books, Stationery & Software

Bookstore
Go **Bookstore**

Bookstore

Budgeting
Go **Budgeting**

Budgeting

Business & Competitive Intelligence
Go **Business & Competitive Intelligence**

Business & Competitive Intelligence

Business Exchange
Go **BusinessEx**

This area is for entrepreneurs, accredited investors, and business managers. It lists ventures seeking capital, mergers & acquisitions, and features chats by new venture experts and entrepreneurs.

Business First of Buffalo
Go **Buffalo**

Buffalo

Business First of Columbus
Go **Columbus**

Columbus

Business First of Louisville
Go **Louisville**

Louisville

Business Intelligence
Go **Intel**

Intel

Business Know-How
Go **Business Know-How**

Business Know-How

Business Know-How Showcase
Go **Business Know-How Showcase**

We will be selecting a different member or business to profile each month. We hope each profile will present a unique perspective, or interesting tips on doing business.

Business Law
Go **Business Law**

A section of The Law Office focused on business related issues.

Business Plan Guides
Go **Business Plan Guides**

Business Plan Guides

Business Services
Go **Business Services**

Business Servic

Business Skills
Go **Business Skills**

Business Skills

Business Software Library
Go **Business Software Library**

Business Software Library

Business Strategy Forum
Go **strategy**

strategy

California
Go **California**

California

Capital District Business Review (Albany)
Go **Albany**

Albany

Career Bookstore
Go **Career-Resources**

Career books and book reviews.

Catering
Go **Catering**

Catering

CCH Entrepreneurial Outfitters
Go **CCH_SOHO**

Information and services for Small Business.

CCI INFO CENTER
Go **Job-Hot-Lines**

Listings of employer job lines by city.

Charlotte Business Journal
Go **Charlotte**

Charlotte

Cincinnati Business Courier
Go **Cincinnati**

Cincinnati

Client Write-up
Go **Client Write-up**

Client Write-up

Clothing Manufacturing Industry
Go **ClothingInd**

Trends & Issues In The Manufacturing of Clothing

Coaching & Counseling
Go **Career-Help**

Individual and group sessions for greater career advancement power.

Cognetics
Go **Cognetics**

Cognetics

Commercial Bankruptcy
Go **Combank**

A section of The Law Office focused on creditor's remedies in bankrupcty proceedings.

Companies For Sale
Go **M&A**

This section lists short descriptions of middle market companies that are available for acquisition and companies that buyers are seeking to acquire.

Compensation
Go **Compensation**

Compensation

Computer
Go **Computer**

Computer

Construction
Go **Construction**

Construction

Consultants
Go **Consultants**

Consultants

Consulting Resource Group
Go **CRG**

CRG

Consumer Protection Law

Go **Consumer Law**

A section of The Law Office focused on consumer protection related issues and topics.

Consumer Research

Go **Consumer Research**

Consumer Research

Continuing Education

Go **CPE**

CPE

Continuing Legal Education

Go **CLE**

CLE

Coopers and Lybrand

Go **coopers**

coopers

CorpTech

Go **CorpTech**

CorpTech

Cost Accounting

Go **Cost Accounting**

Cost Accounting

CPE On-line

Go **CPE On-line**

CPE On-line

Creativity Unleashed

Go **Unleashed**

Creativity Unleashed is a forum dedicated to improving your creativity— whether to make your business more profitable or your life more fulfilled. We're in the business of innovation stimulation!

Credit Card & Payment Systems Forum

Go **CreditCard**

CreditCard

Criminal Law

Go **Crime**

A section of The Law Office focused on criminal law related issues and topics.

Criminal Law Topics

Go **CrimeTopics**

CrimeTopics

D&B Information Services

Go **D&B Information Services**

D&B Information Services

DataTech Software

Go **DataTech Software**

DataTech Software

Dealing with the IRS

Go **Dealing with the IRS**

Dealing with the IRS

Places to Go, Things to See

Debt Collection Abuse
Go **Debt**

Debt

Denver Business Journal
Go **Denver**

Denver

Design Issues
Go **Design Issues**

Design Issues

Development Dimensions International
Go **DDI**

DDI

Disability Legal Issues
Go **DisabilityLaw**

DisabilityLaw

Diversity Management
Go **Diversity Management**

Diversity Management

Dun & Bradstreet Information Services
Go **D&B**

D&B

Education & Professional Development
Go **Education & Professional Development**

Education & Professional Development

Elderly Legal Issues
Go **Agelaw**

Agelaw

Employee Relations
Go **Employee Relations**

Employee Relations

Employment Law
Go **Employmentlaw**

A section of The Law Office focused on employment related issues.

Employment Opportunities
Go **Work-Opportunity**

Job postings and job listings.

Entertainment & Media Law
Go **Entertainment**

A section of The Law Office focused on entertainment law issues and topics.

Entrepreneur's Auditorium

Go **Entrepreneur's Auditorium**

Entrepreneur's Auditorium.

Environmental Issues and the Law

Go **EcoLawgroup**

EcoLawgroup

Environmental Law

Go **Ecolaw**

A section of The Law Office focused on environmental law related issues and topics.

Equipment Testing

Go **Equipment Testing**

Equipment Testing

Events Sign Up

Go **SBA Events**

SBA Events

Executive Reports on Companies & Industries

Go **reports**

Company Reports on 10,000 Public U.S. Companies, 25,000 Private U.S. Companies, and 35,000 International Companies

Expert Service Providers

Go **Forensic**

This is where you find your expert witness.

FYI

Go **FYI**

FYI

Family & Parenting

Go **Family & Parenting**

Family & Parenting

Family Law

Go **Familylaw**

A section of The Law Office focused on family law issues and topics.

Family Life

Go **Minority Business Family**

Minority Business Family

Faulkner & Gray

Go **Faulkner & Gray**

Faulkner & Gray Specialty Business Publishers

Feedback

Go **Feedback**

Feedback

Fessel International
Go **Fessel International**

Fessel International

Financial Audits
Go **Financial Audits**

Financial Audits

Financial Planning
Go **Financial Planning**

Financial Planning

Financial Reporting
Go **Financial Reporting**

Financial Reporting

Find a Lawyer
Go **attorney**

A section of the law office where MSN users can find a lawyer for their particular need in their particular jurisdiction.

Find an Accountant
Go **Accountants**

Accountants

Fine Dining
Go **Fine Dining**

Fine Dining

FIREPOWER!
Go **Careers**

Welcome to the new world of work! If you're wondering about your next career move, you're not alone. Today's world of work includes MANY SURPRISES. The FirePower Career Forum will help you prepare for ALL of them!

Focus Groups In Law
Go **Lawfocus**

This is the part of The Law Office where law is broken down to areas of interest, such as Woman and Law, Taxpayers and Law, Minorities and Law, Gay Legal Issues, and others as the individual forums are created.

Food and Beverage
Go **Food and Beverage**

Food and Beverage

Food Prep Equipment
Go **Food Prep Equipment**

Food Prep Equipment

For the Employee
Go **Employee Law**

A section of The Law Office focused on employment law issues and topics relevant to employees.

For the Employer
Go **Employer Law**

A section of The Law Office focused on employment law issues and topics from the standpoint of the employer.

Franchise Development
Go **Franchise Development**

Franchise Development

Free Speech and the Law
Go **1STAMENDMENT**

1STAMENDMENT

Fund Accounting
Go **Fund Accounting**

Fund Accounting

Furnishings and Fixtures
Go **Furnishings and Fixtures**

Furnishings and Fixtures

Gardening
Go **Gardening**

Gardening

Gay & Lesbian Legal Issues
Go **Gaylaw**

Gaylaw

Geographic Information
Go **Geographic Information**

Regulations and other regional information

Global Designs
Go **Global Designs**

Global Designs

Government Audits
Go **Government Audits**

Government Audits

Graham & Dunn Legal Direct
Go **Graham**

Graham

GreenLight
Go **GreenLight**

GreenLight

Health & Wellness
Go **Health & Wellness**

Health & Wellness

Health Care Law
Go **Health Law**

A section of The Law Office focused on health care law issues and topics.

High School Courses
Go **High School Courses**

High School Courses

Home Business Survival Essentials

Go **Home Business Survival Essentials**

Home-based business owners face all kinds of challenges–mastering marketing, sales and finance, setting up a home office, balancing a business and a life under one roof... Home Business Survival Essentials' articles provide the information you need.

Home Buying and Selling

Go **HomeBuy&Sell**

HomeBuy&Sell

Home Decorating

Go **Home Decorating**

Home Decorating

Home Improvement

Go **Home Improvement**

Home Improvement

Home of the Month

Go **Home of the Month**

Home of the Month

Home Office Computing Magazine

Go **Homeoffice**

Homeoffice

Home Repair

Go **Home Repair**

Home Repair

HomeGuide

Go **HomeGuide**

HomeGuide makes buying, selling, and maintaining a home a snap, providing articles, consumer-to-consumer discussion groups, games, contests, and more. Stop by today and see what we have to offer.

Hospitality Food & Beverage

Go **Hospitality Food & Beverage**

Hospitality Food & Beverage

Hot New Products

Go **Hot New Products**

Hot New Products

HR & the Internet

Go **HR & the Internet**

HR & the Internet

HR Auditorium

Go **HR Auditorium**

HR Auditorium

HR Job Board

Go **HRjobs**

HRjobs

Industry Areas
Go **Industry Areas**

Industry Areas

InfoGenesis
Go **InfoGenesis**

InfoGenesis

Human Resource Professionals
Go **Human Resource Professionals**

Human Resource Professionals

Human Resources
Go **Human Resources**

Human Resources

Hunt Scanlon
Go **Hunt Scanlon**

Hunt Scanlon

Information Systems Audits
Go **Information Systems Audits**

Information Systems Audits

INNterREST Food Service and Lodging Network
Go **ITR**

THE INNterREST provides all organizations and individuals in the Global Hospitality Community with the tools needed to achieve their highest goals on MSN. The INNterREST is designed and managed by PalCom Hospitality Corporation.

Insurance
Go **Insurance**

Insurance

Intellectual Property Law
Go **Patents**

A section of The Law Office focusing on issues relating to intellectual property law issues and topics.

International Franchise Association
Go **Franchise**

Franchise

International HR
Go **International HR**

International HR

International Law

· Go **International**

A section of The Law Office focused on international legal issues and topics.

International Law Offices

· Go **Globallaw**

Globallaw

International Trade

· Go **International Trade**

International Trade

Interviewing & Negotiating

· Go **Interviewing**

Activities to build interpersonal skills in job interviewing and salary negotiating.

Invest Learning

· Go **InvestLearning**

InvestLearning

Issues Archive

· Go **Issues Archive**

Issues Archive

Itex

· Go **Itex**

Itex

Jacksonville Business Journal

· Go **Jacksonville**

Jacksonville

Janet Attard Business Know-How

· Go **Business Know-How**

Your source for facts, success tips, useful business shareware and lively discussions about succeeding in home and small businesses. Managed by Attard Communications.

Jester's Court

· Go **Jester's Court**

Jester's Court

Job Postings

· Go **Recruiters**

Postings of jobs by employers and recruiters.

Job Research

· Go **Job Research**

Job Research

JobQuest
Go **JobQuest**

JobQuest

Jobs & Careers
Go **Jobs & Careers**

Jobs & Careers

Kansas City Business Journal
Go **Kansas City**

Kansas City

Knight-Ridder BusinessBase
Go **Knight-Ridder BusinessBase**

Knight-Ridder BusinessBase

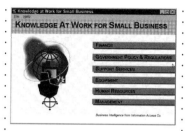

Knowledge at Work from IAC
Go **knowledge**

This is Information Access Co's Forum. It's theme is "Knowledge at Work" and it's designed to be your business information source.

Law
Go **Law**

Law

Law Office Career Center
Go **Lawjobs**

Law jobs

Law Product Vendors
Go **Legal Products**

Legal Products

Law School Library
Go **law library**

law library

Lawyer to Lawyer
Go **Lawyer**

A place for the legal profession. This is where lawyers and paralegals and others within the legal industry can access information particular to their needs.

Legal
Go **Legal**

Legal

Legal Associations
Go **Lawgroups**

Law groups

Legal Issues
Go **Legal Issues**

Legal Issues

Legal Research Center
Go

All your legal research needs will be satisfied here.

Legislative Issues

· Go **Legislative Issues**

   Legislative Issues

LEXIS-NEXIS

· Go **LEXIS-NEXIS**

   LEXIS-NEXIS

Mainstream Access

· Go **MainstreamAccess**

   MainstreamAccess

Mainstream Career Center

· Go **Mainstream Career Center**

   Mainstream Career Center

Mainstream Entrepreneur Center

· Go **Entrepreneur**

   Entrepreneur

Mainstream HR Resource Center

· Go **Mainstream HR Resource Center**

   Mainstream HR Resource Center

Mainstream Learning Center

· Go **Mainstream Learning Center**

   Mainstream Learning Center

Mainstream Personal Development Center

· Go **Mainstream Personal Development Center**

   Mainstream Personal Development Center

Mainstream Resource Center

· Go **HumanResources**

   For employers and job-seekers.

Management Audits

· Go **Management Audits**

   Management Audits

Management Consulting

· Go **Management Consulting**

   Management Consulting

Management Systems & Software

· Go **Management Systems & Software**

   Management Systems & Software

Management Training

· Go **Management Training**

   Management Training

Manpower
Go **Manpower**

Manpower

Manufacturing/ Retail & Technologies
Go **ManRetTech**

This area will service the trade only.

Maritime Law
Go **maritimelaw**

Maritime Law encompasses everything from yachts, to barges, to houseboats, to supertankers and offshore oil exploration equipment. This area will cover administrative seizures, cargo claims and subrogation, charter agreements, collisions, criminal liability.

Market Research
Go **Market Research**

Market Research

Mediation Center
Go **Mediation**

This is where you can resolve your legal conflicts with an independent profession lawyer (in all cases it will be a person who has been a judge in your jurisdiction), so he or she knows the court system in which the case is involved.

Menu Services
Go **Menu Services**

Menu Services

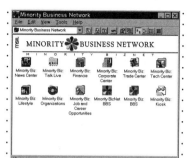

Minority Biz: Corporate Center
Go **Minority Business Corporate**

Minority Business Corporate

Minority Biz: Finance
Go **Minority Biz Financial Services**

Minority Biz Financial Services

Minority Biz: Job and Career Opportunities
Go **Minority Business Opportunities**

Minority Business Opportunities

Minority Biz: Lifestyle
Go **Minority Biz Lifestyle**

Minority Biz Lifestyle

Minority Biz: News Center
Go **Minority Biz: News Center**

Minority Biz: News Center

Minority Biz: Organizations

Go **Minority Biz: Organizations**

Minority Biz: Organizations

Minority Biz: Talk

Go **Minority Biz Conference Center**

Minority Biz Conference Center

Minority Biz: Tech Center

Go **Minority Business Tech Center**

Minority Business Tech Center

Minority Biz: Trade Center

Go **Minority Business Trade Center**

Minority Business Trade Center

Minority Business Corporate Center

Go **Minority Business Corporate Center**

Minority Business Corporate Center

Minority Business Fashion Mart

Go **Minority Business Fashion Guide**

Minority Business Fashion Guide

Minority Business Network

Go **Minority Business**

Minority Business

Minority Business Newsstand

Go **Minority Business Publications**

Minority Business Publications

Minority Business: Commercial Banking

Go **Minority Business Commercial Banking**

Minority Business Commercial Banking

Minority Business: Commercial Banks On-line

Go **Commercial Banks**

Commercial Banks

Minority Business: Financial Planning

Go **Minority Business Financial Planning**

Minority Business Financial Planning

206

Minority Business: Insurance
Go **Minority Business Insurance**

Minority Business Insurance

Minority Business: Investment Banking
Go **Minority Business Investment Banking**

Minority Business Investment Banking

Minority Business: Merchant Banking
Go **Minority Business Merchant Banking**

Minority Business Merchant Banking

Minority Legal Issues
Go **MinorityLaw**

Minority Law

Mortgage Rates
Go **Mortgage Rates**

Mortgage Rates

National Fisheries, Inc.
Go **National Fisheries, Inc.**

National Fisheries, Inc.

Networking Areas
Go **Networking Areas**

Networking Areas

Networking Connections
Go **Job-Networking**

People connections for moving forward on a job search.

New West Consultants
Go **New West Consultants**

New West Consultants

News & Reference
Go **News & Reference**

News & Reference

News from the Far West and Hawaii
Go **Western**

Western

News from the Midwest
Go **Midwest**

Midwest

News from the Northeast
Go **Northeast**

Northeast

News from the Southeast
Go **Southeast**

Southeast

News from the Southwest
Go **Southwest**

Southwest

On the Road
Go **On the Road**

On the Road

207

Orlando Business Journal

Go **Orlando**

Orlando

Pacific Business News (Honolulu)

Go **Honolulu**

Honolulu

PAR

Go **PAR**

PAR

Peer Networking

Go **Peer Networking**

Peer Networking

Personal Bankruptcy

Go **Debts**

A section of The Law Office focused on the individual who is looking at whether filing for personal bankruptcy is an alternative.

Personal Finance

Go **Personal Finance**

Personal Finance

Personal Injury Law

Go **Accident**

A section of The Law Office focused on personal injury legal issues and topics.

Personal Investing

Go **Personal Investing**

Personal Investing

Personality Profiling

Go **Profile**

Self discovery tests and activities. Personality tests.

Photodisc ClipPix Images

Go **photodiscclippix**

photodiscclippix

PhotoDisc Design Tips

Go **Photodisctips**

Photodisctips

PhotoDisc Digital Image Forum

Go **PhotoDisc**

PhotoDisc

PhotoDisc Image Collection

Go **photodiscCollection**

photodiscCollection

PhotoDisc Object Series

Go **PhotoDisc Object Series**

PhotoDisc Object Series

PhotoDisc Sales, Service and Support

Go **Photodiscsales**

Photodiscsales

Pinkerton
Go **Pinkerton**

Pinkerton

Pinkerton Risk
Go **Pinkerton Risk**

Pinkerton Risk

Planning New Career Objectives
Go **Career-Objectives**

Strategies and help for moving forward into a new career direction.

POS Automation
Go **TFIFPOSAuto**

This area will cover Point of Sale Automation for Retailers.

Practice Management
Go **Practice Management**

Practice Management

Private Eye News Alert
Go **Private Eye**

Private Eye

Product and Service Locater
Go **Product and Service Locater**

Product and Service Locater

Production Automation
Go **ProdAuto**

This area will deal with automation deployment strategies for the clothing, shoes and accessories manufacturing industries.

Professional Associations
Go **Professional Associations**

Professional Associations

Professional Development
Go **Professional Development**

Professional Development

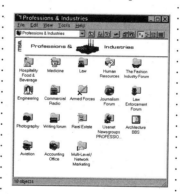

Professions & Industries
Go **Professions & Industries**

Professions & Industries

Profit Center
Go **Profit Center**

Profit Center

Promotions
Go **Promotions**

Promotions

Properties For Sale
Go **Properties For Sale**

Properties For Sale

Public Relations
Go **Public Relations**

Public Relations

Publications
Go **Publications**

Publications

Quick Service Restaurants
Go **ITR QSR**

ITR QSR

R & R
Go **R & R**

R & R

Real Estate
Go **Real Estate**

Real Estate

Real Estate Law
Go **Real Estate**

A section of The Law Office focused on real estate legal issues and topics.

Real Estate Office
Go **RealEstate**

Any and all real estate topics. Those finding items of interest in the Real Estate Office include: home owners, home buyers, other property owners, realtors and other real estate professionals and real estate investors. Step on into the Office and browse.

Realtor's Corner
Go **Realtors**

Realtors

Recipe Development
Go **Recipe Development**

Recipe Development

Recruitment
Go **Recruitment**

Recruitment

Reference Library
Go **Reference Library**

Reference Library

Reference Library
Go **Reference Library**

Reference Library

Relationships
Go **Relationships**

Relationships

Religion and Law
Go **ReligionLaw**

ReligionLaw

Relocation Hotline
Go **Relocation**

Relocation

Resume Postings
Go **Talent**

Opportunities for individuals to post their resumes.

Resume Writing
Go **resume**

Help in writing a winning resume.

Resumes on Computer
Go **Resumes on Computer**

Resumes on Computer

Roper
Go **Roper**

Roper

Sales Training
Go **Sales Training**

Sales Training

San Antonio Business Journal
Go **San Antonio**

San Antonio

San Francisco Business Times
Go **San Francisco**

San Francisco

San Jose Business Journal
o **San Jose**

San Jose

Small Business Administration (SBA)
Go **SBA**

SBA

SBA District Offices
Go **SBA Regional**

SBA Regional

SBA Programs and Services
Go **Program**

Program

SBA Seattle, WA
Go **SBA Seattle**

SBA Seattle

Secrets of Movers & Shakers
Go **SECRETS**

Find out who's making waves in today's business world and learn their secrets to success.

Self Improvement
Go **Self Improvement**

Self Improvement

Services
Go **Services**

Services

Settings International
Go **Settings International**

Settings International

Shopping & Supplies
Go **Shopping & Supplies**

Shopping & Supplies

Silicon Valley
Go **Silicon Valley**

Silicon Valley

Site Location
Go **Site Location**

Site Location

Small Office/Home Office
Go **SOHO**

SOHO

Smart Shopper
Go **Smart Shopper**

Smart Shopper

Society for Creative Anachronism
Go **SCA**

Welcome to the SCA! All ladies, gentlemen and kingdoms are welcome!

Software Demos
Go **Software Demos**

Demos of accounting and tax software

SOHO Advisors
Go **SOHO Advisors**

SOHO Advisors

South Florida Business Journal (Miami)
Go **Miami**

Miami

Special Offers
Go **Special Offers**

Special Offers

Special Reports
Go **Special Reports**

Special Reports

St. Louis Business Journal
Go **St. Louis**

St. Louis

Starting Up
Go **Starting Up**

Starting Up

State Employment Law Resource Center
Go **mleesmith**

mleesmith

Stay Out of Court
Go **COURT**

Recommendations, guidelines and strategies for developing policies and procedures that comply with federal laws and government regulations.

Steak House
Go **Steak House**

Steak House

Strategic Planning
Go **Strategic Planning**

Strategic Planning

Supplies

Go **Supplies**

Supplies

Table-top Ware

Go **Table-top Ware**

Table-top Ware

Table Service Restaurants

Go **itr tsr**

itr tsr

Tampa Bay Business Journal

o **Tampa**

Tampa

Tax Law

o **Tax Law**

A section of The Law Office focused on tax law issues.

Tax Planning

Go **Tax Planning**

Tax Planning

Tax Practice

Go **Tax Practice**

Tax Practice

Tax Research

Go **Tax Research**

Tax Research

Technical Questions

Go **Technical Questions**

Technical Questions

Technical Training

Go **Technical Training**

Technical Training

Telecommuter Survival Essentials

Go **Telecommuter Survival Essentials**

Want to convice your boss to let you work from home? Wondering what's in a telecommuting agreement? Need to know more about how to stay in better touch through technology? These articles contain telecommuting tips and strategies.

Places to Go, Things to See

The Accountant's Forum
Go **F&G Accounting**

F&G Accounting

The Australian Law Office
Go **AussieLaw**

AussieLaw

The Banker's Information Center
Go **Banking**

Banking

The Briefing Room
Go **The Briefing Room**

The Briefing Room

The Bureau of National Affairs
Go **BNA**

BNA

The Canadian Law Office
Go **CanadaLaw**

CanadaLaw

The Fashion Industry
Go **TFIF**

This Forum will Service the Manufacturer, Retailer and the Consumer.

The Law Office
Go **Legal**

The Law Society
Go **Lawsoc**

The Law Society of England and Wales

The Legal Research Center
Go **LRC**

This is where both the professional and layperson find all of their needs met for legal research.

The Magellan Group
Go **Magellan**

Magellan

The Pac-Rim Law Office
Go **PacRimLaw**

PacRimLaw

The People's Network
Go **TPN**

TPN

The U. K. Law Office
Go **UKLaw**

UKLaw

The Yard Sale
Go **YardSale**

YardSale

Thomson Market Edge
Go **Tbox**

Tbox

Time and Billing
Go **Time and Billing**

Time and Billing

Time Management
Go **Time Management**

Time Management

Tools You Can Use
Go **Tools You Can Use**

Practical tools for home-business owners and telecommuters. COMING SOON.

Top Side
Go **Top Side**

Top Side

Training
Go **Training**

Training

Training & Development
Go **Training & Development**

Training & Development

Triangle Business Journal (Raleigh)
Go **Raleigh**

Raleigh

Trivia
Go **Trivia**

Trivia

TRW
Go **TRW**

TRW

TRW Business Services
Go **TRW Business Services**

TRW Business Services

U.S.A. Legal Topics
Go **Topics**

Topics

United Parcel Service
Go **UPS**

UPS

University Courses
Go **University Courses**

University Courses

University of Phoenix
Go **UOP**

UOP

Venture and Entrepreneur
Go **Venture and Entrepreneur**

Venture and Entrepreneur

Visualizing Success
Go **visualize**

This folder contains information and activities to encourage effective use of visualizing or mental imagery during all phases of career/job search.

Wall Street, The Markets, Investing

Go **Wall Street, The Markets, Investing**

Wall Street, The Markets, Investing

What's New

What's New & User's Guide

Go **What's New & User's Guide**

Information about how to move your career forward.

WholeSale Automation

Go **TFIFWSale**

This area will address all issues & strategies of wholesale & distribution automation.

Wills, Probate & Trusts

Go **Wills and Probate**

A section of The Law Office focused on legal issues pertaining to wills, probates and trust issues and topics.

Wise and Wise

Go **Wise and Wise**

Wise and Wise

Women and Law

Go **Womenlaw**

This forum of The Law Office focuses on legal issues related to women.

Work Here

Go **Work Here**

Work Here

World Enterprise Forum

Go **Forum**

This area will feature speakers discussing topics of interest to entrepreneurs, accredited investors and business managers. It will also feature entrepreneurs presenting their venture to other entrepreneurs and experts for feedback from the audience.

World Wide Planning

Go **World Wide Planning**

World Wide Planning

ZPAY Payroll Systems, Inc.

Go **ZPAY Payroll Systems, Inc.**

Find out how Paul Mayer started ZPAY payroll.

Computers and Software

Academy of Learning
Go **MOLIAL_BBS**

MOLIAL_BBS

Administration
Go **MOLIADMIN**

MOLIADMIN

Advising
Go **MOLIADVIS**

MOLIADVIS

Altair Pavilion
Go **Pavilion**

Pavilion

ARIS
Go **MOLI_ARIS**

MOLI_ARIS

ASP Shareware Downloading
Go **ASPFiles**

ASP Shareware and Informational Files.

Association of Shareware Professionals
Go **ASP**

The Association of Shareware Professionals Forum. An organization of Shareware Authors, Publishers, Vendors and BBS Sysops. Shareware information and member shareware files available for downloading.

B.I.T.
Go **MOLIBIT_BBS**

MOLIBIT_BBS

BackOffice News Flash
Go **MSBKOFNEWS**

Get the latest Microsoft BackOffice News, press releases, product scoop, and What's New in the Forum straight from the BackOffice Team.

BBS Sysops Corner
Go **BBS Sysops Corner**

Bookstore
Go **MOLIBOOK**

MOLIBOOK

Broderbund Software
Go **Broderbund**

The Broderbund Software forum is a place where MSN users can find product information, technical support, customer service and game hints for Broderbund programs.

Broderbund Customer Support
Go **Broderbund Customer Support**

Broderbund Customer Support

Broderbund Product Descriptions
Go **Broderbund Product Descriptions**

Broderbund Product Descriptions by category

Broderbund Technical Support
Go **Broderbund Technical Support**

Broderbund Technical Support

CATT
Go **MOLIClass_CATT**

MOLIClass_CATT

CGI Systems
Go **MOLICLASS_CGI**

MOLICLASS_CGI

Chat Events Archive
Go **Chat Events Archive**

Chat Events Archive

Claris Corporation
Go **Claris**

The Claris forum is a full-service support center, providing message boards monitored by Claris Technical Support Staff, technical articles, and an extensive software library.

ClarisWorks Users Group
Go **Claris_CWUG**

This area contains Discussions and Chat areas specific to the ClarisWorks User Group.

Classrooms
Go **MOLICLASS**

MOLICLASS

Cobb's PC Productivity Center
Go **CPCP**

Cobb Group's MSN Beta Forum, featuring Inside

Windows 95 and sample content from other Cobb Group journals covering Microsoft Windows applications.

Computer Games
Go **CompGame**

Computer Gaming Area

Computer Graphics
Go **CompGraph**

Computer Telephony
Go **CTI**

Computer Telephony Integration (CTI). This forum covers topics ranging from simple modems for home users to the Advanced Intelligent Network (AIN) used by Telcos.

Computer Telephony Reference Library
Go **CTI_REF_LIB**

Reference Materials for the Computer Telephony Forum.

Conference Center
Go **CLARIS_Chat**

This Folder contains the Claris Conference Chat room and the conference schedule.

Courses
Go **WORLINK_COURSES**

WORLINK_COURSES

CT User Reviews
Go **CT_User_Reviews**

This folder contains user reviews of Computer Telephony related software, hardware, books, and other items.

CTI Related MSN Forums
Go **CTI_related_forums**

Forums on MSN related to CTI.

DataWiz
Go **MOLI_datawhiz**

MOLI_datawhiz

Dell Computer
Go **Dell**

Dell

Dell Support Bulletin Boards
Go **DellBBS**

DellBBS

Dell File Libraries
Go **DellFiles**

DellFiles

Dell Product Information
Go **DellProdInf**

DellProdInf

Desktop Publishing
Go **DTP**

A forum dedicated to the discussion and sharing of ideas relative to all aspects of desktop publishing, from print media to multimedia authoring, we've got it all!

Developing Visio Solutions

Go **Developing Visio Solutions**

Click here for information on programming with Visio and creating your own custom shapes.

DTP Bulletin Boards

Go **DTPBBS**

DTPBBS

DTP File Libraries

Go **DTP File Libraries**

DTP File Libraries

Educational Software

Go **Educational Software**

Educational Software

Faculty Club

Go **MOLICLUB**

MOLICLUB

Faulkner & Gray

Go **Faulkner & Gray**

Faulkner & Gray

Hardware

Go **HardCo**

IAR

Go **MOLIClass_IAR**

MOLIClass_IAR

Inside Microsoft Windows 95

Go **cobbwin95**

The MSN forum for The Cobb Group's Windows 95 productivity newsletter. Here you can find all the great tips and techniques from Inside Microsoft Windows 95, discuss articles with other readers, post your own tips, and seek help with technical problems.

Institute for Computer Studies

Go **MOLICLASS_ICS**

MOLICLASS_ICS

IS Professionals Info

Go **IS Professionals Info**

IS Professionals Info

220

Library
Go **MOLILIB**

MOLILIB

Macintosh Computers
Go **Macintosh,Mac**

Macintosh,Mac

MapInfo
Go **mapinfo**

mapinfo

MapInfo Products
Go **MapInfo Products**

MapInfo Products

Microcom
Go **Microcom**

Support and information on Microcom modem, LAN access, and software products.

Microsoft
Go **Microsoft**

Microsoft BackOffice and Windows NT Workstation
Go **MSBACKOFFICE**

The Microsoft BackOffice and Windows NT Workstation Forum has been designed to provide useful product and strategy information on the BackOffice family of products. Microsoft BackOffice is the first integrated family of server applications.

Microsoft BackOffice Forum
Go **MSBKOFFICE**

The Microsoft BackOffice forum provides product and strategy information on the Microsoft BackOffice. Microsoft BackOffice is an integrated family of server software built on the Windows NT Server.

Microsoft Certified Professionals
Go **MCP**

MCP

Microsoft Home Online
Go **MSHome**

Microsoft Developer Network
Go **MSDN**

Microsoft Information Sources
Go **msinfo**

msinfo

Microsoft Network

Go **Microsoft Network**

Microsoft Network

Microsoft Office 95 Information

Go **Microsoft Office 95 Information**

Microsoft Office 95 Information

Microsoft Office Family Forum

Go **MSOffice**

This forum features the full family of Microsoft's desktop applications, including Microsoft Office Standard, Microsoft Office Professional, Microsoft

Excel, Word, PowerPoint, Microsoft Access, Schedule+, Microsoft Project, Publisher and Microsoft Works.

Microsoft Online Institute

Go **MOLI**

MOLI

Microsoft Partner Forum

Go **MSPF**

MSPF

Microsoft Press

Go **mspress**

mspress

Microsoft Press News

Go **Microsoft Press News**

Microsoft Press News

Microsoft Press Online Bookstore

Microsoft Project Forum

Go **msproject**

msproject

Microsoft Publisher Forum

Go **MSPub**

MSPub

Microsoft Publisher Technical Services
Go **Microsoft Publisher Technical Services**

Microsoft Publisher Technical Services

Microsoft Sales Information Center
Go **msi**

msi

Microsoft SQL Server Forum
Go **mssql**

The Microsoft SQL Server Forum provides product and strategy information on SQL Server, a scalable high performance database management system designed specifically for distributed client-server computing.

Microsoft TechNet
Go **technet**

technet

Microsoft VC++ Technical Services
Go **Microsoft VC++ Technical Services**

Microsoft VC++ Technical Services

Microsoft Visual Basic
Go **Microsoft Visual Basic**

Microsoft Visual Basic

Microsoft Visual Basic Technical Services
Go **Microsoft Visual Basic Technical Services**

Microsoft Visual Basic Technical Services

Microsoft Visual C++
Go **Microsoft Visual C++**

Microsoft Visual C++

Microsoft Windows 95
Go **Windows**

The Windows 95 forum is the place for information about Microsoft Windows 95.

Microsoft Windows NT Workstation Forum
Go **MSNTW**

The Microsoft Windows NT Workstation Forum provides product and strategy information on Windows NT Workstation, the most powerful desktop operating system for the most demanding business needs.

Microsoft Works Forum
Go **MSWorks**

MSWorks

223

Microsoft Works Technical Services

Go **Microsoft Works Technical Services**

Microsoft Works Technical Services

MS Developer Product Info

Go **MS Developer Product Info**

MS Developer Product Info

MS OS Technology & Strategy 2

Go **MS OS Technology & Strategy 2**

MS OS Technology & Strategy 2

MS Project Chat Histories

Go **MS Project Chat Histories**

MS Project Chat Histories

MSDN Products

Go **MSDN Products**

MSDN Products

MSFT

Go **MSFT**

Microsoft Investor Relations: Information for shareholders and others with a financial interest in Microsoft

Multimedia & CD-ROM

Go **MULTIMEDIA**

The Multimedia and CD-ROM Forum covers all aspects of multimedia applications and peripherals, including video, sound, and, of course, multimedia presentations.

Mustang Software

Go **Mustang**

Mustang Software, Inc. Forum. Product information and technical support for all MSI products including Wildcat! BBS, QmodemPro, and Off-Line Xpress.

NT/NTS Course

Go **Wordlink_NT**

Wordlink_NT

Object Arts

Go **MOLICLASS_OBA**

MOLICLASS_OBA

Off-Line Xpress Info
Go **OLX**

Folder containing information about Off-Line Xpress (OLX) BBS mail reader from Mustang Software, Inc.

Operating Systems
Go **OS**

OS

OS/2 Forum
Go **OS/2**

OS/2

Patches
Go **Patches**

For patches and updates to Broderbund or affiliated software.

PC Magazine
Go **PC Magazine**

PC Magazine

pcAnyWhere
Go **sympca**

pcANYWHERE for Windows V2.0

PERiTAS
Go **MOLIPERITAS_BBS**

MOLIPERITAS_BBS

Plato Auditorium
Go **MOLIPLATO_CHAT**

MOLIPLATO_CHAT

Portable Computers
Go **PortableComp**

Where members can meet to discuss issues relating to laptop, portable, and handheld computers.

Product Catalog
Go **CLARIS_SALES**

The Claris Product Catalog contains information about purchasing Claris Products, pricing for Claris Products, and support from Claris Customer Assistance.

Product Info
Go **Product Info**

Click here for information on various Visio products, features, and product comparisons.

Product Support Forums
Go **WinProdSupport**

WinProdSupport

Publisher News
Go **Publisher News**

Publisher News

Publisher Resources Folder
Go **Publisher Resources Folder**

Open the folder and find BBS's with Clipart, templates and more... .

QmodemPro Info
Go **QmodemPro**

Folder containing information about QmodemPro professional communications software from Mustang Software, Inc.

Ray Dream
Go **ray dream**

> *Ray Dream, Inc.–a new perspective on graphics*

Rumos
Go **Rumos_BBS**

> *Rumos_BBS*

Shareware
Go **Shareware**

> *The shareware forum is a place to find shareware files, talk about shareware and meet other people interested in shareware. A sub-forum is the ASP Forum and you can talk to shareware authors and download ASP shareware files.*

Shareware File Libraries
Go **SharewareFiles**

> *You will find freeware, public domain and shareware files for downloading here.*

Software
Go **SoftCo**

Software Library
Go **CLARIS_LIBS**

> *This area contains files for Claris' FileMaker Pro and ClarisWorks for Window products.*

Solutions Center
Go **Solutions Center**

> *This area contains solutions related to Claris products.*

Student Union
Go **MOLISTU**

> *MOLISTU*

Support Solutions
Go **Symtech**

> *This area contains or will contain folders for various products. Please locate your product and post your questions or comments in that area.*

Symantec
Go **Symantec**

> *Symantec Corporation, Customer Service, Order Information, Technical Support, News and more.*

Symantec C++
Go **SymC++**

> *Symantec C++ Support Area*

Symantec Customer Service
Go **Symcustsrv**

> *Symcustsrv*

Technical Support From ASP Members

Go **ASPSupport**

This is an area that will have ASP Member support BBSs. Users of ASP shareware will be able to contact authors of the ASP that are on-line on MSN in this folder.

The BBS Industry

Go **BBSIndustry**

The MIDI Forum

Go **MIDI**

MIDI

Thomas A. Watson Center

Go **CT_Watson_Center**

Computer Telephony Chat area named for Alexander

Graham Bell's assistant Thomas A. Watson. Mr. Watson invented the switch hook and many other key telephony devices.

Valinor

Go **MOLIclass_VAL**

MOLIclass_VAL

Visio

Go **Visio**

Click here to access the Visio forum. Visio is an award-wnning drag and drop drawing and dia-gramming application for Windows.

Visio Customer Service

Go **Visio Customer Service**

Double click here to access information about how to purchase Visio internation-ally and download a Visio order form.

Visit Microsoft

Go **Visit Microsoft**

Visit Microsoft

What's Hot At MapInfo

Go **What's Hot At MapInfo**

What's Hot At MapInfo

Wildcat! BBS Info

Go **Wildcat**

Folder containing informa-tion about Wildcat! BBS from Mustang Software, Inc.

Windows 95 News and Info (WinNews)

Go **Windows 95 News and Info (WinNews)**

Windows 95 News and Info (WinNews)

Windows 95 Stories

Go **Windows 95 Stories**

Windows 95 Stories

Wordlink

Go **MOLIWL_BBS**

MOLIWL_BBS

Workgroup Institute
Go **MOLIWGI_BBS**

MOLIWGI_BBS

Works Education
Go **Works Education**

Works Education

Works News
Go **Works News**

Works News

Works Overview
Go **Works Overview**

Works Overview

Works Resources
Go **Works Resources**

Works Resources

XTree Gold 4.0 Windows
Go **symxtg**

Supp

Activision
Go **Activision**

This is the place to come for help with Activision products, ordering, game descriptions and answers to Frequently Asked Questions.

Metz Software for Windows
Go **Metz**

The METZ Software forum. Information, technical support and software from METZ Software, Inc.

Mediatrends
Go **Mediatrends**

The Mediatrends Forum is designed to allow members of MSN to learn more about Mediatrends, its products and services. Specifically, the Forum will provide MSN Members with the opportunity to hear about and purchase Mediatrends products, and receive technical support.

Intergraph
Go **Intergraph**

Education and Reference

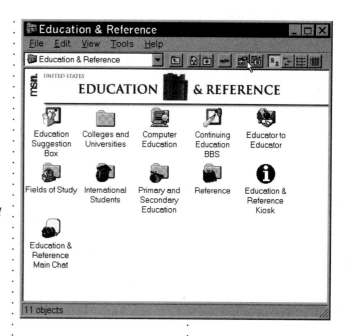

Astronomy & Space

Go **Space**

A forum dedicated to the discussion of and exchange of information on astronomy and the exploration of space.

Educator to Educator

Go **Educator to Educator**

The Educators forum discusses the personnel involved in providing education, including teachers, administrators, coaches, and librarians. Also included are issues such as curriculum choice, discipline, and counseling.

Geology & Geography

Go **Geography**

The Geology and Geography forum discusses the sciences that deal with planetary composition, landforms, and geophysical laws: geology, geography, meteorology, geophysics.

History & Archaeology

Go **History**

Welcome to the History and Archaeology Forums! For views, comments and conversation, click here and let's dig in!

Influential Thinkers

Go **Thinkers**

Thinkers

International Exchange Programs

Go **IntlStuExchg**

This folder contains information on the different organizations that support exchange students. Both non-profit organizations and colleges are listed.

International Language Learning

Go **language translat**

International language tools and resources for translations of one language to another. German to English translation dictionary and programs. English speaking aids.

International Students
Go **IntlStudents**

Welcome! The forum is for all people who would like to know more about International Education and Travel as well as a place to make International acquaintances.

Learning and Translating French
Go **FrenchTools**

This folder contains all programs for learning and translating French.

Learning and Translating German
Go **German**

This folder contains all programs for learning and translating German.

Learning and Translating Japanes
Go **Japanes**

This folder contains programs for learning and translating Japanese.

Learning and Translating Spanish
Go **SpanishTools**

This folder contains programs for learning and translating Spanish.

Philosophy
Go **Philosophy**

A forum dedicated to philosophical discussion.

Philosophy Library
Go **phillib**

phillib

Phone Home Tips & Tools
Go **Phone Home Tips & Tools**

This area contains tips for getting the cheapest rates for making international calls. You can also find different programs that allow voice conversations over the internet service.

Political Reference
Go **Political Reference**

> *This folder is for an ongoing source of information of Political reference files, events, people and places.*

Primary and Secondary Education
Go **Primary and Secondary Education**

> *The Primary and Secondary Education forum is for discussing education up to the 12th grade level, including preschool, extracurricular education and alternative education.*

The Princeton Review
Go **Princeton Review**

> *The Princeton Review*

Reference
Go **Reference**

> *The Reference forum is a place to exchange information and ideas about libraries and reference material, including encyclopedias, dictionaries, thesauruses, and atlases.*

Microsoft Bookshelf
Go **MSbooks**

> *An introductory edition of the award winning Microsoft(R) Bookshelf '95: the new way to look it up!*

Microsoft Encarta
Go **Encarta**

> *Double clicking your mouse on this icon starts the Encarta application, there will be a 10 to 50 second delay until you see the Encarta startup screen. We hope you Enjoy Encarta.*

Home and Family

Age Link Chat
Go **Age Link Chat**

Age Link Chat

Chat Dormitory
Go **Dormitory**

Dormitory

Family Friendly Entertainment
Go **Family Friendly Entertainment**

This area is to encourage and promote wholesome family entertainment.

For Kids Only
Go **For Kids Only**

For Kids Only

For Your Future
Go **For Your Future**

For Your Future

Home and Family
Go **Home**

Forum sysops and branded folder owners will get to write a brief description of their service here.

Home Improvement
Go **House**

Home Schooling
Go **Home Schooling**

Home Schooling

How Does it Work?
Go **How Does it Work?**

How Does it Work?

Kids Adventures
Go **Kids Adventures**

Kids Adventures

Kids and Company
Go **Kids and Company**

Kids and Company

Kids Arts and Entertainment
Go **Kids Arts and Entertainment**

Kids Arts and Entertainment

Kids Home and Family

Go **Kids Home and Family**

Kids Home and Family

Kids News and Weather

Go **Kids News and Weather**

Kids News and Weather

Kids Special Events

Go **Kids Special Events**

Kids Special Events

Kids Sports, Health, and Fitness

Go **"Kids Sports, Health, and Fitness"**

"Kids Sports, Health, and Fitness"

Kidspace Design Forum

Go **Kidspace**

The KidSpace Design Forum will delve into home lifestyle issues as they relate to the young -- from baby space to shared quarters to shared custody. Both parents and kids join forces here to share design ideas that inspire and instruct young people.

Neat Places for Teens on MSN

Go **Neat Places for Teens on MSN**

Neat Places for Teens on MSN

Parenting in the 90's

Go **Parenting**

All about Parenting in today's complex and ever-changing world!

PreTeen Zone

Go **PreTeen**

PreTeen

Save or Spend?

Go **Save or Spend?**

Save or Spend?

Splash Kids

Go **Splash**

Splash Kids is a great place for kids! Check it out.

Teen Forum

Go **Teen**

Teen

Theme Parks!
Go **Theme Parks**

Theme Parks from around the world are covered in this exciting and new forum. From Disney to Sea World to Six Flags...we talk about all of it. We also have many files/photos available in our library.

Work-At-Home Dads
Go **WAHD**

The Work-At-Home Dads forum is the premier online resource for men who work at home and while caring for their children.

Working Mothers
Go **Working Mothers**

Working Mothers

Interests, Leisure, & Hobbies

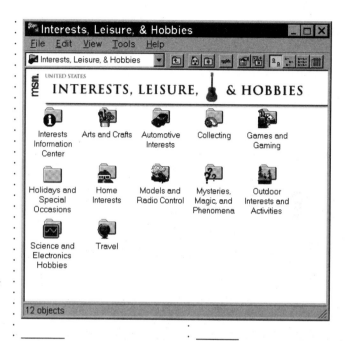

Ale & Lager
Go **craftbeer**

This forum is dedicated to fine Ales and Lagers. Included in this forum among other things is; How to brew them, Q&As about brewing, Chat sessions with Experts in the Ale and Lager world, and how to fully taste and enjoy fine ales and lagers.

Ale & Lager Dining Room
Go **craft brew**

craft brew

Ale & Lager University
Go **lager**

lager

Alien Encounters and UFOs
Go **Aliens**

Alien Beings, past, present and future. Evidence, Implications, Purposes, Nature, Controversies, Rumors, and so forth. Related phenomena: near death experiences, angels, visitations, paranormal experiences, etc.

Aliens in Antiquity
Go **AncientAliens**

Alien visitation in the distant past

Antiques
Go **Antiques**

Antiques

Art and Antiques
Go **A&A**

The place to talk about buying, selling, repairing, storing and dealing with art and antiques.

Arts and Crafts
Go **Craft**

Welcome to Arts and Crafts. This is your online forum for the discussion of Arts and Crafts.

Places to Go, Things to See

Automobilia
Go **automobile**

automobilia; automobile collectibles; automobile miniatures; scale models

Automotive
Go **Automotive**

Automotive Discussions

Automotive Professionals
Go **AutoProfessional**

Area For Automotive Professionals Engaged in Full Time Automotive Employment.

Aviation
Go **Flying**

This is the online home for pilots and anyone who is interested in Aviation! From student pilots to astronauts, renters, owners and even builders, you'll find all kinds of aviation-related discussion and files, here.

Back Issue Comics
Go **Back Issue Comics**

Back Issue Comics

Balloon School
Go **School of Balloons**

Learn to create balloon animals, hats and other things. Book reviews, and source list for balloons.

Balloon Sculpture
Go **Balloon**

Balloon Sculpture Forum

Bar Seating
Go **Bar**

Bar

Baseball Cards
Go **Baseball Cards**

Baseball Cards

Baseball Memorabilia
Go **Baseball Memorabilia**

Baseball Memorabilia

Basketball Cards & Memorabilia
Go **Basketball Cards & Memorabilia**

Basketball Cards & Memorabilia

Bird Watching
Go **BirdWatch**

Dedicated to Birdwatching and related issues.

Books and Paper Collectibles
Go **Rare Books**

Books, paper collectibles, ephemera, rare books.

236

Booth Seating

· Go **Booth Seating**

Booth Seating

Boxes

· Go **Boxes**

Boxes

Boxing Cards & Memorabilia

· Go **Boxing Cards & Memorabilia**

Boxing Cards & Memorabilia

Broderbund Game Hints

· Go **Broderbund Game Hints**

Broderbund Game Hints

Card Sharks

· Go **card sharks**

card sharks

Card Supplies

· Go **Card Supplies**

Card Supplies

Cards & Gifts

· Go **Cards & Gifts ILH**

Cards & Gifts ILH

Coins, Currency and Bullion

· Go **Coins**

Coins; coin collecting; currency; paper money; bullion.

Collectible Card Games

· Go **card games**

Magic: The Gathering; Rage; Star Trek; scrye; wizards.

Collecting

· Go **Collecting**

Collecting

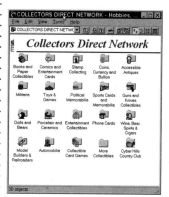

Collectors Direct Network - Hobbies, Collectibles & Antiques

· Go **collectors**

Hobbies; collectibles; antiques. Sports cards, Magic cards, comics, stamps, coins, currency, books, ephemera, memorabilia, automobilia, models, miniatures, militaria, political, guns, knives, dolls, bears, porcelain, ceramics, wine, beer, spirits, cigars, and more.

Comic Attractions

· Go **comic attractions**

comic attractions

Comics

· Go **Comics**

Comics

Comics and Entertainment Cards
Go **Comic Books**

comic books; non-sport cards; entertainment cards; Magic: The Gathering.

Complete Sets - Sports
Go **Complete Sets - Sports**

Complete Sets - Sports

Cultures
Go **Culture**

Culture

Current Alien Phenomena
Go **UFO**

Alien phenomena happening in modern times.

Cyber Space Collectibles
Go **Cyber Space**

Cyber Space

Cyborg 1 Comics
Go **Cyborg1**

Cyborg1

Dartboards
Go **Darts**

Darts

Diebel's Sportsmens Gallery
Go **Diebel**

Cigars, gifts, men's gifts, pipes, tobacco, humidors, cutters.

Dolls and Bears
Go **CDN Dolls**

dolls; bears; doll houses; teddy bears; antique dolls; miniatures.

Entertainment Cards
Go **Entertainment Cards**

Entertainment Cards

Entertainment Cards & Memorabilia
Go **Entertainment Cards & Memorabilia**

Entertainment Cards & Memorabilia

Entertainment Collectibles
Go **movies; music**

movies collectibles; music collectibles; stars; autographs.

EWA Automobilia Center
Go **ewa**

ewa

FaBREWlous Specials
Go **FaBREWlous Specials**

FaBREWlous Specials

Fan Clubs
Go **Magic Fan Clubs**

Magician's Fan Clubs

Fetzer Vineyards

Go **Fetzer Vineyards**

Fetzer Vineyards

Film, Paper, and Darkroom Supplies

Go **Film, Paper, and Darkroom Supplies**

Film, Paper, and Darkroom Supplies

Fishin' Around

Go **FISH**

Saltwater and Freshwater Aquariums

FlashBacks Auctions

Go **FlashBacks Auctions**

FlashBacks Auctions

Flashbacks Memorabilia

Go **flash**

flash

Food, Wine and Cooking

Go **Food**

Welcome to the Food and Wine Forum! Discover a wide variety of recipes and share your personal culinary delight!

Football Cards

Go **Football Cards**

Football Cards

Football Memorabilia

Go **Football Memorabilia**

Football Memorabilia

Future Prospects

Go **AlienFuture**

Future prospects, predictions, messages, trends, and possibilities, given the alien presence.

Games and Gaming

Go **Games**

Talk about all kinds of games here.

Games Chat Rooms

Go **Games Chat Rooms**

Here are the keys to a variety of different chat rooms for 2, 4, 6 and more players. Grab a table and have some fun!

Games Competition Room

Go **Games Room**

Games Room

Gardening

Go **Garden**

The Gardening BBS!

General Automotive

Go **GeneralAuto**

General Automotive Messages and Files. Any Automotive File can be Placed Here!

239

Golf
Go **Golf**

Golf

Guns and Knives Collectibles
Go **gun**

collectible guns; knives; rifles; pistols; sabres.

Gutenberg Auditorium
Go **Gutenberg Auditorium**

Gutenberg Auditorium

Highland Mint
Go **Highland Mint**

Highland Mint

Hobbies
Go **Hobby**

A virtual treasure chest of hobbies.

Hockey Cards & Memorabilia
Go **Hockey Cards & Memorabilia**

Hockey Cards & Memorabilia

Home Interests
Go **Home Interests**

Home interests including Beer Brewing, Food Wine and Cooking, Gardening, Pets, Motorcycles, and Automotive interests.

Hometown Sports
Go **Hometown**

Hometown

ICNN Featured Writers
Go **ICNN Featured Writers**

ICNN Featured Writers

ICNN: Food & Beverage Center
Go **ICNN: Food and Beverage**

ICNN: Food and Beverage

Individual Cards
Go **Individual Cards**

Individual Cards

Internet Magic Highway
Go **MagicHighway**

Your gateway to alt.magic and all of the great web pages on the InterNet.

Juggling
Go **JUGGLE**

This bbs is for general Juggling conversation.

Kids Corner
Go **kidscomedy**

This area is for the discussion of humorous cartoons and art, jokes, puns, limericks, poetry, and stories that appeal to children.

Ladies Room
Go **LadiesRoom**

LadiesRoom

Leming & Sons, Inc.
Go **leming**

leming

Magazines
Go **Magazines**

Magazine discussion.

Magazines and Books
Go **Magazines and Books**

Magazines and Books

Magic and Illusions
Go **Magic**

The Art of Magic and Illusion. Discussions on Magic, Information on Conventions, Sources of Learning, and International Chat with Other Magicians.

Magic BBS's
Go **MagicBBS**

Magic BBS Forums. Discussions on Stage Magic, Closeup Magic, a Magic School, A Magic Calendar of events, Magic Clubs and Fan Clubs, Hat and Hare Chat and Houdini Hall.

Magic Calendar
Go **MagicCalendar**

MagicCalendar

Magic Photo & Video Gallery
Go **MagicPictures**

MagicPictures

Magic School
Go **MagicSchool**

Magic and Illusions School. Magic books list and discussion, file library, and a classroom for magic lessons.

Magic: The Gathering
Go **mtg**

If you're a Magic: The Gathering player, trader, collector, designer, this place is for you.

Manion's International Auction House
Go **Manions**

Manions

Memorabilia
Go **Memorabilia**

Memorabilia

Militaria
Go **Militaria**

military collectibles; militaria; war collectibles.

Model Builders & Railroaders
Go **model**

models; model building; airplane; cars; trains; railroad; scale models

Models
· Go **Models**

Modeling Forum, discussion of model planes, trains, and automobiles.

More Collectibles
· Go **More Collectibles**

miniatures; rubber stamps; black memorabilia.

Motorcycles
· Go **Motorcycle**

Motorcycle Discussion.

Moviecraft Home Videos
· Go **Moviecraft**

Moviecraft

Mr. Mint On-Line
· Go **Mr. Mint**

Mr. Mint

MTG Single Cards
· Go **MTG Single Cards**

MTG Single Cards

Multiversal Trading Company
· Go **multiversal**

multiversal

Mysteries, Magic, and Phenomena
· Go **Mysteries, Magic, and Phenomena**

Discuss Alien and UFO encounters, and their presence thru history. Be entertained in Magic and Illusion, with Juggling and Balloon Scuplture too.

National Sports Collectors Convention
· Go **nscc**

nscc

Needle Arts
· Go **needle**

This is the place to exchange ideas about knitting, weaving, fabric dyeing, beading, dollmaking, needlepoint, cross-stitch and other needle-related arts and crafts you want to talk about.

New Comics
· Go **New Comics**

New Comics

News and Weather
· Go **News**

This category collects news from all other categories into one location, as well as offering clipping services, online periodicals, weather updates, etc.

Non-Smoking Pubs
Go **NonSmoking**

NonSmoking

Ordering Information
Go **Ordering Information**

Ordering Information

Other Sports Cards & Memorabilia
Go **Other Sports Cards & Memorabilia**

Other Sports Cards & Memorabilia

Outdoor Interests and Activities
Go **Outdoor Interests and Activities**

Outdoor Interests and Activities

Owner Maintenance
Go **AutoCare**

Owner Maintenance and Care Files and Messages That Can Save You Money. You Don't Need to Spend $$$ to Keep Your Pride and Joy Looking and Running Like New!

Packs and Boxes
Go **Packs and Boxes**

Packs and Boxes

Packs, Boxes & Sets
Go **Packs, Boxes & Sets**

Packs, Boxes & Sets

Paul & Judy's
Go **PJ**

PJ

Pets
Go **Pets**

Welcome to the Pets Forum!

Phone Cards
Go **Phonecard**

phone cards; telephone cards.

Photography
Go **Photo**

Explore the world of photography in the Photography Forum. Learn all about the equipment, the techniques, and the enjoyment of the images produced.

Photography Equipment
Go **PhotoEquip**

Here you'll find BBS and chat areas covering all kinds of photography equipment including 35mm cameras and lenses, medium and large format cameras, flash, studio lighting, tripods, gadget bags and almost anything you can find in one!

Political Memorabilia
Go **Political**

Political collectibles; politics; political memorabilia; americana; presidents collectibles.

Pool Tables
Go **Pool**

Pool

Porcelain and Ceramics

Go **Porcelain**

Porcelain; ceramics; china; pottery.

Pre-Order Packs & Boxes

Go **Pre-Order Packs & Boxes**

Pre-Order Packs & Boxes

Quilting

Go **quilt**

This area is devoted to all aspects of quilting. We discuss techniques, ideas, horror stories and anything else you want to talk about. The Quilt Studio is the place to swap, do design challenges, contests, community projects and show off our work.

Racing Cards & Memorabilia

Go **Racing Cards & Memorabilia**

Racing Cards & Memorabilia

Registration Office

Go **SU Registrar**

SU Registrar

Reptiles

Go **Reptiles**

Snakes, Lizards, and other reptiles.

Resource Center

Go **AlienResource**

AlienResource

Retail Mall

Go **Retail Mall**

Retail Mall

Retail Mall Card Shops

Go **CCG Retail Mall**

CCG Retail Mall

Rivendell, Inc.

Go **rivendell**

rivendell

Rotman Cards & Memorabilia

Go **rotman**

rotman

Scratching Post

Go **CATS**

Cats Discussion BBS

Scrye Auditorium

Go **Scrye Auditorium**

Scrye Auditorium

Scrye Magazine Electronic Edition

Go **Scrye Mag**

Scrye Mag

Scrye Online

Go **Scrye**

Scrye

Scrye University

Go **SU**

SU

Sewing

Go **sewing**

This is the place to exchange ideas about garment sewing, tailoring, costuming, home decorating and other sewing-related concerns.

Silver Horse Vineyards
Go **Silver Horse**

Silver Horse

Single Cards
Go **Single Cards**

Single Cards

Singles
Go **Singles**

Singles

Special Event Chats
Go **Special Event Chats**

Special Event Chats

Sports Apparel
Go **Sports Apparel**

Sports Apparel

Sports Art
Go **Sports Art**

Sports Art

Sports Cards & Memorabilia Retail Mall
Go **sports sales**

sports sales

Sports Cards and Memorabilia
Go **Sportscards**

Sports cards; sports memorabilia; baseball cards & collectibles; football cards & collectibles; hockey cards & collectibles; basketball cards & collectibles; boxing cards & collectibles; racing cards & collectibles; fan goods; sports autographs.

Sports Cards Etc.
Go **SCE**

SCE

Sports Novelties
Go **Sports Novelties**

Sports Novelties

Stamp Collecting
Go **Stamps**

stamps; stamp collecting.

Starting Line-Ups
Go **Starting Line-Ups**

Starting Line-Ups

Stitch
Go **Stitch**

Stitch is the place to exchange experiences, ideas and techniques about quilting, sewing and other needle-related arts.

Store Information
Go **Store Information**

Store Information

Telephone Booths
Go **Telephone Booths**

Telephone Booths

The Bird's Nest
Go **BIRD**

Pet Birds Discussion BBS

The BreakDown Lane!
Go **AutoRepair**

Automotive Repair Questions and Files

The Disney Parks
Go **Disney**

Disney

The Dog House
Go **DOG**

Dog discussion BBS.

The Magic Source
Go **Magic Source**

Magic Source

The Parts Store
Go **AutoAccess**

Automotive Parts and Accessories Forum and File Area. New Part That Solves a Problem? Good Source of New or Used Auto Parts? An Accessory That You Like? Please Share Your New Knowledge With Millions of Your Fellow Drivers Here!

The Passing Lane
Go **AutoMuscle**

Automotive Performance, Sports Car Files and Messages

The Showroom
Go **AutoShowroom**

New and Used Car Buying, Financing and Insurance. Got a Good Deal. Do You Have The Secret Car Buying Tip? Share Your Good Fortune With Others!

Theme Parks!
Go **Theme Parks**

Theme Parks from around the world are covered in this exciting and new forum. From Disney to Sea World to Six Flags...we talk about all of it. We also have many files/photos available in our library.

Theme Parks! File Library
Go **Attractions**

This folder will contain all of the various files concerning Theme Parks!

Thunder & Lightning Cards International
Go **thunder**

thunder

Toys & Games
Go **Toys**

toy collectibles; toys; antique toys; used toys; games; collectible games; antique games.

Trading Cards
Go **Cards**

A forum for discussing and trading both sports and non-sports trading cards.

Travel
Go **Travel**

General Vacation Travel

246

Trixie's Pub
○ **Trixie**

Trixie's Pub. Public and private chats of all sizes.

rucks, 4X4's and ff Road Vehicles
○ **Auto4X4**

Trucks , 4X4's and Off Road Vehicle Area.

niversity Trading ards
○ **University Trading Cards**

University Trading Cards

Unsold Lots: German
Go **Unsold Lots: German**

Unsold Lots: German

Unsold Lots: Japan and Other Countries
Go **Unsold Lots: Japan and Other Countries**

Unsold Lots: Japan and Other Countries

Unsold Lots: U.S.
Go **Unsold Lots: U.S.**

Unsold Lots: U.S.

Video Games
Go **video**

Everything you want to know about video games here.

Visitor's Center
Go **AlienVisit**

AlienVisit

Wax Boxes _ Sports Cards
Go **Wax Boxes _ Sports Cards**

Wax Boxes _ Sports Cards

Wee Furry Folk
Go **Wee Furry Folk**

Rabbits, hamsters, mice, ferrets, rats, and all other little four legged creatures.

What's Cooking... Online!
Go **Cook**

Looking for a recipe? Nutrition information? Or just a place to chat around the virtual kitchen table? What's Cooking...Online is the place for you!

Wine, Beer, Spirits & Cigars
Go **CDNWine**

wine; winery; wineries; beer; home brew; brewers; cigars; spirits; liquers.

Winery Tours
Go **Winery**

Winery

Wizards of the Coast
Go **WotC**

WotC

WoodWorking
Go **WOOD**

The WoodWorking Forum is the nucleus for all of your woodworking needs. This is a great place to share ideas, get help on techniques, and meet some people that share your interest.

The Internet Center

Core Rules of Netiquette
Go **corerules**

This Media Viewer title is excerpted from the book _Netiquette_ by Virginia Shea. It covers the essential rules of network etiquette. For more information about Netiquette, visit the Netiquette Center (Go word "netiquette"). For other introductory resources,

Internet Center File Libraries

NetNews
Go **NetNews**

NetNews

Newsgroups and Full Access Information
Go **Newsgroups and Full Access Information**

Newsgroups and Full Access Information

The Most Popular Newsgroups
Go **InetTop10**

Here's several very popular newsgroups to get you started. Chosen by your Forum Manager. Submit suggestions to Nate_SrSysop.

Regional and International Newsgroups

Usenet Newsgroups
Go **Usenet Newsgroups**

Usenet Newsgroups

Member Lobby

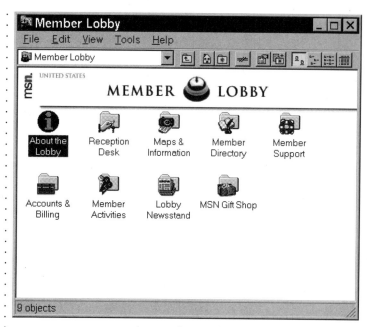

Reception Desk
Go **Reception Desk**

Provides information for new members, including member guidelines, information on network etiquette (netiquette), and a new member chat room.

Maps & Information
Go **MSNMaps**

Provides guidebooks which introduce you to subject areas on MSN, a staffed chat room to ask questions about how to find services, and information on how to find things fast.

Member Directory
Go **MSNDirectory**

Provides information on how to contact members and change your own member information, and member guidelines.

Accounts & Billing
Go **MSNAccounts**

Answers to common questions, including how to change your billing information, what to do if you forget your password, and how to prevent kids from accessing services.

Member Activities
Go **MSNActivities**

Provides current member activities, including promotions, special contests, and other fun activities.

Lobby Newsstand
Go *Contains MSN Today, MSN's headline news, lists of books about MSN, and guidebooks introducing services on MSN.*

MSN GiftShop
Go **MSNGifts**

A place to purchase MSN merchandise and gifts.

Public Affairs

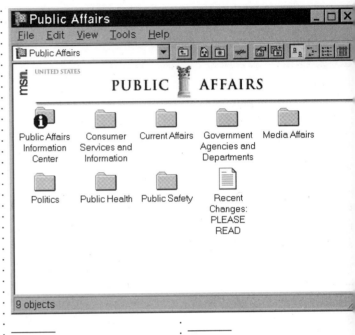

AFF Exchange
Go **Exchange**

The Armed Forces Forum (AFF) Exchange: Where members may purchase, offer for sale, advise of employment opportunities and a host of other options.

Al Gore
Go **Al Gore**

Al Gore

Apparatus & Equipment
Go **Apparatus & Equipment**

Apparatus & Equipment

Archives
Go **Democrats**

Democrats

Armed Forces
Go **AFF**

Information and resources tailored for members of the Armed Forces, their families, and the organizations and business that provide support. All branches of the military represented.

Armed Forces of the World
Go **AFFWorld**

Military Services around the world.

Armed Forces on the Internet
Go **AFFInternet**

Internet Services available on MSN tailored for the Armed Forces Forum.

Australia
Go **Australia**

Australia

Bill Clinton
Go **Bill Clinton**

Bill Clinton

Bob Dole
Go **Bob Dole**

Bob Dole

CA Fire Marshal's Office

Go **CA Fire Marshal's Office**

Subforum for the California State Fire Marshal's Office, Ron Coleman, Fire Marshal.

California

Go **California**

California

Classifieds

Go **fireclass**

fireclass

Court Room

Go **firecourt**

firecourt

Data Bases/ Computers

Go **firedata**

firedata

Department of Health

Go **Department of Health**

Subforum for the EMS and Trauma Division of the Washington State Department of Health. Joe Campo, Director.

Dept. of Natural Resources

Go **Dept. of Natural Resources**

Subforum for the Washington State Department of Natural Resources

Divisions

Go **iafcdivis**

iafcdivis

Emergency in Progress

Go **fires**

Emergencies in Progress will be used in the future to facilitate communications during large scale emergencies. Status Boards combined with Email and Chat rooms will allow officials to keep up to date on all information, decisions and plans during the event.

EMS

Go **EMS**

EMS

Fire Chiefs of British Columbia

Go **Fire Chiefs of British Columbia**

Fire Chiefs of British Columbia

Fire Chiefs of Canada

Go **Fire Chiefs of Canada**

Fire Chiefs of Canada

Fire Prevention

Go **Fire Prevention**

Fire Prevention

Fire Protection Bureau

Go **Fire Protection Bureau**

Subforum for the Washington State Fire Protection Services Division of the Washington State Patrol. Dick Small, Director/State Fire Marshal

Firehouse

Go **firehouse**

Folder containing a large collection of bulletin boards. The meeting place for general exchange of information among firefighters and ems providers.

Firesafe Construction

Go **Firesafe Construction**

Firesafe Construction

France

Go **France**

France

Games

Go **Political Games**

Political Games

General Information

Go **General Information**

Learn here what it takes to become a firefighter or a paramedic or emergency dispatcher. Communicate with the experts, leave your questions and comments.

Germany

Go **Germany**

Germany

GoverNet: The Political Machine

Go **Governet**

Political information and debate

Great Britain

Go **Great Britain**

Great Britain

House of Representatives

Go **Congress**

Congress

Incident Command

Go **Incident Command**

Incident Command

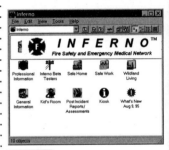

Inferno

Go **Inferno**

The Fire Safety and Emergency Medical Services Forum.

Innovative Comp. Simulation

Go **Innovative Comp. Simulation**

Innovative Comp. Simulation

International Assoc. of Fire Chiefs

Go **goiafc**

goiafc

International/ National

Go **intfire**

The gateway to International and National fire and emergency medical service agencies.

John F Kennedy Auditorium

Go **JFK**

JFK

Journalism World

Go **JW**

For professionals in the field of journalism.

JW For Sale

Go **JW For Sale**

JW For Sale

JW Job Market

Go **JW Job Market**

JW Job Market

JW: The Wire

Go **JW: The Wire**

JW: The Wire

Kid's Room

Go **Kid's Room**

The gateway for children under twelve. Games and educational material related to fire and health safety.

L.A. County Fire Dept.

Go **L.A. County Fire Dept.**

L.A. County Fire Dept.

Law Enforcement

Go **lenf**

A forum for and about law enforcement

Law Enforcement Electronic Forms

Go **lenforms**

Contains electronic forms that can be used to add/ remove your member ID to/from the Law Enforcement Forum mailing list or send electronic mail to the forum moderator.

London Fire Brigade

Go **London Fire Brigade**

London Fire Brigade

Los Angeles City Fire

Go **Los Angeles City Fire**

Los Angeles City Fire

Meeting Rooms

Go **Republican**

Republican

Member Assistance

Go **Member Assistance**

Member Assistance

Military Support Organizations

Go **AFFSupport**

Information and resources available to the entire community of the Armed Forces. Military support groups and organizations.

National Fire Info Council

Go **National Fire Info Council**

Subforum for the National Fire Information Council. The National Fire Information Council is the custodian of the National Fire Incident Reporting System. Visit here with the experts on fire statistics.

National/ Regional Organizations

Go **fireorgs**

fireorgs

Operations

Go **fireops**

fireops

Politics

Go **politics**

Discussions of current political issues.

Post Incident Reports/ Assessments

Go **Post Incident Reports/ Assessments**

Look here for reports on major fire incidents.

Professional Information

Go **goinferno**

"A private, subscription only area for fire and emergency services personnel."

Public Education

Go **Public Education**

Public Education

Public Safety Communications

Go **Public Safety Communications**

Public Safety Communications

Public Service Forum

Go **pubserv**

The Public Service forum is an information source and gathering place for people who are interested in making their communities better places to live.

Public Service Electronic Forms

Go **pubservforms**

"Electronic forms for the organization database, organization calendar, and more."

Responder Magazine

Go **Responder Magazine**

Responder Magazine

Safe Home

Go **Safe Home**

Safe Home

Safe Work

Go **interface**

interface

Seattle Fire Department

Go **Seattle Fire Department**

Seattle Fire Department

Senate

Go **Senate**

Senate

Special Access

Go **firespec**

Private forum for Arson Investigators

State & Local Politics

Go **States**

States

Sunpro Fire Software

Go **sunpro**

sunpro

The Campaign Store

Go **The Campaign Store**

The Campaign Store

The Metros

Go **The Metros**

The Metros

The White House

Go **DC; President**

DC; President

Training

Go **Training**

Training

U.S. Air Force

Go **AFFAir**

AFFAir

Places to Go, Things to See

U.S. Armed Forces
Go **AFFUS**

Armed Forces of the United States. Find in this sub-forum service specific content areas of the U.S. Military.

U.S. Army
Go **AFFArmy**

AFFArmy

U.S. Coast Guard
Go **AFFUSCG**

AFFUSCG

U.S. Marine Corps
Go **AFFMarines**

U.S. Marine Corps sub-forum area in the Armed Forces Forum.

U.S. Navy
Go **AFFNavy**

AFFNavy

United States
Go **gonfic**

The National Fire Information Council is the custodian of the National Fire Incident Reporting System. Visit here with the experts on fire statistics.

WA Assoc. of Building Officials
Go **WA Assoc. of Building Officials**

Subforum for the Washington State Association of Building Officials

WA State Assn of Fire Chiefs
Go **gochiefs**

A private forum for the Washington State Association of Fire Chiefs

Wars & Rumors of Wars
Go **ROW**

Topical discussions and reference to wars fought or likely to be fought.

Washington
Go **Washington**

Folder containing subforums for Washington State fire and EMS organizations.

We the People
Go **WT**

For the people, by the people. A forum for the examination and discussion of federal, state, and local legislation. The positions taken by our elected representatives, and the convictions of those who seek to represent us.

West Region IV
Go **fireassoc**

Privately sponsored or subscription access to fire and emergency medical service organizations.

Western Fire Chiefs
Go **Western Fire Chiefs**

Subforum for members of the Western Fire Chiefs Association

Wildland Living
Go **Wildland Living**

Wildland Living

WSFFA
Go **WSFFA**

Folder for the Washington State Firefighters Association

256

People and Communities

Advice and Support
Go **Advice and Support**

American Greetings
Go **American Greetings**

American Greetings

Astrological Organizations
Go **Astrological Organizations**

Astrological Organizations

Astrology
Go **Astrology**

Astrology

Astrology & Computers
Go **Astrology & Computers**

Astrology & Computers

Astrology Magazines
Go **Astrology Magazines**

Astrology Magazines

Astrology Product Guide
Go **Astrology Product Guide**

Astrology Product Guide

Astrology Software
Go **Astrology Software**

Astrology Software

Astrology, Cycles, & Science
Go **Astrology, Cycles, & Science**

Astrology, Cycles, & Science

Astrology: What About My Chart?
Go **Astrology: What About My Chart?**

Astrology: What About My Chart?

Austria, Germany & Switzerland
Go **Alpine**

Countries where German is spoken and gateway to their forums!

Benelux
Go **Benelux**

Friends of Belgium, Netherlands, and Luxembourg

British Isles
Go **British Isles**

British Isles

Chat Cafe
Go **chatcafe**

Welcome to our chat cafe, composed of many small chat rooms where you can hang out with your pal for intimate conversation.

Divination and Points Beyond
Go **Divination**

Divination

Divination Product Guide
Go **Divination Product Guide**

Divination Product Guide

Divination Software
Go **Divination Software**

Divination Software

Eastern Europe
Go **EasternEurope**

EasternEurope

Eastern Product Guide
Go **Eastern Product Guide**

Eastern Product Guide

Europe
Go **Europe**

Discover the exciting world of Europe!

Financial Astrology
Go **AstroFinance**

AstroFinance

Foundation for the Study of Cycles

Go **Foundation for the Study of Cycles**

Foundation for the Study of Cycles

France (Français)

Go **French**

French

Friends of Austria

Go **Austria**

Austria

Friends of Belgium

Go **Belgium**

Belgium

Friends of Denmark

Go **Denmark**

Denmark

Friends of Finland

Go **Finland**

Finland

Friends of France

Go **Friends of France**

Friends of France

Friends of Germany

Go **Germany**

Germany

Friends of Greece

Go **Greece**

Greece

Friends of Hungary

Go **Hungary**

Hungary

Friends of Ireland

Go **Ireland**

This forum includes the Republic of Ireland and Northern Ireland.

Friends of Italy

Go **Friends of Italy**

Friends of Italy

Friends of Luxembourg

Go **Luxembourg**

Luxembourg

Friends of Netherlands (Holland)

Go **Holland**

Holland

Friends of Norway

Go **Norway**

Norway

Friends of Poland

Go **Poland**

Poland

Friends of Portugal

Go **Portugal**

Portugal

Friends of Russia

Go **Russia**

Friends of Russia Forum! Come and visit the Russians and Russia!

Friends of Spain

Go **Friends of Spain**

Friends of Spain

Friends of Sweden

Go **Sweden**

Sweden

Friends of Switzerland

Go **Friends of Switzerland**

Friends of Switzerland

Friends of the Czech & Slovakia Republics

Go **Czech**

Czech

Friends of Turkey

Go **Friends of Turkey**

Friends of Turkey

Genealogy

Go **Genes**

Genealogy Forum

Generations and Gender

Go **Gender**

Greece & Turkey

Go **Greece & Turkey**

Greece & Turkey

Hungary & Poland

Go **Hungary & Poland**

Hungary & Poland

Karma Kagyu Lineage

Go **Karma Kagyu Lineage**

Karma Kagyu Lineage

KTD Dharma Goods

Go **KTD Dharma Goods**

KTD Dharma Goods

Learning Astrology

Go **Learning Astrology**

Learning Astrology

MacIntosh Astrology Programs

Go **MacIntosh Astrology Programs**

MacIntosh Astrology Programs

Magical Blend

Go **Magical Blend**

Magical Blend

Matrix Software

Go **Matrix Software**

Matrix Software

Meditation Room

Go **Meditation Room**

Meditation Room

Men Online

Go **Men**

Micro States

Go **Micro States**

Micro States

MS-DOS Astrology Programs

Go **MS-DOS Astrology Programs**

MS-DOS Astrology Programs

New Age Art Gallery

Go **New Age Art Gallery**

New Age Art Gallery

New Age Coffee House

Go **NAchat**

NAchat

New Age Forum

Go **New Age**

New Age Journal

Go **New Age Journal**

New Age Journal

New Age Magazines

Go **New Age Magazines**

New Age Magazines

New Age Marketplace

Go **New Age Marketplace**

New Age Marketplace

New Age Media

Go **NAmedia**

NAmedia

New Age Music

Go **New Age Music**

New Age Music

New Age: Books & Music

Go **NABooks**

NABooks

New Age: Buddhism of Tibet

Go **New Age: Buddhism of Tibet**

New Age: Buddhism of Tibet

New Age: Counseling

Go **New Age: Counseling**

New Age: Counseling

New Age: Eastern Concepts

Go **EastConcepts**

EastConcepts

New Age: History & Concepts
Go **TheNA**

TheNA

New Age: Intuition and Creativity
Go **New Age: Intuition and Creativity**

New Age: Intuition and Creativity

New Age: McIver Auditorium
Go **McIver**

McIver

New Age: Start Here
Go **NAstart**

NAstart

New Age: Western Concepts
Go **WestConcepts**

WestConcepts

New Media Product Guide
Go **New Media Product Guide**

New Media Product Guide

Nordic Countries
Go **Scandinavia**

Scandinavia

Organic Wine Shop
Go **wine**

wine

Other Things Tibetan
Go **Other Things Tibetan**

Other Things Tibetan

Parabola
Go **Parabola**

Parabola

People to People
Go **People to People**

People to People

Personal Cardshop
Go **Personal Cardshop**

Personal Cardshop

Planet Out
Go **PlanetOut**

Planet Out is a new, worldwide, online community for lesbian, gay, bisexual and transgendered people. Planet Out is founded by Tom Rielly, co-chair of Digital Queers, to create an engaging, well-edited service which provides a safe, fun home for LGBT people, regardless of whether they're out of the closet.

Po russki
Go **russki**

russki

Points Beyond: Divination and Oracles

Go **Oracles**

Oracles

Points Beyond: Esoteric Schools

Go **Esoteric**

Esoteric

Points Beyond: Invisible Beings

Go **Invisible**

Invisible

Points Beyond: Psychic Arts

Go **Points Beyond: Psychic Arts**

Points Beyond: Psychic Arts

Points Beyond: Ritual & Magic

Go **Ritual**

Ritual

Points Beyond: UFOs and Unexplained

Go **UFOs**

UFOs

Portugal & Spain

Go **Portugal & Spain**

Portugal & Spain

Senior Connection

Go **Sr.**

The Seniors Connection Forum is a social information resource for seniors, for their family and their advisors. It brings together people who want and need to communicate about the joys—and occasional challenges—associated with getting a little older.

Senior's Information Area

Go **Senior's Information Area**

This folder has been set up to give you a place to play while the area is being made wonderful and gorgeous for you. :) Please feel free to post questions and any information as well as ideas for the Senior's Connection here.

Switzerland (in French)

Go **Frenchswiss**

Frenchswiss

Switzerland (in German)

Go **Germanswiss**

Germanswiss

Switzerland (italiano)

Go **Italianswss**

Italianswss

The Astrologers Fund

Go **AFUND**

AFUND

United Kingdom

Go **UKForum**

UKForum

Welcome to Planet Earth Magazine

Go **WTPE**

WTPE

Whole Community

Go **WholeCommunity**

WholeCommunity

Whole Community Product Guide

Go **Whole Community Product Guide**

Whole Community Product Guide

Whole Community: Business

Go **NABusiness**

NABusiness

Whole Community: Communities

Go **NACommunities**

NACommunities

Whole Community: Focus Groups

Go **Focus**

Focus

Whole Community: Home & Family

Go **NAFamily**

NAFamily

Whole Community: Nostalgia

Go **Nostalgia**

Nostalgia

Whole Community: Warning Signs

Go **Warning**

Warning

Whole Earth

Go **WholeEarth**

WholeEarth

Whole Earth Product Guide

Go **Whole Earth Product Guide**

Whole Earth Product Guide

Whole Earth: New Paradigms

Go **Paradigms**

Paradigms

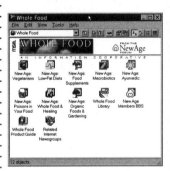

Whole Food

Go **WholeFood**

WholeFood

Whole Food Product Guide

Go **Whole Food Product Guide**

Whole Food Product Guide

Whole Person

Go **WholePerson**

WholePerson

Whole Person Product Guide

Go **Whole Person Product Guide**

Whole Person Product Guide

Whole Person: Creative Arts

Go **NAarts**

NAarts

Whole Person: Education

Go **NAEducation**

NAEducation

Whole Person: Rites of Passage

Go **Rites**

Rites

Whole Person: Self-Transformation

Go **Transformation**

Transformation

Whole Spirit

Go **WholeSpirit**

WholeSpirit

Whole Spirit Product Guide

Go **Whole Spirit Product Guide**

Whole Spirit Product Guide

Windows Astrology Software

Go **Windows Astrology Software**

Windows Astrology Software

Women Online

Go **Women**

WTPE Back Issues

Go **WTPE Back Issues**

WTPE Back Issues

Your Magazine

Go **Your Magazine**

Your Magazine

265

Sports, Health & Fitness

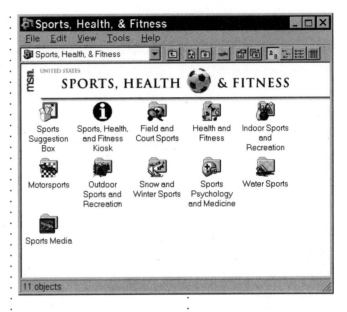

Archery and Firearm

Go **Archery and Firearm**

Sporting aspects of archery and firearms, including hunting, competitive shooting, and paintball, can be discussed in the Archery and Firearms forum.

Arizona

Go **ArizonaNF**

A description of Arizona's National Forest.

Assembly Of Nation

Go **WWA**

WWA

Auto Sport

Go **Auto Sport**

The Auto Sports forum allows for discussion of Formula 1, Indy car, stock car, drag, rally, and offroad racing.

Baseball

Go **Baseball**

The Baseball forum is dedicated to discussions about professional, collegiate, and recreational baseball.

Basketball

Go **Basketball**

The Basketball forum is dedicated to discussions about professional, collegiate, and recreational basketball.

Black Belt Magazine

Go **BB Mag**

BB Mag

BlackBelt Club

Go **blackbelt**

blackbelt

BlackBelt Club Tea House

Go **BBCTH**

BBCTH

Body Building and Weight Training

Go **BodyBuild**

Dedicated to the pursuit of fitness and physique development!

MSN Guide

California
Go **CAUSF**

A description of USFS lands throughout California

Camp Cooking
Go **cookout**

A place to exchange ideas about how to eat well in the wilderness.

Career Opportunitie
Go **nursejob**

This is the area to discuss career opportunities for nurses.

China
Go **China**

China

Clinical Issue
Go **clinical**

This is the area for discussion of nursing clinical issues pertaining to nursing practice and patient care.

Clothing
Go **Clothing**

Clothing

Coaches Corner
Go **Coaches Corner**

Coaches Corner

Colorado
Go **CONF**

A Description of Colorado's National Forests.

Community Center
Go **Community Center**

Community Center

Extreme Sport
Go **Extreme Sport**

The Extreme Sports forum is dedicated to discussion about parachuting, bungee jumping, skating and skateboarding, whitewater sports, extreme skiing, and hanggliding.

Fishing
Go **Fishing**

The Fishing forum is a place to discuss fresh and salt water fishing, fly fishing, and fishing events.

Football
Go **Football**

The Football forum is dedicated to discussions about professional, collegiate, and recreational football.

France
Go **MA France**

MA France

Front Office
Go **Front Office**

Front Office

General Nursing Education

Go **nursgened**

This area is for the discussion of general nursing education including hospital diploma programs, associate degree, baccalaureate, masters, and doctoral degrees as well as specialty certifications and programs.

Golf

Go **golf**

This forum is dedicated to discussion of professional and amateur golf.

Healthcare Professional

Go **Healthcare Professional**

Healthcare Professional

Healthcare Professions Forum

Go **healthpro**

healthpro

Hikes & Trail

Go **Hikes&trail**

Great trails and hikes from all over.

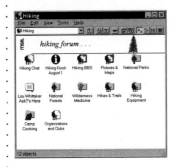

Hiking

Go **Hike**

A place for hikers and everbody interested in the outdoors to connect with other hikers.

Hiking Boot

Go **Hiking Boot**

Hiking Boot

Hiking Equipment

Go **Equipment**

A source for information on outdoor equipment. Reviews, opinions, facts and comparisons.

Hockey

Go **Hockey**

The Hockey forum is dedicated to discussions about professional, collegiate, and recreational hockey.

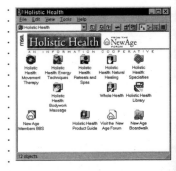

Holistic Health

Go **HolisticHealth**

HolisticHealth

Holistic Health Product Guide

Go **Holistic Health Product Guide**

Holistic Health Product Guide

Holistic Health: Bodywork Massage
Go **Massage**

Massage

Holistic Health: Energy Technique
Go **EnergyTech**

EnergyTech

Holistic Health: Movement Therapy
Go **Movement**

Movement

Holistic Health: Natural Healing
Go **NaturalHealing**

NaturalHealing

Holistic Health: Retreats and Spa
Go **Retreat**

Retreat

Holistic Health: Specialties
Go **HealthSpec**

HealthSpec

ICNN Adult Nutrition
Go **ICNN Adult Nutrition**

ICNN Adult Nutrition

ICNN Geriatric Nutrition
Go **ICNN Geriatric Nutrition**

ICNN Geriatric Nutrition

ICNN Pediatric Nutrition
Go **ICNN Pediatric Nutrition**

ICNN Pediatric Nutrition

ICNN Personal Nutrition
Go **ICNN Personal Nutrition**

ICNN Personal Nutrition

ICNN Sports Nutrition
Go **ICNN Sports Nutrition**

ICNN Sports Nutrition

ICNN: Adolescent Nutrition
Go **Adolescent Nutrition**

Adolescent Nutrition

ICNN: Health Misinformation Watch
Go **Health Misinformation Watch**

Health Misinformation Watch

ICNN: Nutrition and Pregnancy
Go **Nutrition and Pregnancy**

Nutrition and Pregnancy

ICNN: Nutrition Center
Go **Nutrition**

Nutrition

Idaho
· Go **IdahoNF**

A description of all the National Forests in Idaho.

Israel
· Go **Israel**

Israel

Japan
· Go **Japan**

Japan

Karate
· Go **Go Karate**

Go Karate

Karate/Kung Fu Illustrated Magazine
· Go **kki Mag**

kki Mag

Korea
· Go **Korea**

Korea

Law, Politics, and Ethics
· Go **nurselaw**

This area is for the discussion of law, politics, and ethics as it pertains to nursing practice.

Living with Long-Term Illnes
· Go **longterm**

A self-help forum for those living with long-term illnesses such as lupus, myasthenia gravis, diabetes.

MA Training Magazine
· Go **MA Training**

MA Training

Martial Art
· Go **Martial Art**

Martial Art

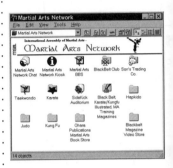

Martial Arts Network
· Go **MartialArt**

Within this fee-based forum you can chat with your MA friends world-wide; talk with movie stars in our SikeKick Auditorium; talk with Masters & Grand Masters about your personal progress; and purchase uniforms, videos, equipment, etc (discounted!).

Mexico
 Mexico

Mexico

Michigan
 MINF

A description of Michigan's National Forest.

Midwest
 MidwestNF

A description of the National Forests in the midwest.

Minnesota
 MinnesotaNF

A description of the three National Forests in Minnesota.

Montana
Go **Montana**

Montana

Motorboat Sport
Go **Motorboat Sport**

The Motorboat Sports forum deals with power boating and motorboat racing.

Motorcycle Sport
Go **Motorcycle Sport**

"Motorcycling, motocross, and motorcycle road racing can be discussed in the Motorcycle Sports forum."

National Forest
Go **usf**

A description of United States Forest Service Lands throughout the country.

National Park
Go **NP**

A description of our National Parks.

Nevada
Go **USFSNV**

A description of all the National Forest Lands in Nevada.

New England
Go **NENF**

A Description of New England's National Forests.

New Mexico
Go **NMF**

A description of National Forest lands in New Mexico.

Nurses Lounge
Go **nurselounge**

This area is for casual discussion between nurse colleagues.

Nursing Conference
Go **nurseconference**

This area is for the distribution of information about nursing conferences and meetings.

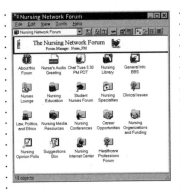

Nursing Continuing Education

Go **nursconted**

This area is for the discussion and download of continuing education programs for nurses. All programs on the forum are ANCCCA internationally accredited and can be applied for contact hours towards continuing education required for licensure.

Nursing Education

Go **nursingeducation**

This area is for the discussion and distribution of nursing education materials for general nursing and continuing education. Continuing education programs will be available for purchase and download when the system officially launches in the fall.

Nursing Media Resource

Go **nursemedia**

This area is for the discussion and distribution of nursing and health-care related media resources.

Nursing Network Forum

Go **Nursing**

The Nursing Network Forum is a computer-based one-stop professional mall for nurses for the discussion of the clinical, legal, ethical, political, and psychological aspects of nursing, in addition to information about media resources, conferences, and education.

Nursing Organizations and Funding

Go **nursorganization**

This is the area where information about nursing organizations and funding will be posted.

Nursing Specialties

Go **nursespecialtie**

This is the area to discuss different nursing specialties including hospital nursing, community and public health nursing, psychiatric nursing, maternal-child, nursing administration, nurse educators and practitioners and other nursing specialties.

Nutrition

Go **Nutrition**

Nutrition

Oregon

Go **ORUSF**

A description of USFS lands throughout Oregon.

Organizations and Club
Go **club**

A list of hiking organizations and clubs.

Pack
Go **Pack**

Pack

Parents' Place
Go **Parents' Place**

Parents' Place

Pictures & Map
Go **Map**

Hiking Maps. This description to be completed later.

Rainbow Publication
Go **Rainbow**

Rainbow

Recovering: One Day at a Time
Go **recovery**

recovery

Rugby
Go **Rugby**

The Rugby forum is dedicated to discussions about professional, collegiate, and recreational rugby.

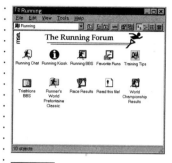

Running
Go **running**

An area for all running enthusiasts, from coaching, to competing to spectating.

Russia
Go **Russia**

Russia

Sailing
Go **Boat**

The Sailing forum is a place for connecting with other sailors and discussing sailing equipment, techniques, and competitions.

Sexuality
Go **sexy**

For the exploration of your sexuality, experiences and gaining knowledge!

Skiing and Snowboarding
Go **Skiing and Snowboarding**

The Skiing and Snowboarding forum is dedicated to the exchange of information and ideas about cross country skiing, downhill skiing and snowboarding, and extreme skiing and snowboarding.

Sledding

Go **Sledding**

The Sledding forum discusses bobsledding, luging, dogsledding and mushing, and recreational sledding.

Sleeping Bag

Go **Sleeping Bag**

Sleeping Bag

Soccer

Go **Soccer**

The Soccer forum is dedicated to discussions about professional, collegiate, and recreational soccer.

Son's Trading Co.

Go **MA Store**

MA Store

South

Go **SouthernNF**

A description of National Forests in the Southern States.

Sports Media

Go **Sports Media**

Sports Media

Sports Psychology and Medicine

Go **Sports Psychology and Medicine**

The Sports Psychology and Medicine forum discusses the prevention and treatment of injuries and the mental aspects of competition.

Student Nurses Forum

Go **nursestudent**

This area will be for student nurses around the world to exchange information, and network with one another.

Survivor

Go **Survivor**

Forum where survivors of alcoholism, cancer, long-term illness, and other personal trauma can meet for discussion and support.

Tae Kwon Do

Go **TKD**

TKD

Tent

Go **Tent**

A cornucopia of information about tents.

The DisAbilities Forum

Go **ABLECAFE**

Cafe' Access is a place where people can gather to discuss whatever issues they like. This is an equal-access for all area!

Utah

Go **Utah**

Utah

Washington
○ **WAUSF**

A description of all the USFS lands in Washington-ton

Whole Health
○ **WholeHealth**

WholeHealth

Wilderness Medicial Library
○ **Wilderness Medicial Library**

How to treat common medical problems in the wilderness.

Wilderness Medicine
○ **wildmed**

A resource area for keeping healthy and surviving injury in the wilderness.

Women's Cancer Forum
Go **wocan**

Women sharing their experiences & concerns as cancer patients, as survivors, and as care givers for friends and family with cancer.

Wrestling
Go **Wrestling**

Wrestling

Wyoming
Go **WYNF**

A description of Wyoming's National Forests.

Youth Sport
Go **Youth Sport**

Youth Sport

Science and Technology

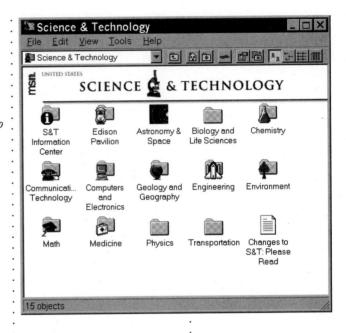

AI Resource Corner
GO **AIResource**

An area for member exchange of information on professional organizations, conferences, workshops, publications, and other activities and resources in artificial intelligence.

AI Techniques
GO **AI Techniques**

Usenet newsgroups pertaining to specific artificial intelligence subject areas and techniques.

Amateur RADIO
GO **HAM**

Discussions on HAM Radio such as HF, Packet, Scanners and Amateur TV.

American History
GO **america**

america

Archaeology
GO **Archaeology**

Grab your picks and shovels and let's dig in!

Artificial Intelligence
GO **AI**

The Artificial Intelligence Forum covers areas such as artificial life, neural networks, genetic algorithms, expert systems, virtual reality, fuzzy logic, language processing and other areas. Professionals, practitioners, and beginners are welcome.

Astro Libraries
GO **Astrolibs**

Libraries for images, programs and astronomy text files.

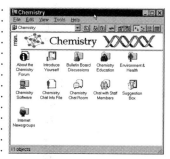

De Briefing Chat Rooms
GO **Brief**

> *A place where you are debriefed after coming in from the cold.*

Astronomy & Space
GO **Space**

> *A forum dedicated to the discussion of and exchange of information on astronomy and the exploration of space.*

Chemistry
GO **Chemistry**

> *The Chemistry Forum is devoted to chemistry, biochemistry, and the related subjects of toxicology and molecular biology.*

Edison Pavilion
GO **ScienceEvents**

> *The Edison Pavilion contains the Edison Auditorium and other rooms used for guest chats and other Science & Technology special events.*

Engineering
GO **Engineering**

> *The Engineering forum is open to all Engineering Professionals, Students and enthusiasts. All Engineering disciplines, skills and interests are welcome here!*

Bistro Chat Lounge
GO **bistro**

> *bistro*

Chemistry Education
GO **School**

> *School*

Electronics
GO **Electronics**

> *The Electronics forum is a place to exchange information about consumer electronics and other electronic technologies.*

Engineering & Technical Resources
GO **EngRes**

> *EngRes*

Chemistry Software
GO **Chemistry Software**

> *Chemistry Software*

Engineering BBS World
GO **EngBBSWorld**

This is an area in the Engineering Forum which contains Engineering BBS's which are dedicated to various different branches of Engineering.

Engineering Conference Center
GO **EngCon**

This area is for special presentations, lectures and seminars. The Engineering Forum is scheduling these events.

Engineering Design Center
GO **EngDesCtr**

This is an Engineering Virtual Work Center.

Environment
GO **EnviroChem**

EnviroChem

Flamingo Chat Lounge Room
GO **flamingo**

flamingo

Health & Environmental Chemistry
GO **ChemHealth**

ChemHealth

History and Archaeology
GO **History**

Welcome to the History and Archaeology Forums! For views, comments and conversation, click here and let's dig in!

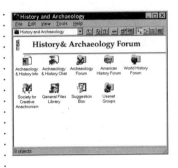

Industrial Robotics
GO **industrialrobo**

Industrial Robotics & Industrial Electromechanical Technologies.

Midnight Rendezvous (Spy Chat)
GO **adul**

Where spies and gals and guys come in from the cold for companionship and to exchange secrets.

MSN Related Areas
GO **MSNEngRel**

This folder is in the Engineering Forum, it contains numerous shortcuts to other Engineering related areas on the MSN.

Orient Express Chat Lounge
GO **Orien**

The Orient Express offers safety and privacy for the weary. Each coach is unique and finely crafted for your relaxation.

Physics
GO **Physics**

Physics

Psychology
GO **Psychology**

Psychology

Robosources
GO **robosources**

*Robotics resources, books,
part suppliers, video tapes,
software, historical
information, art, music,
pictures, toys, career
opportunities.*

Robotics
GO **TRILEX**

*Robotics & Electrome-
chanical Technology. This
area covers both industrial
and hobby applications,
servo mechanisms, fluid
control systems, encoders,
transducers, PLC's, open-
loop & closed loop systems,
feedback systems, program-
mable controllers.*

Rose Garden Chat Lounge
GO **rose**

rose

Runsterbot (under 18)
GO **runster**

*Young Adults (18 and
under) experimenting,
designing, and building
robots. Hobby and contest
style robotics.*

Index to the MSN Guide

Places to Go, Things to See

M.S.N Guide

Places to Go, Things to See

Index

Symbols

:-(80
:-) 80
:-> 80
:-O 80
:-o 80
;-) 80
<G> 79
<g> 79

A

access numbers
    choosing 45
        backup number 46
        primary number 46
Add to Favorite Places toolbar button 60
address books 75
    maintaining separate 38
    specifying for MSN 38
addressing options 38
alt newsgroups 162
Ask Questions Here chat room 82
Attached Files view in BBSes 97
attaching a file to a BBS
    message 96, 102
Auto Answer light 39
Automatic Disconnect Interval 49
Automatically decompress files
    option 111

B

Babbage Auditorium 82
Backspace key 56
banners 54
baud rate 40
BBSes 86–113
    attachments 96
    Conversation view 89
    conversations 89
        collapsing messages 93
        expanding messages 92
        following 89
        opening entire 93
    folders 89
    messages 89
        adding attachments 102
        copying graphics from another
            application 101
        copying text from another applica-
            tion 101
        embedding existing objects 103
        embedding objects 102
        entering text 99
        formatting text 99
        forwarding 98
        importing graphics 100
        importing text 100
        importing text from a text file 101
        marking as read 97

        marking multiple 97
        new 98
        opening 93
        posting 97
        printing 95
        reading offline 104
        sending 104
        sorting 95
        symbols 89
    navigating 92
    refreshing 95
    replying to messages 97
    returning to your place 94
    saving messages 96
    sorting conversations 95
    unread messages 89
    using the keyboard 93
    viewing only messages with attach-
        ments 97
    what are 86
BRB 79
BTW 79
Bulletin Board System. *See* BBSes

C

Calendar of Events 83
Call waiting, disabling 48
Carrier Detect light 39
Categories button 52

Index

Index

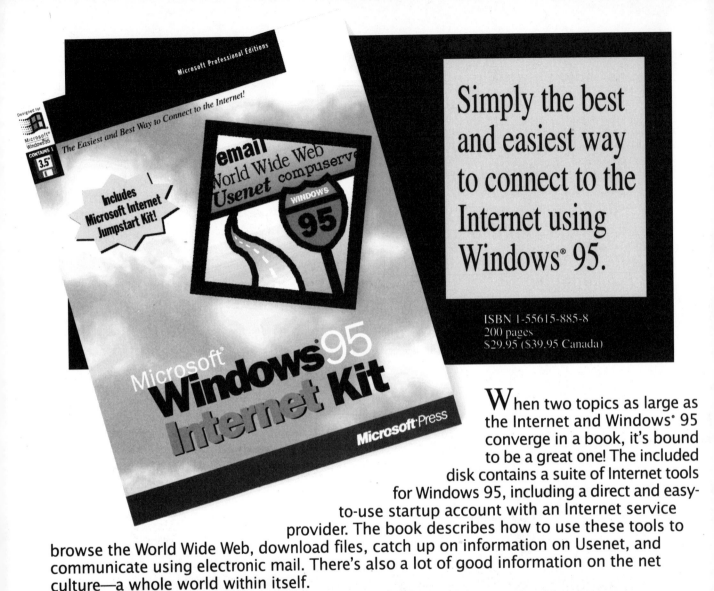